# THE PIONEERS:
# EARLY AFRICAN-AMERICAN LEADERS
# IN PINE BLUFF, ARKANSAS

Freedmen, Newly Freed, and First/Second Generation, Born from 1833-1892

## BETTYE J. WILLIAMS

First edition

**For Information Contact**
Dr. Bettye J. Williams, Founder
PO Box 2435
Pine Bluff, AR 71613
(870) 718-0191
www.oakandivymuseum.com

Location of Museum
5224 Highway 79 South
Pine Bluff, AR 71603

Cover Photos: Walter "Wiley" Jones, Ferdinand "Ferd" Havis, and Professor Joseph Carter Corbin

Archway Publishing books may be ordered through booksellers or by contacting:

Archway Publishing
1663 Liberty Drive
Bloomington, IN 47403
www.archwaypublishing.com
1 (888) 242-5904

ISBN: 978-1-4808-7191-5 (sc)
ISBN: 978-1-4808-7192-2 (e)

Library of Congress Control Number: 2019918635

Print information available on the last page.

Archway Publishing rev. date: 1/21/2020

To the Ancestors in the South.

# Contents

# ILLUSTRATIONS

# ACKNOWLEDGMENTS

Upon the completion of this book, which is the first of many, I wish to express my gratitude to the countless who have been of invaluable assistance to me as I moved forward on a vision that I think is still long overdue—that is, giving recognition to African American leaders of generations past who shaped this city, county, and state in productive, dynamic ways. To all, both named here and unnamed, who contributed in any ways to Oak and Ivy: African American Museum and Cultural Center, thank you.

To my siblings and their spouses, Evester Louise Darrough (deceased) and James Darrough Sr.; Shirley M. Williams; Dr. Brenda F. Graham; Dr. Margarette A. Williams and Lewis J. Williams; Charles L. Williams (deceased); N. Lucille Gilkey; Sterlin D. Williams and Priscilla Williams; Ted W. Williams; Robin N. Baylark; Sonnya N. Adams and Dwight Adams Sr., thanks for immeasurable love and inspiration through the years. To all my nephews, nieces, great-nephews, great-nieces, aunts, uncles, cousins, and friends, thanks for love, respect, talk, and always a "sweet" place. To close here, to my dear parents, Eunice and Dorothy Mae Willingham Williams, thanks for life and love. I "still owe you both."

## Board of Directors

Bettye J. Williams, PhD    Founder/President
Janine Jamison    Vice President
Peggy Tidmore-White    Secretary
Sonnya N. Adams    Treasurer
Naomi L. Jolaoso    Historian

## Executive Council

Donna Barnes

Dr. Barbara Grayson

Dr. Paul Lorenz

Kimberly Williams

Kelly Bryant

Dr. Calvin Johnson

Dr. Brenda Martin

Henry Golatt

Mary M. Jones

Kymara H. Seals

## The Public Program and Ground Breaking: Proclamations, Greetings, and Encouragement

The Honorable Debe Hollingsworth, Mayor of Pine Bluff
The Honorable Shirley M. Washington, Mayor-Elect of Pine Bluff
The County Judge, the Honorable Dutch King
The County Judge-Elect, Rev./Dr. Henry "Hank" Wilkins
The Honorable Senator Stephanie Flowers, Esquire
The County Sheriff, the Honorable Gerald Robinson
Frederick H. Reed; Dr. Martha A. Flowers, MD; Rev./Dr. L. K. Solomon; Rev. Ronald S. Laurent; Rev. Melvin G. Graves; Dr. Brenda F. Graham; Naomi Lawson Jolaoso; Janice L. Roberts; Bobby Dandridge; Glenda Foots; Valencia Fields; Jimmy Cunningham Jr.; Donna Cunningham; Henri Linton Sr.; and Chancellor Laurence and Mrs. Veronica Alexander at UAPB

## Founding Donors

Dwight and Sonnya N. Adams; Josephine Adams; Barbara Akins; Doris Marie Alexander; Chancellor Laurence and Mrs. Veronica Alexander; Edna Allen; Donna Barnes; Robin N. Baylark; Bunia Baxter; Evelyn Alexander Benjamin; Rev. Jerrold D. Brantley; Sammie E. Brantley; Charles L. Brown and Stella Brown; Drs. James and Josephine Bell; Sam and Versa L. Berry; Evelyn Jean Blunt; Dr. Mary Brentley; Dorothy Chapman Brown; Rachel Covington-Banks; Gail P. Butler; Pauline A. Chandler; Jessie M. Clemmons; Dr. Viralene J. Coleman; Bonita Corbin; Mildred Cross; Juanita Currie; Donna Cunningham; Albert and Shirley Carey; Doris Dansby; Alton Davis; Huey and Jo Ann Davis; Vandora Demery; Terrence and Lyska J. Dilworth; Sekethia Dilworth; Annette Dove and TOPPS Inc.; Jewel and Leroy Edwards Sr.; Dr. Joanna P. Edwards; Dr. Lois J. Faucette; Dr. John and Mary Y. Flowers; Dr. Martha A. Flowers, MD; Stephanie Flowers; Esquire; Annie B. Ford; Margaret S. Gatson; N. Lucille Gilkey; Doris Goolsbye; Lola D. Gordon; Dr. Brenda F. Graham;

Earnestine F. Grant; Mary F. Grant; Dr. Barbara A. Grayson; Jacqueline L. Green; Cora A. Hansberry-Cloird; Helen Hasan and the Muslim Women Association of Little Rock; Jeanette Hence; Vickie A. Hicks; Sharon D. Hildreth; Ben and Doris Holmes; Risie Howard; Vivian S. Howard; Yvonne Humphrey; Melliglory Jackson; John and Shirley Jacob; Lucille Jasper; Naomi Lawson Jolaoso; Brenda V. Johnson; Ollie D. Johnson; Ollie King; Etta M. Kuykendall; Joe and Betty J. Lacy; Rev. Ronald and Mrs. Cathryn D. Laurent; Naomi N. Lawson; Dr. Irene K. Lee; Tonya Lemon; Wilbert and Birlee Lever; Mary C. Liddell; Dr. Paul Lorenz; Dr. Michael and Mary M. Lynch; Dr. Brenda Martin; Shawn C. Mitchell; Ummil K. Mohammed; Rudy and Mary A. Morgan; Nettie Morrison; Eddie and Sharon H. Nicholson; Tina Owens; Gregory and Marceinia Peoples; Pine Bluff Alumnae Chapter of Delta Sigma Theta Sorority, Incorporated; Pine Bluff Branch of the National Association of University Women (NAUW); Rev. Kerry Price Sr. and the Breath of Life Church; Yolanda Prim; Drs. James and Ezora J. Proctor; Frederick H. Reed; Linda J. Richardson; Janice Roberts; Dora J. Sanders; Kymara H. Seals; Stephanie D. Shavers; Jennifer Smith; Linda L. Simmons; Dr. Paul and Hazel A. Smith; Idell W. Snowden; Rev. L. K. and Mrs. Vera Solomon; Sharon L. Stephens; Gloria Stoudamire; Dr. Grace Tatem; Joyce Bracy Vaughan; Valerie Vaultz; Dr. Jewell Walker; Frank and Shirley Washington; Amanda M. Wells; Herman and Daisy Wells; Janice Wesley; Dr. Janette R. Wheat; Claudette White; Rev. Clifton R. White and Peggy Tidmore-White; Charles Lewis Williams (deceased); Kimberly Williams; Mr. Lewis and Dr. Margarette A. Williams; Shirley M. Williams; Sterlin and Priscilla Williams; Ted W. Williams; Bobbie Willingham; Odis and Joyce Willingham; Markeith Woods, and James and Arlene R. Woody.

## Collections, Artifacts, and Gifts to Oak and Ivy Museum

Rev. Clifton R. White and Mrs. Peggy Tidmore-White Collection; the Thomas Family Collection of Clairborne Parish, Louisiana; the Dennis Biddle Collection; Dr. Michael Hurst Collection; Edward Fontenette and the John Brown Watson Memorial Library Gift; Lillie Mae Carter; Billie Jean Keeble; Lola Gordon; Martin Piano Company; Carrie Scott's Antiques of Pine Bluff; and Cleovis and Arwiarda Whiteside.

## Special Thanks

Evester Louise Williams Darrough, my sister, who believed in the vision of a museum—from its inception (now deceased); Dr. Brenda F. Graham, professor, School of Education, Concordia University, Chicago, for the "Strategic Plan"; Annette Howard Dove and TOPPS Inc. for inspiration; Henry Golatt and staff at UAPB Business Support Incubator and Office Complex; *Pine Bluff Commercial* journalists and staff; *Sea Life* publisher and staff; Mr. Edward Fontenette, director, Audrey Long, and the staff at the John Brown Watson Memorial Library at UAPB; Jana Mitchell, reference, research and genealogy manager with Jessie Hammond and other staff at Pine Bluff/Jefferson County Central Library; Founder/Dr. Margarette A. Williams and staff at Ephesus Christian Bible Bookstore; Jimmy Cunningham Jr. and Donna Cunningham, authors; Mr. Henri Linton, professor emeritus and University Museum director, and the staff at the University Museum and Cultural Center, UAPB; Staff at the Arkansas History Commission, Little Rock; the Butler Center of the Central Library System, Little Rock; Rev./ Dr. L. K. Solomon, Pine Bluff pastor emeritus and author; Janice L. Roberts, Pine Bluff; Rev. Kerry Price Sr., pastor, Breath of Life Church, Pine Bluff; Dr. Ruth Roberts, Little Rock; Marshall Kelley, manager and funeral director, Brown Funeral Home; Judy Miller, owner of Miller's Funeral Home; and Roy Hearn, owner of P. K. Miller Cemetery.

## Methodology

The purpose of *Pioneers: Early African American Leaders in Pine Bluff* is to provide the reader with resource material. My attempt was not to distill or interpret—simply present the historical data for readers to reflect upon. The book follows the usual procedure for historical study: collection of primary and secondary data, interpretation, and synthesis. Records, catalogs, bulletins, newspaper information, magazine access, journal notes, dissertations, library indices, and digital data—just to mention a few—were obtained from many sources. Seeking Pine Bluff and/or Jefferson County history almost two centuries ago was a daunting feat. Some information researched was found to be imprecise, unclear, and even inaccurate. Finding information about the past with pictures was most challenging. For some illustrations, I used vintage postcards, especially those printed before 1923, which are in the public domain. As a visual record of the past, postcards offered a better pictorial documentation of culture and architecture than perhaps most other sources. Often, a postcard was the only example of people, streets, buildings, and cars in color in this research.[1]

## Permissions

Grateful acknowledgment is made to the following for permission to reprint previously published and previously unpublished material.

Reed Architectural Firm of Pine Bluff. Grateful appreciation extended to Frederick H. Reed, a member of the American Institute of Architects. The original drawing of Oak and Ivy: African American Museum and Cultural Center unveiled in Pine Bluff, on Saturday, August 10, 2013.

Original photo by Baker. New York: Dodd, Mead and Company, 1896, by the Century Company. John Wilson and Son, Cambridge, USA. Photo, signature, and poem by Paul Laurence Dunbar. Grateful appreciation to Rev. Clifton R. White for sharing the "poet's image" from his 1896 first edition copy of Dunbar's volume of poetry.

*Pine Bluff Commercial*, "UAPB Founding Father Honored with a Headstone on Memorial Day," Sunday, June 2, 2013, 2B.

*Pine Bluff Commercial*, "New Museum to Showcase Black History in Arkansas," Sunday, August 11, 2013.

*Sea Life*, a newsmagazine published by the *Pine Bluff Commercial*. "Pine Bluff Welcomes New Museum," September 2013.

# INTRODUCTION

*Fashion your dress for the future in the realities of the past.*

—Anonymous

Oak and Ivy: African American Museum and Cultural Center will give origin to a facility that will highlight the African American heritage in Pine Bluff and the state of Arkansas. Through its exhibitions, public programs, publications, media, and related activities, Oak and Ivy Museum seeks to provide content, context, and perspective on the history, legacy, and experiences of African Americans—past and present. Placing the vision of the museum in its broader perspective, the aim is not to build Oak and Ivy Museum to celebrate Black history solely for African Americans; rather, the museum will be a place for all to see how the African American experience has affected and shaped the lives of everyone in Pine Bluff and the state. The museum will be an important cultural addition to the Pine Bluff landscape.

Pine Bluff was incorporated in 1839. In the 1840s, a vast multitude of African Americans from Mississippi, Alabama, Tennessee, South Carolina, and North Carolina arrived in town. They came with talent and skills. Almost never "talked about these days," the lives of pioneering Blacks and their civic attainments are woven into the fabric of Pine Bluff's past history and now. The city owes much of its early progress to the resourcefulness of early African Americans who were talented, competitive, and Republican. In spite of "separate and unequal" rulings, they became farmers, educators, politicians, and businesspersons. In a town where cotton was the major economy at the time, African Americans became craftsmen—creating frontier furniture, cast iron skillets, plows, and locks.

In documentation format emphasizing remembrance and understanding in chronological and topic order of ancestral indebtedness, this book is a historical summary of nineteenth- and early twentieth-century African American achievers who were born between 1833 and 1892 and who lived in Pine Bluff for some time. Although some information shared within this book is scanty, perhaps incomplete, or even inaccurate as given by chroniclers to researchers, this book of pioneering and early African American leaders will open minds and eyes to the history of a race of people whose biographies and personal contributions have been neglected, effaced, and overlooked by most mainstream historians in Pine Bluff and the state through the decades. Using narration, archival images, photos, and some interviews with descendants, spouses, and/or other kin relations, this book will document the rich legacy of a century of African American farmers, ministers, lawyers, politicians, administrators, educators, and painters. For many of the African American forebears mentioned in the grouping above, their signal vision for Pine Bluff—and for many other small towns in Arkansas—has not been valued or shared with the public. Politically, their civic undertaking as nineteenth- and early twentieth-century Republicans has been muted. During the latter two decades of the nineteenth century and into the twentieth century, Republicans favored abolition of slavery, education and the establishment of schools for the newly freed, and oversaw Reconstruction in the South. To the preceding, a selected list of Jefferson County and Pine Bluff's social, civic, and business leaders—both European and Jewish—during the early nineteenth and twentieth centuries will be included.

As citizens, we cannot tell the Pine Bluff story, or the Jefferson County story, or even the Arkansas story without telling the African American version as well. Oak and Ivy Museum will tell that story through its many programs and wide-ranging events. The museum will recount the remarkable biography of leaders who braved obstacles to promote the city. Presenting the complex picture—that is, providing the entire scope of the African American story—is precisely what Oak and Ivy Museum will do. For certain, the museum will be a place where young people, adult residents, and guests can learn how generations of African Americans helped make this city, state, and nation remarkable. Oak and Ivy Museum was incorporated on December 3, 2012, and is a tax-exempt public museum under section 501(c) (3) of the Internal Revenue Code, Section 170.

Bettye J. Williams, PhD

*Photo of Paul Laurence Dunbar*

# Brief History of Pine Bluff

Pine Bluff was founded by Europeans on a high bank of the Arkansas River. It is located in the southeast section of Arkansas in the Arkansas Delta with the Arkansas Timberlands region to its immediate west. Its topography is flat with wide expanses of farmland. Agriculture is the mainstay in Pine Bluff. The leading products include cotton, soybeans, cattle, rice, poultry, timber, and catfish. Pine Bluff is served by a network of five United States and five state highways. The United States highways are Interstate 530 (formerly part of US 65); US Route 63; US Route 79; US Highway 270; and US Highway 425. Oak and Ivy Museum is located on US Highway 79 South.

Before incorporation in 1839, Pine Bluff was Quapaw country, nestled by heavily forested tall pine trees overlooking the Arkansas River. The Quapaws signed away the land that became Jefferson County, relinquishing their title to all the lands they claimed in Arkansas. They moved west. Some years later a few of the Indians returned to the city. Joseph Bonne, a fur trader and trapper of French and Quapaw ancestry, settled on this Arkansas bluff in 1819. His home is located in the earliest part of Pine Bluff, a few blocks from the Jefferson County Courthouse and on the bank of Lake Saracen, which occupies a former channel of the Arkansas River, abandoned in 1908. UAPB's archaeologist, John H. House, has unearthed artifacts about Pine Bluff, which include ceramic and glass fragments, hand-forged nails, and remains of wells, cisterns, and privies from the pre-Civil War era.[2] Other settlers joined Boone. In 1829, Thomas Phillips claimed land in Pine Bluff. On August 13, 1832, Pine Bluff was chosen as the county seat. Pine Bluff Town was named on October 16, 1832, and incorporated January 8, 1839. In the 1840s, there were about fifty residents in Pine Bluff Town. The Arkansas River served as a port for travel and shipping.[3] From 1832 to 1838, Pine Bluff was situated on the "Trail of Tears" waterway as thousands of Native Americans were forcibly removed from the southeast part of the United States to the state of Oklahoma. From 1832 to 1858, Pine Bluff also served as a waterway route for hundreds of Indian Seminoles and Black Seminoles who were forcibly removed from their land.

The first clear record of African Americans in Arkansas is from 1721. A vast multitude arrived in the 1840s and 1850s from Mississippi, Alabama, Tennessee, South Carolina, and North Carolina. Although they were slaves, many escaped the hard labor of the fields through their resourcefulness, talent, and skills. They became craftsmen—creating frontier furniture, cast iron skillets, plows, and locks. By the outbreak of the Civil War, Pine Bluff was prospering with wealth built on the crop of cotton cultivated on large plantations by enslaved African American laborers. By 1860, Pine Bluff had one of the largest slave populations in the state. Jefferson County was second in the state for cotton production. Union troops under Colonel Powell Clayton arrived in Pine Bluff on September 17, 1863, to protect the city from Confederates who were terrorizing the citizens. Confederate General J. S. Marmaduke tried to expel the United States Army in the Battle of Pine Bluff, October 25, 1863, but was repulsed by Union soldiers and former slaves.

Because of Union forces, Pine Bluff attracted many refugees and freedmen after the Emancipation Proclamation. After the war, freed slaves worked with the American Missionary Society to start schools for Blacks. By September 1873, Professor Joseph Carter Corbin opened Branch Normal College of the Arkansas Industrial University. Founded as Arkansas's first Black public college, today it is UAPB.

Around 1866, an altercation in a refugee camp between Blacks and Whites launched the city into a grim atmosphere, when more than twenty-four Black men, women, and children were found lynched. Toward the end of the nineteenth century, African Americans became suspicious of practically everything happening in the South. Many Blacks were attracted by the appeal of the "Back to Africa" movement and many purchased tickets or sought information on immigration to Liberia. Most of the emigrants came from Jefferson, St. Francis, Pulaski, Pope, and Conway counties.[4]

Pine Bluff entered the "Golden Era" in the 1880s with cotton production and river commerce. This latter venture helped the city draw industries and public institutions. The lumber industry grew in the

1880s and 1900s.[5] Wiley Jones, a freedman who achieved wealth by his own business, built the first mule-driven street car in 1886. From 1936 to 1938, the Works Progress Administration (WPA) through the Federal Writers Project initiated an effort that distinguished Pine Bluff. Writers were sent throughout the South to capture oral histories of former slaves still alive at the time. Upon completion of the project, Arkansas residents had contributed more oral slave histories—about 780—than any other state in the South. Black citizens in Pine Bluff/Jefferson County contributed more oral interviews of Arkansas-born slaves than any other city/county in the state. Pine Bluff is a valuable storehouse of oral slave narrative material.[6]

The 1960s brought boycotts and demonstrations demanding an end to segregated public facilities in Pine Bluff. Civil Rights demonstrators held sit-ins at the Pines Hotel, Woolworth's, and Walgreen's.[7] Violence directed at the protests resulted in the fire-bombing of a church and the shooting of civil rights activists. Many of the demonstrators arrested were students enrolled at AM&N. National figures were enlisted, and many such as Stokely Carmichael (SNCC), Dick Gregory, and James Farmer (CORE) arrived in the city to help bring about change. The NAACP, local churches, and community activists assisted the demonstrators by organizing rallies and campaigns—contributing money for bails, transportation, media purposes, and others; purchasing toiletries for those jailed weeks at a time; and anything else necessary for expediency. Many Black churches purchased, prepared, and delivered food in large trays for arrested demonstrators because activists would not eat the prepared jail food. Voter registration drives in the city increased Black political participation. Student protests and NAACP participation eventually led to reforms in public accommodations in Pine Bluff. Irene Holcomb became the first African American alderwoman on the City Council.

Pine Bluff offers an excellent opportunity for residents and visitors to see the history of the area covering the past two hundred years. With a total of thirteen murals painted since 1992 by renowned international artists, Pine Bluff is being known as the "City of Murals." Located on the corner of Second and Main streets, the UAPB Mural traces the school's history from 1875 to 1972. It was painted by Robert Dafford, of Lafayette, Louisiana. It shows the traditions and heritage at Branch Normal College, located in a rented frame building on the corner of Sevier and Lindsey Streets, with Professor J. C. Corbin in charge.

- The Founder, J. C. Corbin, is pictured in the upper right.
- Mechanical arts was one of the disciplines promoted at Branch Normal. The top left shows a mechanical arts class. The man whose portrait appears on the top left section is the first president of AM&N, Dr. John Brown Watson. He established many of the traditions of the college and managed with other administrators and faculty to get the multipurpose concept of education adopted and implemented.
- The next pane to the right shows what appears to be one of the first of the Branch Normal classes in the two-story brick structure, erected in 1882 by state funds on a fifty-acre plot in Pine Bluff.
- The next pane to the right shows the barn that was the first building on the site that is now UAPB. The large pane below shows how Branch Normal looked when it was first opened.
- Also pictured are Isaac Fisher, Jefferson Ish, Robert Malone, and F. T. Venegar; all made significant contributions to the advancement of the college.
- With Dr. Lawrence A. Davis Sr., the official seal of present-day UAPB reflects its heritage.
- UAPB opened a $3 million business incubator in downtown Pine Bluff. The city offers an excellent opportunity for residents and visitors to see the history of the area covering the past two hundred years.

In 2005, Mr. Carl Redus became the first African American mayor in the city's history. On March 22, 2016, Mrs. Shirley M. Washington was elected the first female African American mayor in the city.

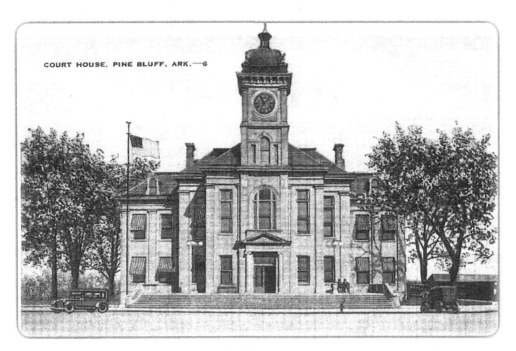

COURT HOUSE, PINE BLUFF, ARK.—6

*Pine Bluff Courthouse*

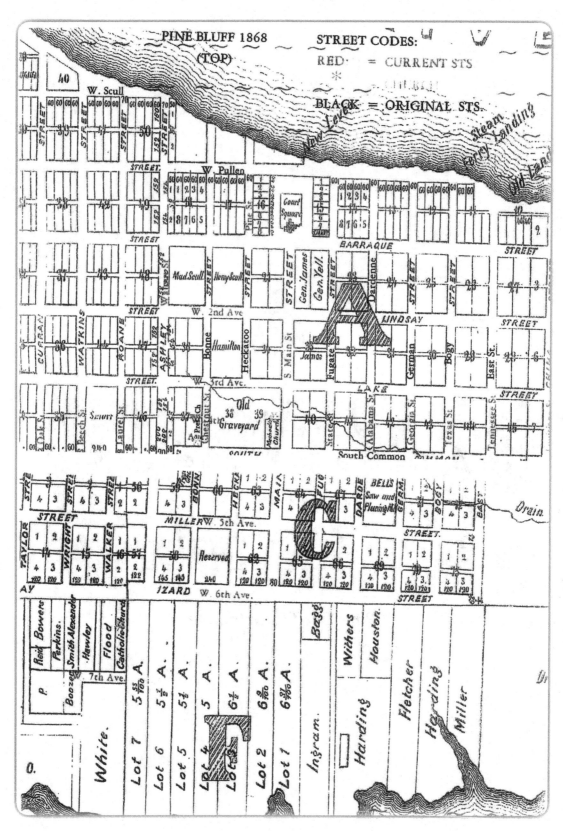

*1868 Map of Pine Bluff*

# Naming the Museum

Written in 1893, *Oak and Ivy* is the first book of poetry written by Paul Laurence Dunbar. Published by a small firm in Dayton, Ohio, *Oak and Ivy* consists of fifty-six poems. The slave and plantation experiences of Dunbar's Kentucky parents influenced the writing. Included in the book are "Ode to Ethiopia" and "Sympathy." *Oak and Ivy* constitutes both a history and a celebration of African American life. Recognizing the literary input of the slim book of poetry as the predecessor to twelve books of poetry, four books of short stories, five novels, and a play, I am indebted to Dunbar, who became a powerful interpreter of the African American experience in literature and song. Dunbar's early success was promoted and praised, first by schoolmates Wilbur and Orville Wright, and, second, by William Dean Howells, a leading critic associated with *Harper's Weekly* and the *Atlantic Monthly*. Reared in the Arkansas town named Stamps, Maya Angelou said that Dunbar's works had inspired her "writing ambition." The title of her first autobiography, *I Know Why the Caged Bird Sings* (1969), is the first line in Dunbar's poem "Sympathy." Establishing a national reputation, he was the first Black poet to earn national distinction and acceptance.

**Paul Laurence Dunbar**

Oak and Ivy Museum is named in his honor. Born in Dayton, Ohio, at 311 Howard Street, Dunbar (1872–1906) is regarded as America's first great Black poet. He was the son of Joshua and Matilda Murphy Dunbar. He wrote his first poem at six years old, recited his first poem at nine, and published his first poem in the *Dayton Herald* at fourteen years old. Graduating from Dayton Central High School in 1891, where he was the only African American in his class, he was the president of the literary club, editor in chief of the school's newspaper, and the class poet. Months following the publication of *Oak and Ivy*, he was invited to recite at the

1893 Columbian Exhibition (World's Fair) in Chicago, where he sold copies of *Oak and Ivy* and met Frederick Douglass, who praised the book and provided Dunbar with a job in the Haitian pavilion at the fair. Dunbar would be closely associated with Douglass, James Weldon Johnson, and Booker T. Washington. He would travel to London to recite and write poetry. Upon his return to the United States, he was honored with a ceremonial sword by President Theodore Roosevelt. He received a clerkship at the Library of Congress in Washington, DC. By 1895, his poems began appearing in the *Century*, the *New York Times*, the *Lippincott's Monthly*, the *Atlantic Monthly*, the *Saturday Evening Post*, and the *Denver Post*. In 1898, he married Alice Ruth Moore, a teacher and author from New Orleans. Shortly thereafter, while living in Washington, DC, and consulting for the Library of Congress, he suffered from tuberculosis (lung disease) and the alcohol prescribed for the illness. His steadily deteriorating health caused him to return to his mother's home in Dayton, where he died on February 9, 1906, at the age of thirty-three. He was buried in Woodland Cemetery in Dayton. Dunbar was one of the first African American literary figures to garner critical acclaim on a national level and the first Black author to support himself solely through his works.

*Left:* This is a photo of Paul Laurence Dunbar in 1890, three years before publishing his first volume of poetry, *Oak and Ivy* (1893). *Right:* At her home in Dayton, Ohio, is the poet's mother, Matilda Murphy Dunbar. She recited stories in dialect to him of her experiences as a slave. His parents were Joshua and Matilda Dunbar, both migrated to Ohio.

*Paul Laurence Dunbar and Matilda Murphy Dunbar*

# OAK AND IVY MUSEUM

The Mission Statement

The mission of Oak and Ivy African American Museum and Cultural Center is to acknowledge and celebrate through programs and other forms of distribution the religious, literary, historic, and artistic creativity of African Americans in Pine Bluff, Jefferson County, and the state of Arkansas by collecting, exhibiting, interpreting, and preserving objects and documents in ways that increase understanding and knowledge of the African American culture and heritage.

The Vision

- Oak and Ivy Museum curates, promotes, and protects the artistic and cultural treasures of Arkansas' African American community.
- Oak and Ivy Museum is dedicated to learning, developing, and improving services in Pine Bluff, Arkansas, and surrounding cities.
- Oak and Ivy Museum values collecting, preserving, exhibiting, and interpreting the African American experience.
- Oak and Ivy Museum inspires people of all ages to explore and discover the role of African Americans in shaping the history of Arkansas.
- Oak and Ivy Museum provides a location for sharing community events and social gatherings.
- Oak and Ivy Museum supports community initiatives.
- Oak and Ivy Museum is inviting to people of all ages and backgrounds.

Dr. Bettye J. Williams
FOUNDER

**Contact Us**
Oak and Ivy Museum
P.O. Box 2435
Pine Bluff, AR 71613
(870) 536-3073
bjw1998@cablelynx.com

SKETCH by REED ARCHITECTURAL FIRM Pine Bluff, Arkansas

Taking its place on 3.6 acres, the museum is located at 5224 Highway 79 South,
Pine Bluff. Two miles south of Watson Chapel High School.

*Sketch of Oak and Ivy Museum by Reed Architectural Firm*

# The Founder of Oak and Ivy Museum

Oak and Ivy African American Museum and Cultural Center

*Bettye J. Williams, PhD, Educator*

Bettye J. Williams was born in Pine Bluff, the second daughter of the late Eunice and Dorothy Mae Willingham Williams of Bookman, Arkansas, in Grant County. Williams received formal schooling at Townsend Park High School, graduating in 1964. Having been the first Agricultural, Mechanical & Normal College (AM&N), now the University of Arkansas at Pine Bluff (UAPB) student-teacher to integrate the Little Rock Public School System, she completed the Bachelor of Science degree in English in 1968, and was honored with a Graduate Fellowship while desegregating the Graduate English Program at Pittsburgh State University in Kansas.

Williams started teaching at AM&N College in September 1969. In 1970, she earned a master of science degree in English at Pittsburgh State University. After teaching twenty years, she was selected a 1990 Indiana University of Pennsylvania (IUP) Graduate Scholar. From 1990 to 1993, she pursued a Doctor of Philosophy degree in American literature with concentrations in women's literature, African American literature, and the Western novel. In 1992, she was among ten African Americans in the United States to receive a $30,000 National Dissertation Fellowship to complete the PhD work. She is named in the *Cambridge Who's Who of World Achievement*, *International Who's Who of Contemporary Achievement*, and *Dictionary of Notable Women*. She has published chapters and articles in *African American Literature: A Biographical Bibliographical Study*; *CLA Journal*; *Oxford Companion to African American Literature*; *African American Literature, A Biographical and Bibliographical Study, 1745–1945*; *Cyclopedia of Literary Characters*, revised edition; *Masterplots II: Juvenile and Young Adult Literature*; *Magill's Guide to Science Fiction and Fantasy Literature*; *Arkansas Journal*; *Studies in the Humanities*; and *The Journal of the National Association of University Women*.

Travel is a way of gaining a deeper understanding of a country. As a part of the King Fahad Program for Middle East Studies at the University of Arkansas in Fayetteville in 1997, Williams was invited by the university to spend the summer in Saudi Arabia (Jeddah, Dhankran, and Riyadh) and Amman, Jordan. The preceding program was created by President William "Bill" Clinton and the country of Saudi Arabia. In 1998 and 2000 respectively, Williams was invited by the J. William Fulbright Foreign Scholarship Board to teach American literature in Zimbabwe (Africa) and Seville, Spain. As a UAPB faculty member participating in the Fulbright-Hayes Summer Abroad Program in 1999, she toured Israel and Jordan (Tel-Aviv, Jerusalem, the Old City of Jerusalem, Jericho, Nazareth, Cana, Tiberias, Cesarea, Bethlehem, Rehovot, Dimona, Ein Avdat, Eilat, Arad, and Amman). In March 2010, the trustees of the Oxford Round Table invited her to lecture on Zora Neale Hurston along with thirty-seven other speakers throughout the world. Traveling to Monrovia, Liberia, in February 2012, she assisted in chartering the first African branch of the National Association of University Women. Located in Harper City, Liberia, the branch is named the Maryland Harper City Branch. On July 15, 2012, she retired as a Professor and Interim Chair, Department of English, Theatre and Mass Communications at UAPB. After forty-three years of university teaching, she devotes her service and time to the nonprofit sector.

Williams' service to the community includes president, sectional director and national second vice president to the Pine Bluff Branch, the South Central Section, and the national organization of the National Association of University Women (1989–2014); vice president and president to the Pine Bluff Alumnae Chapter of Delta Sigma Theta Sorority (2004–10); the NAACP; the National Council of Negro Women; and New Town Missionary Baptist Church. On December 3, 2012, she became the founder and president of Pine Bluff's first Black museum—Oak and Ivy African American Museum and Cultural Center. The museum will honor past achievers and celebrate the rich legacy of African Americans in Pine Bluff, Jefferson County, and Arkansas.

*The Land*

# First Letter to Subscribers

## OAK AND IVY: AFRICAN AMERICAN MUSEUM AND CULTURAL CENTER

*Incorporated on December 3, 2012*
oakandivymuseum.com

5224 Highway 79 South
P. O. Box 2435
Pine Bluff, AR 71603

June 10, 2013

Bettye J. Williams, Ph.D.
Founder/Executive Director
(870) 536-3073
bjw1998@cablelynx.com

Dear Contributor:

Written by Michael Masser and Linda Creed and originally recorded by George Benson in 1977, "The Greatest Love of All" was popularized by successful singer, Whitney Houston. She sang "The Greatest Love of All" with a forceful directness that gave its message of self-worth an astounding vibrancy. The song became an international hit around 1986, topping the charts around the world. It spent three weeks at No 1 on the *Billboard Hot* 100 Chart. The lyrics describe struggle and great challenge. Yet in the midst of immediate perils and obstacles, the chronicler suggests being strong whether you succeed or fail.

"The Greatest Love of All" and *Oak and Ivy Museum* offer a compelling vision of African American creativity and pride, spiritual devotion, and cultural integrity–meshed smoothly. The mission of *Oak and Ivy Museum* is to collect, preserve, and teach the African American experience so that you never forget, and *the children* will have the tools they need to remember:

> *I believe the children are our future*
> *Teach them well and let them lead the way*
> *Show them all the beauty they possess inside*
> *Give them a sense of pride to make it easier*
> *Let the children's laughter remind us how we used to be.*

In its exhibitions and educational programs adapted for diverse age groups, *Oak and Ivy Museum* will provide context and perspective on the journey of African Americans in Pine Bluff–and the state of Arkansas. We want to break new ground by bringing stories to life that have not been adequately told.

The first clear record of African Americans in Arkansas is from 1721. A vast multitude arrived in the 1840s and 1850s from Mississippi, Alabama, Tennessee, South Carolina, and North Carolina. Although they were slaves, many escaped the hard labor of the fields through their resourcefulness, talent, and skills. They became craftsmen–creating frontier furniture, cast iron skillets, plows, and locks.

Before incorporation in 1839, Pine Bluff was Quapaw country, nestled by high, heavily forested bluffs overlooking the Arkansas River. The Quapaws signed away the land that became Jefferson County and moved West–some years later a few of them returned to the city.

Let's list a few African American pioneers. Born in Ohio in 1833, Joseph Carter Corbin was the most scholarly graduate of the 19th century. Migrating to Arkansas as a reporter for the *Arkansas Republican* and elected State Superintendent of Public Education, Corbin served as Chairman of the Board of Trustees of the Arkansas Industrial Institute (now the University of Arkansas). In the performance of duties, he recommended a college "for the education of the poor classes"and Branch Normal College (later A.M.& N., now the University of Arkansas at Pine Bluff) was founded. In 1875, Corbin became the founder and

(over please)

2

principal, remaining at the college until 1902. He was an active member of the Prince Hall Masons in Arkansas.

During the 1880s, ex-slave and wealthy Republican businessman, Wiley Jones, helped open the Colored Industrial Institute (later named St. Peter's School). By 1895, Jones had bought a saloon, collected race horses, accumulated a race track, started the first mule-drawn streetcar system (now known as the Pine Bluff Transit), and purchased land for a resort town called White Sulphur Springs (now known as Sulphur Springs). At the time of his death on December 7, 1904, Jones was the richest African American in Arkansas, with an estate worth more than $300,000. He is buried in his own cemetery west of Bellwood Cemetery (now known as Miller's Cemetery).

Other pioneers to remember and celebrate are William H. Zackary, who began teaching music in 1906 and retired 69 years later at the age of 95. With his horse-drawn carriage, Moses Offord started the first taxi in 1905. Chicago-born Nettie Hollis opened Pine Bluff's first beauty salon-cosmetology school in 1906 and operated the business for 40 years. In 1951, Janie Townsend was the first African American woman to have her own radio show. The preceding is amazing–and there are many more.

As a public, charitable, non-profit organization, *Oak and Ivy Museum* will open minds and eyes. Might I add. We are not building *Oak and Ivy Museum* to celebrate Black history solely for African Americans. Rather, this museum will be a place for all to see how the African American experience has affected and shaped the lives of everyone in Pine Bluff. It will be an important cultural addition to the Pine Bluff landscape.

What we do not have and need are the funds required to construct the building. We need to raise hundreds of thousands of dollars in private donations from friends, businesses, churches, and organizations–like you. Reed Architectural Firm of Pine Bluff will reveal the design concept to the public–this summer.

*Oak and Ivy Museum* is a tremendous opportunity. It is a tremendous challenge. And it is something Pine Bluff needs. Much work still remains to be done before we can open the museum in 2015. A four-acre tract of land has been acquired. Your gift helps raise the walls and the roof beams.

"The Greatest Love of All" will come alive to our *children* and *grandchildren*: . . . *Teach them well* . . . *Show them all the beauty they possess inside* . . . *Give them a sense of pride.* As a beacon of learning, *Oak and Ivy Museum* will engage *the children*, educate *the children*, and inspire *the children* with remembrance and understanding.

Join with others to see this dream become a reality. Thank you.

All the best,

*Bettye J. Williams*

Bettye J. Williams, Ph.D.
Founder/Executive Director

Bettye J. Williams

# First Public Program
Oak and Ivy Museum

THE PUBLIC PROGRAM
## OAK AND IVY
**African American Museum & Cultural Center**
Incorporated December 3, 2012

UAPB Business Support Incubator & Office Complex
615 South Main Street
Pine Bluff, AR 71601
Saturday, August 10, 2013
10:00 a.m. – 11:30 a.m.
Dr. Brenda F. Graham, Presiding
Melrose Park, IL

Opening Remarks
**Meditation**                   Reverend Ronald S. Laurent
Pastor, First Baptist Church, Holly Grove, AR

**Greetings / Proclamation**
The Honorable Debe Hollingsworth, Mayor of Pine Bluff
The Honorable Reverend Dr. Henry "Hank" Wilkins
The Honorable Senator Stephanie Flowers

**Images and Reflections of African Americans in Pine Bluff**
Mrs. Naomi N. Lawson
Mrs. Naomi L. Jolaoso

**Oak and Ivy Museum: The Mission and Vision**
Dr. Bettye J. Williams, Founder/Executive Director

**Oak and Ivy Museum: The Architectural Design**
Mr. Frederick H. Reed
*Member of the American Institute of Architects*
Reed Architectural Firm
Pine Bluff, Arkansas

Question & Answer Period
**Closing Prayer**                   Rev
Pastor, First Bap

REFRESHMENTS

The Mission and Vision
of *Oak and Ivy Museum*

Bettye J. Williams shared that *Oak and Ivy Museum* is a symbol of new life and new opportunities to grow and learn. Guests of the museum will be guided to a more revealing glimpse of the legacy of pioneering African Americans in Jefferson County and Pine Bluff. Historical presentations will be made with care and respect and in linkage with other institutions, including the home, the church, institutions of learning, and the community.

*Below:* A member of the American Institute of Architects, Frederick H. Reed is a celebrated architect in Pine Bluff, the county, and the state. He designed the Reynolds Building, among many others. To the invited guests at the occasion of the public program, his remarks were as follows: "The museum will occupy a little more than 13,000 square feet on a four-acre parcel of land, south of Watson Chapel High School, on U.S. Highway 79. The cost to construct the building is $2.5M."

(The Public Program and a man, Frederick H. Reed)

16

## THE GROUND BREAKING

### OAK AND IVY

**African American Museum & Cultural Center**
Incorporated December 3, 2012
5224 Highway 79 South
Pine Bluff, AR 71603
Saturday, August 10, 2013
1:00 p.m. – 2:30 p.m.

Ms. Janice L. Roberts, Presiding
Pine Bluff, AR

| | |
|---|---|
| Opening Remarks | |
| Invocation | Reverend Melvin G. Graves |
| | Pastor, New Town Baptist Church |
| Greetings / Proclamation | |
| The County Judge, The Honorable Dutch King | |
| The County Sheriff, The Honorable Gerald Robinson | |
| Special Recognitions | |
| Dr. Bettye J. Williams, Founder/Executive Director | |
| Musical Selection | Mrs. Glenda Foots |
| Address | Reverend Dr. L. K. Solomon |
| | Pine Bluff Pastor Emeritus and Author |
| Ground Breaking Litany | Led by Reverend Melvin G. Graves |
| | (see back of program) |
| Breaking of Ground | Led by Reverend Dr. L. K. Solomon |
| | (see back of program) |
| Musical Selection | Mrs. Glenda Foots |
| Closing Prayer | Reverend Melvin G. Graves |
| | Pastor, New Town Baptist Church |

## GROUND BREAKING LITANY

**LEADER:** "Lift up your heads, ye everlasting doors." We are here in honor and praise of God, in dedication of the site of Oak and Ivy: African American Museum and Cultural Center.

**PEOPLE:** Just as "the Lord builds up Jerusalem," so the Lord allows us to build and mark our witness in the state of Arkansas, in Pine Bluff/Jefferson County on 5224 Highway 79 South.

**LEADER:** The Lord has blessed us mightily and calls us to praise and worship. This museum shall promote the literary, historic, and artistic expressions of objects and documents in the collection.

**PEOPLE:** Gracious Lord, as we rededicate ourselves and come to break this ground to further the work of Oak and Ivy Museum, we do this in obedience, out of love, and in praise of Thee.

**LEADER:** The need for the Word in the world and building Christian community support our efforts today. In linkage, Oak and Ivy Museum will serve as a teaching resource to the community, state, and nation on African American religion, literature, music, anthropology, economics, and related fields.

**PEOPLE:** May we remain as enthusiastic as we are today throughout the construction and continuity of Oak and Ivy Museum.

**ALL:** As prophets and priests of old built altars to the glory of God, today we break ground to raise Oak and Ivy Museum. Let us do our part to build you up through word and deed as we witness to the world.

## THE GROUND BREAKING

**LEADER:** Today, we begin another chapter of our understanding of God's plan and will for Pine Bluff and Jefferson County. We are here to break the ground where we will construct Oak and Ivy: African American Museum and Cultural Center. We prayerfully anoint this ground as hallowed and sacred to the mission of the museum. May we be faithful to support the completion of this dream. In Jesus' name, we bless this ground and the mission of the museum.

*Turning the Sod*

**LEADER:** We have taken the first step toward the erection of this museum. May the blessing of God be evident throughout the entire building process.

The Ground Breaking Program

PINE BLUFF

# COMMERCIAL

*'First in Southeast Arkansas'*

SUPER SAVINGS

Inside Today's Paper ...
$16,589 in Circular Savings
$85.50 in Coupon Savings

SUNDAY, August 11, 2013 — 133rd Year, No. 99 — 24 Pages — $1.25

# New museum to showcase black history in Arkansas

By Michael S. Lee

Oak and Ivy is the title of the first volume of poetry by Paul Laurence Dunbar, considered to be the first black poet in the United States to gain national recognition and fittingly is also the name chosen for a new museum of Arkansas black history.

The official groundbreaking ceremony for the Oak and Ivy African American Museum & Cultural Center was held Saturday afternoon in Pine Bluff.

The brainchild of Bettye J. Williams, the museum will occupy a little more than 13,000 square feet on a four-acre parcel of land just south of Watson Chapel High School on U.S. 79. It is tentatively scheduled for completion by the end of 2014.

"When I went into this venture 15 years ago I didn't know that 2013 would be the year that construction began," Williams said during a Saturday morning public program about the new museum held at the University of Arkansas at Pine Bluff Business Support Incubator. "The museum is a symbol of new life and of new opportunities to grow and understand the legacy of pioneering blacks in Jefferson County and Pine Bluff. The mission of Oak and Ivy is to educate the public about African-American history in Pine Bluff."

Williams said the historical presentation will be done with care and respect and in linkage with other institutions including the home, the church, institutions of learning and the community.

"We will explore African-American history through music, anthropology, economics and in many other ways," Williams said. "Even though I spent 12 years teaching

*Please see MUSEUM on 7A*

## MUSEUM

(continued from Page 1A)

literature and rhetoric I will still be teaching at Oak and Ivy."

The morning program had the feel of a family reunion of sorts with several of Williams' relatives in attendance, including her sister Brenda F. Graham, who acted as the presiding officer.

"It is a blessing that is coming to Pine Bluff and Jefferson County with the Oak and Ivy African American Museum & Cultural Center," Graham said.

Rev. Ronald Laurent is the pastor of First Baptist Church in Holly Grove.

"I grew up on the west side of Pine Bluff across the highway," Laurent said. "It's called Blake Street now but it was the highway to us when we were growing up. We lived on dirt roads and had outside facilities but we had a sense of who we were and where we had come from. Family, school and church was all intertwined when we were growing up. It all came together. We

the native American tribes who lived here to the expansion of the western frontier to the Civil War," Flowers said. "Up until now the quilt of Arkansas and American history has been missing an important piece and that is the contributions of African-Americans. The Oak and Ivy museum will go a long way towards addressing this absence."

Pine Bluff Mayor Debe Hollingsworth read from an official proclamation marking Aug. 10 as Oak and Ivy African American Museum and Cultural Center Day in the city.

State Rep. Henry "Hank" Wilkins IV added his voice of support for the museum.

"I would like to express my thanks for Dr. Williams' vision," Wilkins said. "This will be a great addition to the culture and heritage of Pine Bluff."

Naomi L. Jolaoso provided a bit of living history by giving a brief

18

# Dedication of the Land
## Oak and Ivy Museum

*Top: Ground Breaking*: Rev./Dr. L. K. Solomon; The Honorable Dutch King, County Judge for Jefferson County; Rev. Ronald Laurent; The Honorable Stephanie Flowers, Esq., Arkansas State Senator; Kenneth Fisher; Dr. Brenda F. Graham; Valencia Fields; Frederick H. Reed, Architect; Dr. Bettye J. Williams, Founder; and Rev. Melvin G. Graves. Photo by Earnestine Grant, Pine Bluff.

*Seated: Dedication: Front row:* ___, ___, Janice L. Roberts; *Second row*: Peggy Tidmore-White; ReEvelyn Jones; *Third row*: Leroy Edwards, Sr.; Jewell M. Edwards, and Markeith Woods. Not shown are Representative from the Jefferson County Sheriff's Department, Glenda Foots, Marceinia Peeples, Robin Baylark, Zion Graham, Yvonne Humphrey, and Sharon Nicholson. Photo by Earnestine Grant, Pine Bluff.

# PINE BLUFF WELCOMES NEW MUSEUM

STORY MICHAEL LEE
PHOTOS WILLIAM HARVEY

Oak and Ivy is the title of the first volume of poetry by Paul Laurence Dunbar — considered to be the first black poet in the United States to gain national recognition — and fittingly is also the name chosen for a new museum of Arkansas black history.

The official groundbreaking ceremony for the Oak and Ivy African American Museum & Cultural Center was held recently in Pine Bluff.

The brainchild of Bettye J. Williams, the museum will occupy a little more than 13,000 square feet on a four-acre parcel of land just south of Watson Chapel High School on U.S. 79. It is tentatively scheduled for completion by the end of 2014.

"We will explore African-American history through music, anthropology, economics and in many other ways," Williams said. "Even though I spent 42 years teaching literature and rhetoric I will still be teaching at Oak and Ivy."

Top, Dr. Bettye J. Williams speaks about the new Oak and Ivy Museum.

Above, Peggy Tidmore-White, Mary and Michael Lynch.

Left, Rev. Ronald S. Laurent and Janice L. Roberts enjoy the event to celebrate the groundbreaking of the new museum..

*Top:* Dr. Bettye J. Williams holding the microphone at the first public program of *Oak and Ivy Museum*, Saturday, August 10, 2013, at the UAPB Business Support Incubator & Office Complex, Pine Bluff. Eminent speakers were (*back row*) The Honorable Reverend/Dr. Henry "Hank" Wilkins; Mr. Frederick H. Reed, Architect for *Oak and Ivy Museum*; (*second row*) Reverend/Pastor Ronald S. Laurent, First Baptist Church, Holly Grove, Arkansas; The Honorable Debe Hollingsworth, Mayor of Pine Bluff; and The Honorable Senator Stephanie Flowers, Esq.; *foreground:* Dr. Brenda F. Graham, Professor, School of Education, Concordia University, River Forest (Chicago), Illinois, *presiding. Courtesy, Sea Life Magazine* October 2013, p.37. Michael Lee, journalist, and William Harvey, photography.

## Allow Oak and Ivy Museum

to be your repository for recollections, reminiscences, memoirs, memories, group history, and collectibles.

| | | |
|---|---|---|
| | LETTERS & CORRESPONDENCES | |
| RESOLUTIONS DOCUMENTS YEARBOOKS ANNUALS CATALOGUES PROGRAMS | GREEK ORGANIZATIONS  Programs/Events Stored | CLASS PICTURES SCHOOL PICTURES  PHOTOS  ORIGINAL DRAWINGS  PAINTINGS |
| FACILITY for the STORAGE of  CHURCH HISTORY/PROGRAMS  ARCHIVAL SPACE for NON-PROFIT GROUPS & FAMILY HISTORY | NEWSPAPERS MAGAZINES JOURNALS PAMPLETS DISSERTATIONS | OTHERS |

# Exhibition

This museum will exhibit thousands of book titles, artifacts, documents, and portraits by and about the experiences of African Americans in Pine Bluff, Jefferson County, and the state of Arkansas. Oak and Ivy Museum will stand strong in Pine Bluff, creating an atmosphere for promoting the impressive history of the city.

*Stamps*

# Stamps

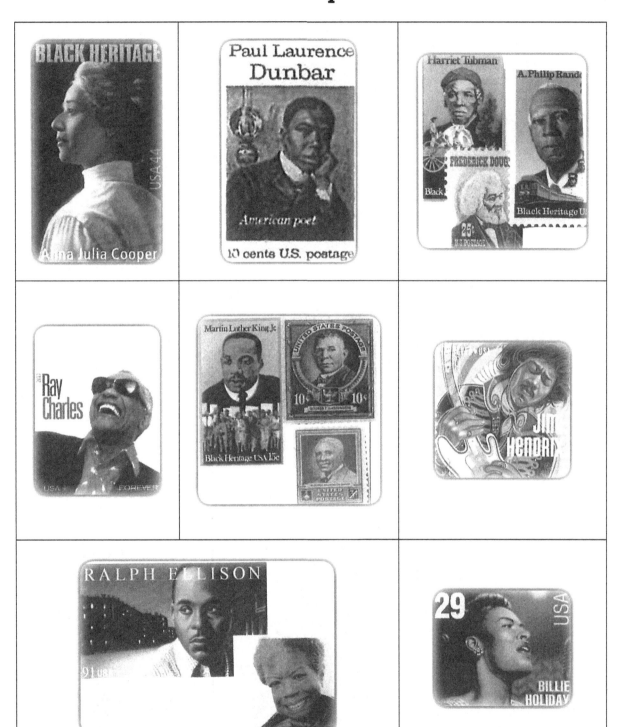

# Oak and Ivy Museum
## *Reading List*

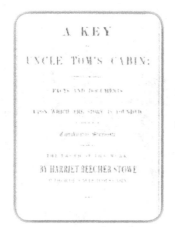

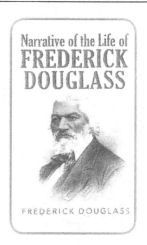

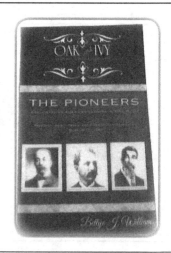

# Oak and Ivy Museum
## *Reading List*

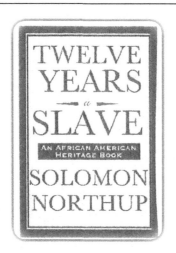

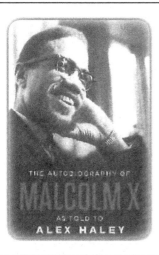

# Oak and Ivy Museum
## *Reading List*

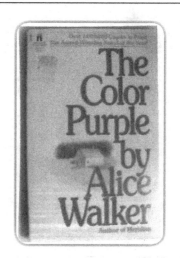

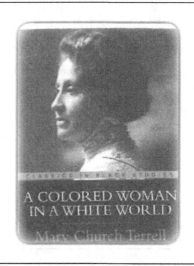

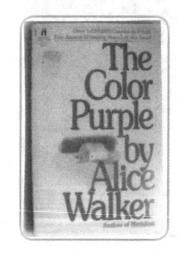

# Oak and Ivy Museum
## *Reading List*

# Oak and Ivy Museum
## *Reading List*

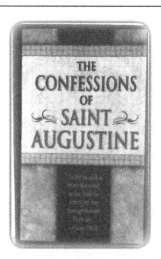

# Oak and Ivy Museum
*Reading List for Children*

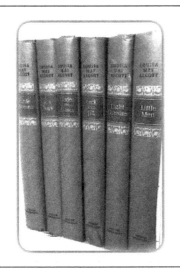

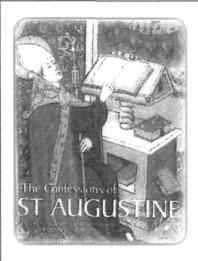

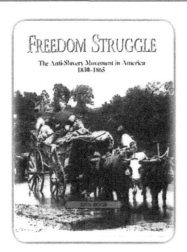

# Oak and Ivy Museum

## *List of Lois Lenski's Books for Children*

*Left to right*: Lois Lenski, Newberry Award-Winning author and illustrator of *Strawberry Girl*, wrote books about the South. These books appeal to children 8-12 years of old. Most of the books were published by the J. B. Lippincott Company of Philadelphia.

| | |
|---|---|
| *Houseboat Girl* | 1957 |
| *Strawberry Girl* | 1945 |
| *Judy's Journey* | 1955 |
| *Mama Hattie's Girl* | 1953 |
| *Judy's Journey* | 1955 |
| *Blue Ridge Billy* | 1946 |
| *Houseboat Girl* | 1957 |
| *We Live in the South* | 1952 |

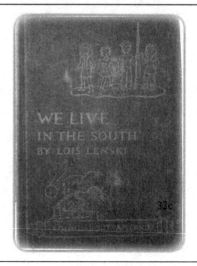

## Sewing Machines and Quilts

*Row 1, left to right*: Original Singer Treadle Sewing Machine that still sews, 1925 model. The Monkey Wrench quilt pattern, burgundy and pink. Quilted by Idell Williams Snowden, Natchitoches, Louisiana, 2014. *Row 2, left to right*: 1954 Singer foot pedal sewing machine, original heavy duty gear drive. Original Singer Treadle sewing machine head.

*Left:* Celebrated quilter, Serena Wilson, in conversation with Bettye J. Williams at the Arts and Science Center, Pine Bluff, Arkansas, November 11, 2004. Williams' mother, Dorothy Mae Willingham Williams, and maternal grandmother, Aislee Monts Willingham, were quilters. Aislee Willingham migrated to Grant County from South Carolina with her parents, Mr. & Mrs. Monts (Ada) during the first decade of the 20th century.

## *Black Family Album Quilt, 1854*

*Above*: This *Black Family Album Quilt* was stitched by Sarah Ann Wilson, New York or New Jersey, 1854. It is made of cotton, 85" x 100". Stephen Score Collection. Collection America Hurrah Antiques, New York City. Photographed by Schecter Lee.

This quilt was illustrated in the *Index of American Design*. It is an unusual quilt, for all the figures are executed in black fabric which indicates that they were probably members of the quilter's family. Unless the quilt is stitched by members of a *quilting bee* (commonly called community quilts), pictorial quilts are rare. In this quilt, each block is different, and each exemplifies a clean, folk-like design. All the figures face the viewer adds to its overall greatness. Motifs include three houses and many birds and animals, including a lion, a boar, a deer, a swan, and a fish in a pond. The familiar heart-and-hand motif is in the last block. The sashing between the applique' blocks is pieced. There is superior and intricate stitching in the quilt. The unique double-scalloped border with applique' details and the beautiful bias binding on each of the scallops are visible. The quilt is listed in *America's Glorious Quilts*, Dennis Duke and Deborah Harding, eds. Beaux Arts Editions. Hugh Lauder Levin Associates, Inc., China, 1987, p. 26.

## *Civil War Presentation Appliqué Album Quilt and Other Traditional Patterns*

*Above*: This *Civil War Presentation Applique' Album Quilt*, 1850, is of unknown origin. It is made of cotton, linen, and wool, 83" x 78". The Shelburne Museum. Shelburne, Vermont. Gift of Electra Havemeyer Webb. Photography courtesy of the Shelburne Museum. Each of the blocks in this presentation album quilt is signed by the makers. While many of the designs, such as the oak medallion, tulips, or rose wreath, are typical of popular nineteenth-century quilt patterns, others like the playing puppies or rooster were probably derived from commercial hooked rug designs. The vase of flowers was perhaps copied from a ladies' periodical or a decorator's book. The more original contributors to this quilt chose to commemorate a special person (the seated figure of Abraham Lincoln), an event (the Lincoln-Douglas Debate), or a place (their own home). The quilt is listed in *America's Glorious Quilts*, Dennis Duke and Deborah Harding, eds. Beaux Arts Editions. Hugh Lauder Levin Associates, Inc., China, 1987, p. 267.

*Above:* Using the *Round the World* pattern, which is a traditional diamond design, Idell Williams Snowden, Natchitoches, Louisiana, pieced this polyester quilt for Bettye J. Williams in 2014. Polyester fabric was popular in the 1950-1970s for both clothes and quilts. Photographer, Bettye J. Williams.

*Memories and Collectibles*

*Above*: An anatomically-correct doll, dressed in a romper dress attire with matching bonnet designed and made by Willie Mae Warfield, Pine Bluff, August 2001; popular between 1948-1957, a McCoy brand, Hattie McDaniel "Aunt Jemima" Cookie jar—purchased in Pine Bluff, on December 19, 2006, after 25 years of searching for one, $89, original; *below*: one-of-a-kind carnival glass swag lamp made into a desk lamp; and popular costume jewelry on a decorative dowel from San Jose Los Cabos, Mexico.

*Below:* Made entirely of cotton more than 160 years ago, this pre-Civil War quilt belonged to a Pine Bluff resident who wanted her family member's quilt saved for future generations to enjoy. The pattern is unknown. Purchased in 2015 by Bettye J. Williams. Photographer, Bettye J. Williams.

## *Memorabilia*

*Top left:* Mammy and Butler artifacts with a watermelon and other Black artifacts; a bejeweled oil lamp; three vintage watches—the middle Swiss watch was won by Dorothy M. Williams at a Rabbit Foot Show, at Hestand Stadium in September 1955. *Row 2:* three different vintage smoothing irons; lye soap made with lard, water, and lye. *Row 3:* a lovely, embroidered purse and an appealing vintage lizard handbag.

## *Memories and Collectibles*

*Top Row, left to right:* vintage 1940s Black clowns, salt and pepper shakers, teapot shaped; an anatomically correct doll, dressed in a christening attire designed and made by Willie Mae Warfield, Pine Bluff, August 2001; *below*: 1920s Chesterfield cigarette package; corn whiskey in a hand-made corn cob basket trimmed with corn; vintage manual typewriter with original ribbon and documents; vintage Prince

Albert crimp cut, long burning pipe and cigar tobacco tin can; two vintage lawn jockeys concrete statues with lantern holders; European colonists and slaves from Africa introduced the watermelon to the New World—the fruit is thought to have originated in southern or tropical Africa; and assorted tea sets—*Blue Garland* pattern, made in Bavaria, Germany, by Johann Haviland; Hertel Jacob pattern from Bavaria, Germany, and a tea set from Poland.

## *Furniture Collectibles*

*Column 1, left to right:* 1905 antique upright mahogany, three pedal piano; maple wood roll top desk; *Column 2, left to right:* mahogany Duncan Phyfe beveled glass China cabinet; antique Victorian Seth Thomas movement shelf clock that retains original glass with gold painted design featuring the pendulum under an arch, dated 1900—clock is a working one which chimes on the hour and the half hour; antique English oak, beveled mirror carved tree stand/coat rack with drawer and shelf. *Column 3, left to right:* antique Wernicke drawer oak library card index file cabinet.

# Coins

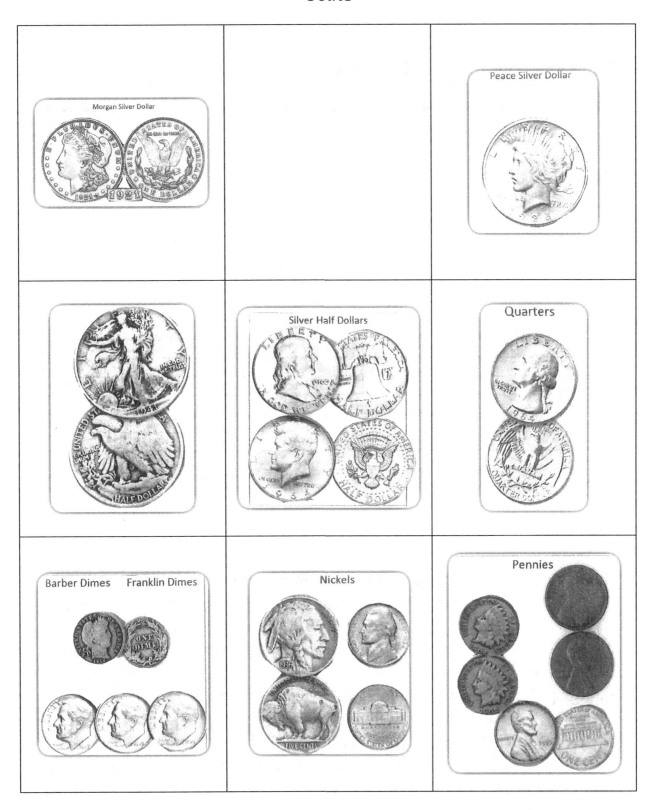

# Reflections on the Early Years [1833-1925]

## Population Statistics

| Year | State of Arkansas Population[8] | Arkansas Slave Population[9] | Jefferson County Population[10] | Jefferson County Slave Population[11] | Pine Bluff Population[12] | Pine Bluff Free Slaves[13] |
|---|---|---|---|---|---|---|
| 1810 | 1,062 | 188 | | | | |
| 1820 | 14,273 | 1,617 | | | | |
| 1830 | 30,388 | 4,576 | | | | 141 |
| 1840 | 97,574 | 19,935 | 2,566 | 1,010 | | 465 |
| 1850 | 209,897 | 47,100 | 5,834 | 2,621 | 460 | 608 |
| 1860 | 435,450 | 111,115 | 14,971 | 7,147 | 1,396 | 144 |
| 1870 | 484,471 | | | | 2,081 | |
| 1880 | 802,525 | | | | 3,203 | |
| 1890 | 1,128,211 | | | | 9,952 | |
| 1900 | | | | | 11,496 | |
| 1910 | | | | | 15,102 | |
| 1920 | | | | | 19,280 | |
| 1930 | | | | | 20,760 | |

In 1832, Pine Bluff became the county seat of Jefferson. The land in the county was developed as large cotton plantations, with fronts on the river for transportation. Plantations were dependent on the labor of enslaved African Americans, who comprised the majority of the population in the county well before the Civil War. As the Arkansas enslaved population grew, slaves also constituted a larger and larger portion of the total population, growing from 11 percent in 1820 to 25 percent by 1860. In 1889, Jefferson County included Altheimer, Bankhead, Cornerstone, Dexter, Double Wells, English, Fairfield, Faith, Garretson's Landing, Greely, Greenback, Grier, Humphrey, Jefferson, Kearney, Linwood, Locust Cottage, Macon, Madding, New Gascony, Noble's Lake, Nubia, Pastoria, Pine Bluff, Plum Bayou, Rainey, Red Bluff, Redfield, Rob Roy, Sleeth, Swan

Lake, Toronto, Wabbaseka, and Williamette.[14] Cities, towns, and unincorporated areas in Jefferson County currently are: Pine Bluff, White Hall, Sulphur Springs, Redfield, Jefferson, Altheimer, Wabbaseka, Humphrey, Sherrill, Ferda, Lake Dick, and Midway.

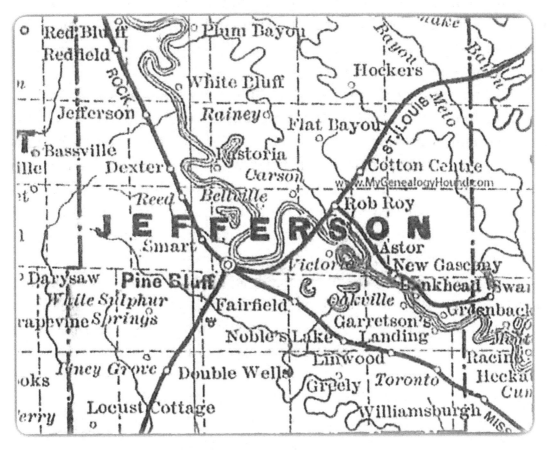

*Map of Jefferson County*

## SLAVERY IN ARKANSAS AND JEFFERSON COUNTY

In Arkansas, slaveholding and cotton plantation were especially concentrated in the fertile river bottom lands of eastern Arkansas' Mississippi River Delta and in southern Arkansas' Gulf Coastal Plain, which together held 74 percent of the state's enslaved population by1860. The Federal Census of 1860 shows 12,131 slaves (11 percent) belonged to White families owning from one to four slaves. More than fifty-one thousand slaves (46 percent) worked on large estates owned by the 9 percent of Arkansas slaveholders, who possessed from twenty-five to over five hundred slaves. In this latter group, slaves had less direct contact with their owners, and the disparity in living conditions was much greater.[15] On the large plantations, where enslaved people had more autonomy, slave communities began to develop and flourished. African tribal-influenced religious rites were observed as well as traditional folk medicine, and West African folk stories involving animals such as "Brer Rabbit" and "Tar Baby." Plantation enslaved communities functioned as extended families. In the 1870s, Arkansas instituted a system of slave patrols to prevent slaves from wandering from their plantations without a pass.

Held involuntarily as property by slave owners who controlled their labor and freedom, people of African ancestry drove the Arkansas plantation economy until long after the Civil War. White settlers who moved into Arkansas brought enslaved property with them to work the area's rich lands, and slavery became an integral part of local life. One in four White Arkansans either owned slaves or lived in families that did. Many White settlers benefited from slavery, as leasing slaves was not an uncommon practice in Arkansas and the South. However, most slave owners possessed only a few slaves. By law, a slave was subject to all laws involving personal property. Like cattle, horses, or other types of possessions, slaves formed part of the owner's estate. This meant slaves had no legal identity of their own, making it impossible for them to engage in contractual relations for labor, business, or even marriage. Heirs inherited slaves upon an owner's death.[16] Although most Arkansas slaves lived in rural areas on farms or plantations, there were some urban slaves. They were used simply as help: cooks, maids, nurses, houseboys, gardeners, stable boys, and coachmen.[17]

Enslaved people were always controlled. Throughout the South, laws provided for punishment of slave who broke laws. Called "Black Codes," these laws restricted slave movement, required passes to leave the home plantation, limited the rights of slaves to assembly, and prohibited their possession of firearms. An 1825 law created the slave patrol, which enforced and policed the countryside punishing slaves found off farms or plantations without a pass. The slave patrol searched for runaways and watched for slave revolts. The majority of slaves did not see their condition as benevolent. Newspaper advertisements placed by owners indicate the dissatisfaction of slaves with their condition. Whipped for impudence, disobedience, and a refusal to work, many Arkansas slaves made attempts to escape, and some were successful.

*Cotton Field and Bales of Cotton*

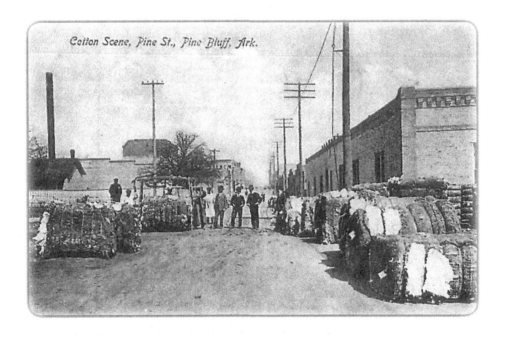

SCENE AT PINE BLUFF STATION, ARKANSAS.—[From a Sketch by H. J. Lewis.]

*Bales of Cotton and Cotton Pickers*

*Top:* Bales of cotton in Pine Bluff.
*Bottom:* In the 1950s, cotton pickers leaving Pine Bluff traveling by truck across the old bridge on the Arkansas River to pick cotton in the towns of Sherrill, Altheimer, and Wabbaseka.

## NAMES AND NAMING OF SLAVES

African Americans have always cared about their names.[18] Enslaved mothers (or both parents) named their own children although in numerous instances slave owners took the liberty. Slaves refused to name their children until the ninth day after birth. Slaves had surnames, and they usually identified themselves by the name of the first owner. Known only by their given name, the surname was infrequently used and rarely recorded. Name connections joined African American families with their forebears. Names with clear African origins are: Affy, Ah-affoe, Quaco, Quack, Quashee, Squash, Kofi, Phiba, Cudjo, Juba, and Sethe. Although they never wholly disappeared, African names receded after the turn of the nineteenth century. Even though most slaves could not read, they often wanted to see their names written down in the family Bible. Besides Adam and Eve, many were given the names of Old and New Testament patriarchs, prophets, kings, and disciples, such as: Abram, Isaac, Israel, Moses, Joshua, Samuel, Elijah, Elisha, Amos, Daniel, David, Solomon, Matthew, Mark, Luke, Peter, Simon, Thomas, Andrew, John, Stephen, Paul, James, and Timothy. Some slave women were called: Miriam, Sarah, Hagar, Esther, Ruth, Rebecca, Rachel, Leah, Mary, Elizabeth, and Lydia. Imposed on slave children by their owner were classical names. Enslaved parents would Africanize such Latin names as Caesar, Hercules, Cato, Bacchus, Scipio, Hector, and Jupiter. The Latin names did not survive the Civil War. Many other naming methods can be listed: (1) attributions for the pleasure of the owner; (2) literary characters; (3) gemstones; (4) flowers; (5) day, month, location designations; (6) attributions such as "friendly," or "patience" as in Sojourner Truth; (7) identified beyond their given name such as Mammy, Ole Mammy, "aunt" (older female slave), "uncle" (older male slave), and "boy." A slave male parent was never called "father." Prior to the Civil War, White southerners could not address any African American by the title Mr. or Mrs. Enslaved people were not permitted to say *sister* or *brother* to each other.

After the Civil War, slaves took surnames or openly announced those they already had. They called those names "entitles." Seeking friendship and protection "in a dangerous world," as they called the period, many adopted their master's surname or that of a local notable. In such cases, the desire was to capitalize on the close connection the name suggested.

Newly freed men took particular surnames to establish a historical link with their own family. Or they went back in time to take the name of the first master they ever had or the first whom they could remember as having been a decent man. In some cases, nationalistic names such as Washington, Lincoln, and Grant were borrowed. Many chose names that celebrated their new status, such as Freeman, Freeland, and Justice. Others, following an ancient European tradition, borrowed surnames from their crafts, trades, skills, surroundings, appearances, and personalities. Carter was a drayman; Mason, a bricklayer; Green, a gardener; Bishop a preacher; Cook, a domestic; Wheeler, a wheelwright; and Taylor, a tailor. Some identified themselves by their pigment and origin and took names like Brown, Coal, Africa, and Guinea. Surnames reflected attempts for respectability. In addressing Whites whom they knew intimately, such as those for whom they worked, African Americans called them by the first name but only if it was preceded by Mister, Missus, or Miss as in "Yes, suh, Mister William" or "Yes, ma'am, Miss Caroline."

## SLAVE SALES

Congress outlawed the International Slave Trade in 1807. In the South, economic benefits almost always outweighed considerations of family ties for landowners. Because of the high premium placed on male slaves, Black men were the most likely to be parted from their families. Many slave owners considered the basic family unit to be comprised of mother and children; thus, husbands and fathers could be and were easily replaced. Many a slave woman was assigned a new husband by her master. Male children were also frequently taken from slave mothers. An enslaved mother and her daughter were the least likely to be disturbed through a sale. Study shows that more than 35 percent of marriages were dissolved by masters as a result of slaves being sold away from the family home. [19] Yet, the possibility of separation was an ever-present threat to every member of a slave family. When a master died, his slaves might be distributed among his heirs or sold off to multiple buyers. When a planter's child was born or married, he or she might receive the gift of a Black attendant. Mothers were taken from their own children to nurse the offspring of their master. The preceding mothers were called "wet nurses." Single mothers and children necessitated communal parenting, focused on maternal figures. Older women no longer useful as field hands—called "aunts" or "grannies"—often cared for children too young to work the fields. Slaves took risks to maintain relationships, sneaking away to visit relatives on neighboring plantations. They faced abuse in order to protect their kin, and they accepted responsibility for the welfare of children who were not their own. Extended families offered physical and emotional support. After *Emancipation*, newly freed slaves traveled the roads of the South and placed advertisements in newspapers in efforts to reunite with family members.

Uncle Mark Thrash
Born near Richmond, Va. Dec. 25, 1820. Died Dec 17, 1943 at his residence in Chickamauga National Military Park only 8 days before his 123rd. birthday. He was married 5 times and the father of 29 children. Coat shown was presented to him by General Grant.

*Uncle Mark Thrash*

## SLAVE MARRIAGES

Marriage was a legal contract. Enslaved people could not legally marry. State laws considered them property and commodities, not legal persons who could enter into contracts. Slave marriages had neither legal standing nor protection from the abuses and restrictions imposed on slaves by owners. Until 1865, when slavery ended in the United States, African

Americans could not legally marry.[20] As they could do nothing without the consent of their owners, slaves had to get permission to marry. Most planters encouraged their slaves to marry. It was believed that married men were less likely to be rebellious or to run away.[21] Some owners assigned partners, forcing people into relationships they could not have chosen for themselves. Couples who resided on different plantations were allowed to visit only with the consent of their owners.

If a slave man or woman wished to marry, a party would be arranged some Saturday night among the slaves in the quarters. Slaves generally married without the benefit of clergy. The marriage ceremony in most cases consisted of the slaves simply getting the master's permission and moving into a cabin together. The ritual consisted of the pair jumping over a stick/broom. However, formal ceremonies were generally observed for house servants. In such cases, a white minister or a Black plantation preacher performed the ceremony, and a large feast and dance in the quarters followed, honoring the couple. The groom wore ordinary clothes. The bride wore the cast-off clothes of the mistress or clothes made by other slaves. The ceremony could/did include "jumping the broom." When a slave married someone from another plantation, the master of the wife owned all the children.[22] If no children were born within a year or so, the wife was sold.[23] It was in the interest of plantation owners for women to have children. Childbearing started around the age of thirteen, and by the age of twenty, the women slaves would be expected to have four or five children.

*An enslaved couple*

## HEALTH OF SLAVES

While working on plantations, many slaves faced serious health problems. Improper nutrition, unsanitary living conditions, and excessive labor made them more susceptible to diseases than their masters. The calories in the diet of a slave were sufficient to maintain the slave's body weight and normal health. The average daily intake of an adult slave was between twenty-five hundred to three thousand calories. In terms of nutrition, the diet was not adequate. Although their diet included bread, vegetables, fruits, and meats (squirrels, rabbits, raccoons), more than four-fifths of their calories came from sweet potatoes, corn, cornbread, sorghum, and pork (bacon). This diet was low in iron and important vitamins. Intestinal diseases were also problems for the slaves. Diseases such as anemia (due to inadequate iron) and rickets (inadequate vitamin D) were caused by malnutrition. Human excretions in the water supply caused cholera, diarrhea, typhoid, tuberculosis, influenza, and hepatitis.

Enslaved people died from diseases such as tuberculosis, pneumonia, typhoid fever, and diarrheal diseases, which gained a foothold in weakened and undernourished bodies and had their roots in filth and poverty. For a long time, White indifference and Black powerlessness crippled efforts to improve the conditions breeding disease in Black enclaves. Not all but many White officials preferred to view the disproportionate death rates of Blacks as confirmation of the biological and moral inferiority of African Americans. [24]

Owners often tried to cure their ill slaves before they sent the slaves to a doctor. Planters wishing to save money relied on their own self-taught skills and the help of their wives to address the health care needs of slaves. Some of the enslaved developed or retained from African heritage their own brand of care, complete with special remedies, medical practitioners, and rituals. A slave who became ill meant loss of working time or death, an even greater loss. Given the cost of slaves and their importance to plantation economics, planters organized slave hospitals to treat their serious health problems. [25]

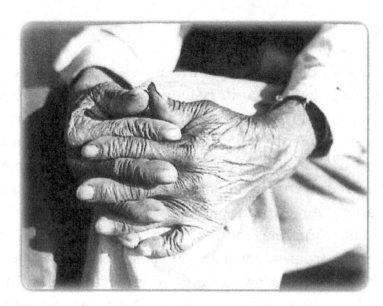

*Hand of a Worker*

## Negro Spirituals: Slave Songs

African American spirituals, also known as *Negro Spirituals*, were a familiar part of the home and worship worlds of slaves. These spirituals or songs related to personal experiences. They can be categorized as plantation songs, sorrow songs, jubilee songs, liberation songs, or protest songs. They emerged from a mix of brutal conditions on plantations and the "call and response chant" of the African culture. Originating during the slavery years in the United States [1600–1870], the songs (1) expressed a yearning for a better life; (2) expressed identification with biblical patriarchs; (3) named the slave owner's deceit and hypocrisy; (4) announced the need for a closer walk with God; (5) identified Satan's treachery; (6) proclaimed the prospect for heaven; and (7) expressed hope for the future. Love, grace, mercy, judgment, death, and eternal life were among the themes embedded in the songs. They reveal the slave's struggle for freedom and survival.

| Negro Spirituals | Negro Spirituals |
| --- | --- |
| "Deep River" | "Sometimes I Feel Like a Motherless Child" |
| "O Peter, Go Ring Dem Bells" | "The Lonesome Valley" |
| "Listen to the Lambs" | "Swing Low, Sweet Chariot" |
| "I'm a Trav'ling to the Grave" | "Go Down, Moses" |
| "It's a Me, O Lord Standin' in the Need of Prayer" | "Steal Away" |

| | |
|---|---|
| "My Way's Cloudy" | "Hard Trials" |
| "Heav'n, Heav'n Goin' to Shout All over God's Heav'n" | "I Don't Feel No-Ways Tired" |
| "Nobody Knows the Trouble I've Had" | "Ev'ry Time I Feel the Spirit" |
| "I'm a Rolling" | "Wait Till I Put on My Crown" |
| "Jesus on the Waterside" | "Didn't My Lord Deliver Daniel" |
| "Roll, Jordan, Roll" | "Wrestle on, Jacob" |
| "I've Been in the Storm So Long" | "I Want to Be Ready" ("Walk in Jerusalem Just Like John") |
| "My Way's Cloudy" | "The Gospel Train" |

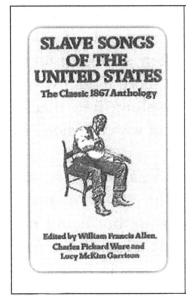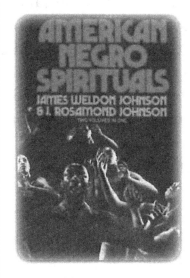

*Negro Spirituals*

## "FREE PEOPLE OF COLOR"

At first, "Free People of Color" (also called free Blacks) referred to persons of mixed African and European descent who were not enslaved. They often achieved education and some measure of wealth. Throughout the slave societies of the Americas [the Caribbean, South American slave societies, and New Orleans with the southern area of Louisiana], some White males took advantage of the power relationship to use female slaves sexually. Sometimes this latter group had extended relationships of concubinage. [26] Some European fathers might acknowledge the concubinage and their children. Some were common-law marriages of affection. Slaveholders were more likely to free their mixed-race children of these relationships than they were to free other slaves. They also sometimes freed the enslaved

51

women who were their concubines. Masters might free their slaves for a variety of reasons, but the most common was family relationships between masters and slave. Slaves also achieved their freedom by purchasing it. Some masters hired out their slaves and allowed them to keep a portion of their earnings. From money saved, slaves did buy their freedom. Relatives already freed purchased the freedom of another. A few slave owners freed slaves who revealed slave conspiracies or uprisings.

Many people living as free did not have formal liberty papers. Many times they were runaways who hid out in towns among "free people of color." They maintained a low profile. Yet, they were always at risk of losing their freedom. Southern law allowed jailers to sell "free people of color" if they could not prove their freedom. Most "free people of color" were women and were light-skinned. Free Blacks often secretly taught urban slaves to read and write, as urban slaves had more mobility and less supervision than slaves on plantations. City-dwelling free Blacks worked to buy the freedom of family members, many of whom resided in rural Arkansas. [27]

The number of "free people of color" in Arkansas was always small. They were viewed with suspicion and distrust by the White majority. "Free people of color" were permitted to own real estate but could not vote or testify against White people in the courts. Only a handful of free Blacks owned slaves. The number of "free people of color" in Pine Bluff before the Civil War was small, reaching a maximum of 608 in 1850; two-thirds were mulattoes, suggesting blood ties to the Whites who manumitted them. Most Arkansas free Blacks lived in rural areas, notably Marion County.

Arkansas adopted a law in 1842 prohibiting the immigration of any additional "free people of color" into the state after March 1, 1843. Mounting tensions during the 1850s led to the enactment of a measure in 1859 expelling all free Blacks over the age of twenty-one years from Arkansas. Those remaining after January 1, 1860, would be sold into slavery.[28] The Federal Census of 1860 disclosed 144 free Blacks still lived in Arkansas.

## THE REPUBLICAN PARTY OF THE NINETEENTH CENTURY

The Republican Party emerged in 1854, to combat the Kansas-Nebraska Act, which threatened to extend slavery into these territories. The party was pro-business, supported banks, the gold standard, railroads, and high tariffs to protect factory workers—thereby growing industry faster. The party stood against the extension of slavery and for slavery's abolition. Supporters of the party were Northern White Protestants, businessmen, small-business owners, professionals, factory workers, farmers, and Blacks. The Republican Party had almost no presence in the South.

By 1858, the Republican Party had enlisted former Whigs and former Free Soil Democrats to form majorities in nearly every Northern state. With the election of Abraham Lincoln in 1860 and the party's success in guiding the Union to victory and abolishing slavery, the Republican Party came to dominate the national political scene until 1932. In 1863, President Lincoln signed the *Emancipation Proclamation*, which declared slaves in rebelling states to be "forever free" and welcomed them to join the Union's Army and Navy. Because of President Lincoln's leadership and the Republican Party's stand in the abolition of slavery, the party is sometimes referred to as the "Party of Lincoln."

One of the era's [1870s] most heated debates was the question of party affiliation. Although practically all Black voters voted the Republican ticket throughout Reconstruction, by the 1880s, many were disillusioned with the Republican Party. With radical Republicans retiring or dying, the party appeared to have sold its antislavery soul in the interest of big business. Some African Americans changed parties.[29] By 1900, Blacks were depoliticized—and disfranchisement was in motion.

## Pine Bluff Republican Party Representatives

*Left:* Ferdinand Havis. *Right*: John Gray Lucas. Both were active in the Republican Party in Pine Bluff and Arkansas. Havis was the Arkansas representative to the National Republican Convention several consecutive years.

## THE CIVIL WAR

In the words of President Abraham Lincoln, the Civil War brought to America "a new birth of freedom." Some 650,000 men died in the Civil War, which included 260,000 Confederates, more than one-fifth of the adult male population in the South. At the war's outset, the Lincoln administration insisted that restoring the Union was its only purpose. But slaves by the thousands abandoned plantations and traveled to Union lines. It was at this time that the President made the slavery issue a war aim—a decision announced in the *Emancipation Proclamation* of January 1863. The *Emancipation Proclamation* authorized the enlistment of African American soldiers.

No African American actually fought for the Confederate States of America. Slaves were sometimes used to help construct earthworks or other military fortifications and were used as cooks, or as servants to Confederate officers, but they were not permitted to enlist. The Confederacy was in opposition to slaves bearing arms and encouraged those serving under their command to treat "armed Negroes and their officers as runaway and insurrectionists."

Throughout the Civil War, over five thousand (an exact number cannot be determined) former slaves in Arkansas joined the Union Army. They escaped bondage and made their way to Union Army encampments. Perhaps thousands died from malnutrition and disease in fetid, unsanitary, hastily constructed "shanty towns" and settlements. Owners of slaves could draft one-fifth of the slaves to work for the government. For the Union cause, slaves did not engage in battle, for they were not given weapons. They were used to cook, clear roads, drive wagons, and build structures.

In Jefferson County, Pine Bluff came to serve as a Union stronghold. The Battle of Pine Bluff was fought on October 25, 1863, around eight o'clock in the morning. Colonel Powell Clayton sent a company of cavalry toward Princeton Pike, which ran into Confederate General John S. Marmaduke's men advancing. Marmaduke led twenty-five hundred men in an attack on 550 Federal troops under the command of Clayton. Protecting the court square and fighting from behind a breastwork of cotton bales erected by three hundred slaves, Clayton warded off the Rebels for five hours. James R. Talbot, superintendent of contrabands for the Union Army, credits the former slaves with courageous action:

> None of them had ever before seen a battle, and the facility with which they labored and the manly efforts put forth to aid in holding the place excelled my highest expectations, and deserves the applause of their country and the gratitude of the soldiers.[30]

The Confederacy, under a flag of truce, came forward demanding surrender. Marmaduke withdrew rather than risk heavy losses. Clayton slowly retreated back into Pine Bluff. The Confederate forces were repulsed, leaving Pine Bluff in Union hand. After failing to take the square by force, Marmaduke's soldiers attempted to burn out the Union forces. A number of stores and other buildings were burned along with the bulk of the Federal army's supplies during the battle. Although no fierce fighting took place in Pine Bluff during the Civil War, the four-year conflict badly hurt the town. It rebounded quickly, and improved means of transportation to the fertile agriculture and timbered area during the 1870s to the 1890s brought about a remarkable increase in population, which stood at 11,496 by 1900.

By the end of the Civil War, some two hundred thousand African American soldiers served in the Union army and navy. Leaving the plantation in 1865, many newly freed persons had little more than their freedom. Some were given a wagon and mule team, furniture, and "sacks of spare ribs and backbones." New freedmen reunited families separated under slavery, established their own churches and schools, sought economy autonomy, and demanded equal and political rights. What most wanted was land for their families, a church to attend, and a school to educate the children. Even as enslaved people, African Americans maintained strong family ties. Slave marriages had no legal standing. After the Civil War, tens of thousands of the newly freed legalized their marriage unions before the army, the Freedmen's Bureau, and the local government. Many former slaves believed that their years of free labor gave them a claim to land. "Forty acres and a mule" became their cry.

Whites were reluctant to sell to African Americans, and the federal government's decision was not to redistribute land in the South. Only a small percentage of freedmen became landowners. Most rented individual plots of land or worked for wages on White-owned plantations. The system was called "sharecropping," which dominated Arkansas and the South for generations. Both White and African American farmers came to depend on local merchants for credit. A cycle of debt ensured, and the promise of economic independence faded for the Black farmer. Monthly wages for African Americans were only $10 for men and $5 for women in 1866. Even these wages were not low enough to suit some Whites, and Blacks all over the South were arrested for minor offenses and bound out as apprentices for nominal fees.

Founded in Syracuse, New York, in 1846, the American Missionary Association (AMA) was a nondenominational abolitionist society dedicated to providing education and political rights to African Americans. The AMA founded more than five hundred schools and colleges for the freedmen of the South during and after the Civil War, spending more money for that purpose than the Freedmen's Bureau of the federal government. In Arkansas, the AMA focused its efforts on providing education to freed men and women, seeking to train them to survive in the antebellum South. Prior to the Civil War, the AMA worked with the Freedmen's Aid Society to promote the abolitionist cause, refusing to allow slaveholders as members or to accept funds from unknown sources. As slaves were freed during the Civil War, the AMA altered its mission to making provisions for them. More than five hundred churches and schools were set up by the AMA to help acculturate the newly freed slaves. Churches and most of the schools were initially led by White men and women (more information on the AMA in the school section of this book). [31]

*Bales of Cotton in Pine Bluff*

*Above*: Map of Free and Slave States in the United States and Arkansas. This is an original 1857 Map of the United States showing the Free and Slave States. The dark green states are the Free States. The light green are the Free "Territories," which were not yet states. The red states were Slave Importing States, and the pink states were Slave States that exported slaves. *Below*: Map showing African American percentage of the population in each county in Arkansas as of 2010. Percentages in red indicate that the county has a higher percentage of African Americans than the statewide average of 15.4 percent. All statistics are U. S. Census Bureau figures. Map created by Mike Keckhover. *Courtesy of Encyclopedia of Arkansas.*

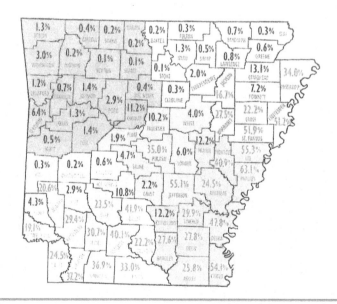

*Map of Free and Slave States and Blacks in Arkansas: 2012*

## RESOLUTIONS

—— PASSED BY THE ——

# CONVENTION OF THE PEOPLE OF ARKANSAS,

On the 20th day of March, 1861.

We, the people of the State of Arkansas, in convention assembled, in view of the unfortunate and distracted condition of our once happy and prosperous country, and of the alarming dissensions existing between the northern and southern sections thereof, and desiring that a fair and equitable adjustment of the same may be made, do hereby declare the following to be just causes of complaint on the part of the people of the southern States against their brethren of the northern, or non-slaveholding States.

1. The people of the northern States have organized a political party, purely sectional in its character; the central and controlling idea of which is hostility to the institution of African slavery, as it exists in the south ern States, and that party has elected a President and Vice President of the United States, pledged to administer the government upon principles inconsistent with the rights, and subversive of the interests of the people of the southern States.

2. They have denied to the people of the southern States the right to an equal participation in the benefits of the common territories of the Union by refusing them the same protection to their slave property therein that is afforded to other property, and by declaring that no more slave states shall be admitted into the Union. They have by their prominent men and leaders, declared the doctrine of the irrepressible conflict, or the assertion of the principle that the institution of slavery is incompatible with freedom, and that both cannot exist at once, that this continent must be wholly free or wholly slave. They have, in one or more instances, refused to surrender negro thieves to the constitutional demand of the constituted authority of a sovereign State.

3. They have declared that Congress possesses, under the constitution, and ought to exercise, the power to abolish slavery in the territories, in the District of Columbia, and in the forts, arsenals and dock-yards of the United States, within the limits of the slaveholding States.

4. They have, in disregard of their constitutional obligations, obstructed the faithful execution of the fugitive slave laws by enactments of their State legislatures.

5. They have denied the citizens of southern States the right of transit through non-slaveholding States with their slaves, and the right to hold them while temporarily sojourning therein.

To redress the grievances hereinbefore complained of, and as a means of restoring harmony and fraternal good will between the people of all the states, the following amendments to the constitution of the United States are proposed:

1. The President and Vice President of the United States shall each be chosen alternately from a slaveholding and non-slaveholding state—but, in no case, shall both be chosen from slaveholding or non-slaveholding states.

2. In all the territory of the United States now held, or which may hereafter be acquired, situate north of latitude 36 deg. 30 min., slavery, or involuntary servitude, except as a punishment for crime, is prohibited while such territory shall remain under territorial government. In all the territory now held, or which may hereafter be acquired, south of said line of latitude, slavery of the African race is hereby recognized as existing, and shall not be interfered with by Congress, but shall be protected as property by all the departments of the territorial government during its continuance. And when any territory, north or south of said line, within such boundaries as Congress may prescribe, shall contain the population requisite for a member of Congress, according to the then federal ratio of representation of the people of the United States, it shall, if its form of government be republican, be admitted into the Union on an equal footing with the original States, with or without slavery, as the constitution of such new State may provide.

3. Congress shall have no power to legislate upon the subject of slavery, except to protect the citizen in his right of property in slaves.

4. That in addition to the provisions of the third paragraph of the second section

they shall have the right, in their own name, to sue the county in which said violence, intimidation, or rescue was committed, and to recover from it, with interest and damages, the amount paid by them for said fugitive slave. And the said county, after it has paid said amount to the United States, may, for its indemnity, sue and recover from the wrong doers or rescuers, by whom the owner was prevented from the recovery of his fugitive slave, in like manner as the owner himself might have sued and recovered.

5. The third paragraph of the second section of the fourth article of the constitution, shall not be construed to prevent any of the States from having concurrent jurisdiction with the United States, by appropriate legislation, and through the action of their judicial and ministerial officers, from enforcing the delivery of fugitives from labor to the person to whom such service or labor is due.

6. Citizens of slaveholding States when traveling through, or temporarily sojourning with their slaves in non-slaveholding States, shall be protected in their right of property in such slaves.

7. The elective franchise and the right to hold office, whether federal, State, territorial or municipal, shall not be exercised by persons of the African race, in whole or in part.

8. These amendments, and the third paragraph of the second section of the first article of the constitution, and the third paragraph of the second section of the fourth article thereof, shall not be amended or abolished without the consent of all the States.

That the sense of the people of the United States may be taken upon the amendments above proposed.

*Resolved, By the people of Arkansas in convention assembled,* That we recommend the calling of a convention of the States of the federal Union, at the earliest practicable day, in accordance with the provisions of the fifth article of the constitution of the United States.

2. *Resolved further,* That the President of this convention transmit to the President and Congress of the United States, and to the Governors and legislatures of

### Census of 1860

| No. | States. | Free Population. | Slave Population. | Total | Per Centage of Slaves |
|-----|---------|-----------------|-------------------|-------|------------------------|
| 1 | South Carolina | 301,271 | 402,541 | 703,812 | 57.2 |
| 2 | Mississippi | 354,700 | 436,696 | 791,396 | 55.1 |
| 3 | Louisiana | 376,280 | 333,010 | 709,290 | 47.0 |
| 4 | Alabama | 529,164 | 435,132 | 964,296 | 45.1 |
| 5 | Florida | 78,686 | 61,753 | 140,439 | 43.9 |
| 6 | Georgia | 595,097 | 462,232 | 1,057,329 | 43.7 |
| 7 | North Carolina | 661,586 | 331,081 | 992,667 | 33.4 |
| 8 | Virginia | 1,105,192 | 490,887 | 1,596,079 | 30.7 |
| 9 | Texas | 421,750 | 180,682 | 602,432 | 30.0 |
| 10 | Arkansas | 324,323 | 111,104 | 435,427 | 25.5 |
| 11 | Tennessee | 834,063 | 275,784 | 1,109,847 | 24.8 |
| 12 | Kentucky | 930,223 | 225,490 | 1,155,713 | 19.5 |
| 13 | Maryland | 599,846 | 87,188 | 687,034 | 12.7 |
| 14 | Missouri | 1,067,352 | 114,965 | 1,182,317 | 9.7 |
| 15 | Delaware | 110,420 | 1,798 | 112,218 | 1.6 |
| | | 8,289,953 | 3,950,343 | 12,240,296 | 32.2 |

*1861 Arkansas State Convention*

## RECONSTRUCTION

In the generation after the end of Reconstruction [1867–1877], the southern states deprived African Americans of their right to vote and ordered that public and private facilities of all kinds be segregated by race. Thus, most African Americans remained locked in a system of political powerlessness and economic inequality. Called *boy* (a designation used for an adult African American), *uncle,* or *aunt,* African Americans "got to know their place." The expression never, never, never uttered aloud from African Americans about their invisibility and powerlessness was, "Let the white folk with their wealth and sin go to Hell."

Racism is deeply rooted in the American past. *Negrophobia* became a southern obsession. The bright hopes raised by *Emancipation* and Reconstruction rapidly faded into an increasingly hostile environment marked by lynchings, race riots, disfranchisement, and new Jim Crow laws. Most Americans turned their backs, and both political parties, as well as all three branches of the federal government, abdicated responsibility for the protection of the rights of the African American. In the nineteenth century, the division of *Homo sapiens* into races was based on a multitude of physical criteria. Facial angles, bone structure, hair texture, skin color, and cranium size were all used to classify mankind. Blacks were pictured as less than human.[32]

## BACK-TO-AFRICA MOVEMENT AND RECONSTRUCTION IN PINE BLUFF

The American Colonization Society (AMS) was an early advocate of the idea of resettling African-born Blacks Back to Africa. Founded in 1816, it was composed of philanthropists, clergy, and abolitionists who wanted to free African slaves and their descendants and provide them with the opportunity to return to Africa. The other group favoring the back-to-Africa movement was the slave owners of the South, who feared "free people of color" and wanted to expel them from America. In 1847, the AMS founded Liberia and designated it as the land to be colonized by Black people returning from the United States. The back-to-Africa movement began to decline but revived again in 1877, at the end of Reconstruction.

Especially in the 1870s, the Reconstruction era [1866–1877] brought progress and challenges for African Americans. As Republicans, Blacks were elected to city offices and the state legislature for the first time in history as the heavily Black Pine Bluff/Jefferson County electorate stretched its political options. Several African American businesses were opened including banks, bars, and barbershops. However, with the adoption of Jim Crow laws by the State of Arkansas, the atmosphere became grim for Black Pine Bluff toward the end of the nineteenth century when the Democratic Party was restored. The 1880s was a time when many Blacks in the South faced violence from groups such as the Ku Klux Klan. It [the 1890s] was a time when racism reached its peak, and the greatest number of lynchings in American history took place. The Liberian government promised twenty-five acres of free land for each immigrant family or ten acres to a single adult. African American residents purchased tickets and/or sought information on emigration. Arkansas had 650 emigrants depart to Liberia, more than any other state in the United States. Most of the emigrants came from Jefferson, St. Francis, Pulaski, Pope, and Conway counties.[33]

Back-to-Africa" Movement

Above: African American missionaries from Arkansas photographed in New York City on their way to Liberia in 1898. *Below:* New York City. Colored Refuges from Arkansas awaiting transportation to Liberia at the Mount Olivet Baptist. Church. *Courtesy of Library of Congress Prints and Photography Division.*

## LYNCHINGS IN PINE BLUFF

Without judicial due process, lynching was group violence perpetrated predominately on African Americans but also on Jews, immigrants, homosexuals, and criminals. For our discussion here, this portion will focus on the lynchings of African Americans. The peak decades in Arkansas were the 1860s to the 1930s, when 318 documented lynchings occurred; 231 victims were African Americans.[34] As property, slaves were rarely lynched. The end of the Civil War brought social disorder when justice was lacking and criminals frequently went free or were given light sentences. Some of the common reasons given for lynchings were: (1) economic competition for land, (2) intimidation (social control), sexualized affairs (protecting White womanhood), and (4) racial cleansing. Appearing in Arkansas in 1868, the Ku Klan Klux was the most notorious perpetrator of lynchings. Lynching was on the rise in the 1880s throughout the South, and Black newspapers deplored its rise and condemned its participants. The 1890s witnessed the worst period of lynchings. The record understates many instances of mob violence. Many lynchings were not recorded in Pine Bluff newspapers. Pure numbers do not convey the brutality of this ghastly crime, which continued—without report—in Pine Bluff well into the 1950s.

Outrageous as it was, the accounting which follows is a disgusting realization of how lynching reached high intensity in a small town. On February 14, 1892, John Kelley was lynched in Pine Bluff for the murder of W. T. McAdams, an agent for the Obest Brewing Company and a highly respected Pine Bluff citizen. At the time, Pine Bluff was the second largest city in Arkansas. The Black population in Jefferson County was 73 percent, and there were a number of prominent African American landowners and merchants. The city boasted a Black newspaper, as well as the state's only college for African Americans, Branch Normal College. According to the *Arkansas Gazette*, on the night of February 9, 1892, Kelley and several other accomplices allegedly murdered McAdams. At 10:30 p.m., McAdams was walking near his home when someone hit him over the head with a dray pin. He screamed, alerting his wife. He then died of his wounds. When his body was found, his pistol and a small amount of money were missing. By the evening of February 10, 1892, officials were looking for Kelley. According to the *Arkansas Gazette*,

> If the parties obtain enough evidence to fix the murder on the parties arrested, there will be no need of a trial, as the citizens here are very indignant, and they would make an example at once of the guilty parties ... The frequent murders of white men by negroes in this county of late have aroused the community to a high pitch of excitement.[35]

Kelley was captured in Rison (Cleveland County) on February 14, 1892. A mob of two hundred armed men met the train with him at 9:00 p.m. The mob stopped the train and took Kelley as a prisoner, marching him up the Main Street to the courthouse. The size of the mob had risen to one thousand. While the crowd yelled, a rope was put around Kelley's neck, and he was taken to the courthouse steps and given a chance to speak. He denied his guilt. The crowd hanged him from a telephone pole that stood directly across from the courthouse. After he was strung up, more than one hundred bullets were fired at him. [36] On the same night, Gilbert Banks (named Blanks or perhaps Culberth Harris rather than Gilbert Banks) was taken from the cell and given the opportunity to speak. He denied being with Kelley at the time of the murder. He was then hanged from the same telephone pole as Kelley, and even more shots were fired this time. Because it was Sunday night, large crowds of churchgoers, many of them women, were trapped downtown after church and witnessed these gruesome murders.[37] The *Arkansas Gazette* of February 16, 1892, reported,

> The mob was composed of some of our best citizens, and no masks were used, and everything transpiring could be seen by the bright lights and the moon.[38]

Pine Bluff was not defined as a "sundown town," a designation for locales between 1890 and 1968 that drove out their African American population or took steps to forbid Blacks from living in them. Such towns marked their city limits with signs reading, "Nigger, don't let the sun go down on you in _____"[39] Some towns used the "red line" marker to limit African American movement.

PINE BLUFF, February 10.—One of the most atrocious crimes in the history of this county was committed in the city last night.

Mr. W. T. McAdams, agent for the Obest Brewery Company at this place, and one of Pine Bluff's most highly respected citizens, left the city for his home, on State street, between Seventh and Eighth avenues, last night about 10:30 o'clock.

THE DEATH BLOW.

When within a few feet of his gate he was struck in the back of the head with a heavy dray pin, by some unknown person. He screamed and fell dead. His wife heard his screams and immediately came out, but could see no one but her husband, who was lying where he had fell. She summoned some neighbors and had his body carried in the house.

THE POLICE

were notified at once, and they started to work on the case.

This morning they arrested Gilbert Banks and another negro man named Smith, also two negro women, on suspicion, as they were seen

HANGING AROUND

the neighborhood before and after the murder.

Mr. McAdams has always been a law-abiding citizen, and robbery was evidently the motive for the crime, as his pistol and several dollars in silver were taken from his pockets.

A LYNCHING POSSIBLE.

If the parties obtain enough evidence to fix the murder on the parties arrested, there will be no need of a trial, as the citizens here are very indignant, and they would make an example at once of the guilty parties.

WAITING FOR THE MURDERER.

At 8 o'clock tonight a crowd of over 1,000 men assembled on Court Square awaiting the arrival of the Altheimer train, it being reported that officers Kilpatrick and Price were returning from Altheimer with John Kelly, the negro who waylaid and murdered J. T. McAdams last night. The report proved false. The people were quiet but determined, and had Kelly been brought in he would have been lynched in front of the court house. The officers went as far as Argenta, but say they found no trace of Kelly. Deputy Sheriffs leave tonight for Helena, which is his home.

COMMITTED WITHOUT BAIL.

Gilbert Banks, charged as an accessory, was committed without bail. He has made no confession implicating himself, but says he met Kelly last night, and he had a pistol and $5, which he snatched from a drunken white man. The pistol described corresponds with the one owned by McAdams.

THE COMMUNITY AROUSED.

The frequent murders of white men by negroes in this county of

The newspaper article attached here appeared in the *Arkansas Gazette*, February 16, 1892, The article was entitled, "A Fatal Blow."

# BLACK JOURNALISM AND BLACK NEWSPAPERS

The close of the Civil War brought something new to journalism in the South. Because the White press was not an available medium for African Americans, newly freed Blacks established their own press. African American newspapers appeared in such major southern cities as New Orleans, Nashville, Augusta, Charleston, and Baltimore. Many of the early Black newspapers were short-lived. Black editors began publication during the Reconstruction era in an effort to achieve: (1) certain political ends, (2) promote harmony and good will between Whites and Blacks, (3) instruct and educate the race, and (4) defend the newly acquired rights of Black Americans. From 1865 to 1876, the federal government attempted to legislate political, economic, and social equality for southern Blacks. At the same time, White southerners organized politically to express their hostility and contempt for the radical Republican programs and laws. Through violence, intimidation, corruption, and economic pressure, the southern press restored Democratic rule, in the name of "white supremacy," to the South in 1876.[40] During Reconstruction, the Black press in the South voiced support for the Republican Party and its program of racial equality. Black papers printed accounts of brutality and outrages on Blacks and defended the race's newly acquired social and political rights against attacks by the Democratic press.

By 1891, African American newspapers were blossoming around the country. Historians of the Black press differ on how many existed at the beginning of the 1880s, but some estimate that there were more than 150 by 1890. When the illiteracy rate among African Americans was about 70 percent at the time, some believe that as many as 1,184 Black papers were launched between1865 and 1900. So many newspapers appeared that in 1890, a group of Black editors convened in Indianapolis to found their own National Afro-American Press Association, and T. Thomas, Fortune [New York] was elected chairman.[41]

## Pine Bluff Black Newspapers

| Newspapers | Founder or Editor | Date of Publication |
|---|---|---|
| *Pine Bluff Weekly Echo* | Jesse C. Duke | 1889–1900 |
| *Weekly Echo-Progress* | | 1900 |
| *Arkansas Colored Catholics* | | 1899–1902 |
| *Baptist Organ* | | 1882–83 |
| *Negro Spokesman* | | 1938–58 |
| *Pine Bluff Weekly Herald* | | January 13, 1900 to 1907 |
| *Arkansas Republican* | | 1850–18?? |
| *Republican* | Started by S. P. and Ferd Havis. | 1880–85. Suspended in 1885. It changed its name to the *Hornet*, with Jessie C. Duke as editor. |
| *Daily Commercial* | | 1895–97 |
| *Morning Courier* | | 1897–19?? |
| *Pine Bluff American* | | 1850–18?? |

| Pine Bluff Courier | | |
|---|---|---|
| Hornet | Jesse C. Duke | 1887–88. See information on the *Republican*. |
| True Reformer | Started by White Americans, continued by Black Republicans[42] | Suspended in January 1885 |

## Social Stratification in the African American Population, 1880–1915

This next section is a view of class structure among African Americans before the Civil War and after World War I.[43] Social stratification among African Americans appeared before the Civil War. Among the enslaved, there were distinctions between house servants and skilled artisans on the one hand and field laborers on the other—the preceding distinctions were to a large extent associated with skin color, and that was carried over into freedom. In the antebellum North, a group of artisans, barbers, tradesmen, higher types of personal and domestic servants, caterers, coal dealers, and other businessmen constituted an upper class. In the principal southern cities [Atlanta, Washington, DC, Charleston, St. Louis, and New Orleans] where there were free Blacks of mixed ancestry, social distinctions were based on skills, income, and family background. The elite families were those who possessed considerable property and could claim aristocratic White ancestry or the absence of the tradition of slavery. For some time after *Emancipation*, free Blacks and their descendants enjoyed a higher social status than the freedmen. In rural areas, a pattern developed ranging from farm laborers through share tenants and cash renters to landowners. Around 1898, the upper class consisted of a handful of ministers, teachers, blacksmiths, carpenters, shoemakers, tailors, restaurateurs, barbers, retail merchants, postal employees, clerical workers, and some domestic workers. Some towns included physicians, lawyers, and building contractors. In general, the artisans and entrepreneurs listed previously depended on the White market. The rest of the population were lower-class laborers. Just before World War I, besides the leading ministers, teachers, and a rare doctor or lawyer, the upper class consisted of a few carpenters and mechanics, and somewhat below them barbers, coachmen, cooks, draymen, blacksmiths, tailors, postal employees, coal dealers, and hotel owners. In the 1920s, there was a disappearance of entrepreneurs who catered to the White market. A newer class of entrepreneurs became dependent on the African American market. Some entrepreneurs—mostly newspaper publishers, and undertakers, some grocers, barbers, and beauty shop owners—had always depended on the African American market.

## JIM CROW SEGREGATION

African Americans were familiar with the customs, habits, and etiquette of the South. [44] Black people placed restrictions on their children in order to keep them alive. A familiar catchphrase was, "I get humiliated and insulted often, but I never get used to it. It is new each time and stings and hurts more and more." Jim Crow came to the South in an expanded and rigid form between 1890 and 1915. White fears mounted between 1880 and World War I. Blacks were sent to the Jim Crow car, the back of the bus, the side of the theater, and the side window of a restaurant.

When Blacks showed evidence of independence and assertiveness, those in power acted to ensure the permanent political, economic, and social subordination and powerlessness of African Americans. In *Trouble in Mind: Black Southerners in the Age of Jim Crow* (1998), Leon F. Litwack writes,

> Whites systematically disfranchised Black men, imposed rigid patterns of racial segregation, manipulated the judicial system, and sustained extraordinary levels of violence and brutality. Also the findings of science and the learned professions and the dissemination of dehumanizing caricatures reinforced and comforted whites in their racial beliefs and practices. Professors, especially historians, mis-educated by giving a prescribed version of reality. (219)

Some who enjoyed through their deferential behavior a reputation in the community as "good niggers" were often businessmen, clergymen, and professionals along with trusted ones of lesser economic stature. The previous list of African Americans was permitted to vote. For others, disfranchisement took one or a combination of many mechanisms: (1) intimidation and force; (2) poll tax; (3) property ownership; (4) a literacy, educational, or understanding test as in providing a reasonable interpretation of any section of the *Constitution* and "How old was Christ when He was born?"

(5) residency requirements; and (6) the notorious *grandfather clause*. Yet, "Blacks were not submissive, less willing to subject themselves to the whims and demands of others, less willing to compromise . . . . They were thought by many whites to be childlike, lazy, slow moving, sloppy workers, with a propensity for theft and absenteeism . . . . Blacks could not work to the satisfaction of whites . . . . Blacks found ways to exploit."[45]

Many of the segregation statues were enacted in the 1890s and the early twentieth century. In 1896, the *Plessy v. Ferguson* ruling was sustained.[46] The "separate but equal" doctrine became the constitutional basis for segregation. Everything in the South was separated: public transportation, public parks, hospitals, asylums, homes for orphans and the aged, special needs persons, prisons, taverns, inns, and churches. Some hospitals denied admission to African Americans altogether. Laws required that nurses took care of their own race. Most schools were separated.[47] Signs [Colored or White] were seen throughout the landscape: over the entrances to parks, theaters, boardinghouses, waiting rooms, restrooms, and water fountains. Theaters had separate ticket windows and seating for African Americans. Balconies were called "buzzard roost" or "nigger heaven." Some stores forbade Black women from trying on dresses, hats, and shoes before purchasing them. African Americans were excluded from most amusement parks, roller skating rinks, bowling alleys, swimming pools, and tennis courts. In cities and towns, segregated residential patterns were legally sanctioned. Black areas were designated as "darktown" or "niggertown." Jim Crow was thorough: public school textbooks, Jim Crow Bibles on which to swear Black witnesses in court, separated telephone booths, windows in banks, elevators, and many others. The laws made no exceptions among Blacks based on class or education. Those in power had no thought as to how they insulted and degraded Black men and women. Blacks were helpless to check White oppression. Parents and children were forced to watch family members humiliated and abused with no opportunity to afford them protection or to retaliate. Blacks had to respond in a manner that was deferential. However, there were a few places where the races could mix: grocery stores, post offices, and banks.

Young African American males made up a large proportion of convictions for theft, gambling, assault, disorderly conduct, and vagrancy. They also comprised the bulk of the convict labor supply. Rather than dispatch convicts to plantation farms, African Americans would be used on county chain gangs for road construction and maintenance. Convict lease and chain gangs stood as constant reminders to Blacks of their vulnerability and subordination. In communities across the South, Blacks came to perceive the law and its enforcers as an outside and alien force,[48] an intrusive and repressive agency against which appeals for fairness and impartiality, and humane and just treatment were all but useless.[49]

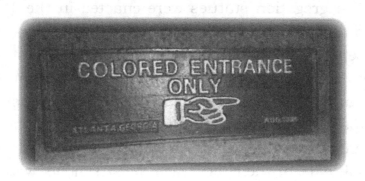

## Jim Crow Segregation in Pine Bluff

On Saturdays in Pine Bluff (called "town") when African Americans shopped for weekly provisions, consumers from Princeton Pike, Grady, Gould, Dumas, Altheimer, Wabbaseka, Humphrey, and Stuttgart were expected to follow local customs and use accommodations designated for Colored. The Greyhound Bus Lines, the Continental Trailways Bus Lines, and other smaller bus stations in Pine Bluff catered to a policy of separate services for Blacks. In 1920, a sign, "Colored Section Pine Bluff," hung on the outside of Union Station in Pine Bluff, designating the section of the railroad depot where African Americans were required to stand to wait to board the train—and then onto a specifically designated "Colored Only" railroad car.[50] The Saenger Theatre and the Malco, Pine Bluff's early movie theaters, had separate balconies designated for "Colored." Black movie goers entered the movie and purchased tickets in separate spaces in the building. The early drive-in movie refused African Americans admittance entirely. Besides Jones Park (built by Wiley Jones) and Townsend Park (founded in the early 1950s, honoring William Townsend, an African American educator), there were no "Colored" parks where either "Colored" visitors or residents could relax in the open air. In offices both public and private, Black secretaries were often stationed behind a black or gray metal file cabinet. Many secretaries were often placed behind a curtain or screen in the rear of the office. All schools in the Pine Bluff Public School System were separated. Catholic African American students attended Colored Industrial Institute, later named St. Peter's Catholic School. Besides the faculty and Black students at St. Peter's Catholic School, the Pine Bluff Public Library, located on Fifth Street, did not offer book service to African American students and patrons in the city—nor the district schools. During the 1950s, the Branch Library—built across the street from Merrill High School—gave service to Black elementary pupils. During the school day, a bookmobile filled with incredible titles offered reading opportunities for African American students. For both city and district schools, African American public school administrators received cast-off furnishings and secondhand books to be given to their pupils. Blacks nowadays recall drinking from separate water fountains at S. H. Kress and Company. White physicians had separate waiting rooms for their White and Colored clients. The specified Colored waiting room was generally in a room behind both the White clients and the secretary's desk. Almost all African American physicians and dentists leased space in the Masonic Temple during the early decades of the twentieth century. The first African American birth at Davis Hospital was remembered to be in 1949. In the 1960s, the Pine Bluff NAACP chapter announced a boycott of local department stores that did not serve African Americans at their lunch counters. The boycotted stores included F. W. Woolworth 5 and 10 Cent Store, and J. J. Newberry 5c, 10c, and $1.00 Store, both businesses located on Main Street.[51]

## BLACK-OWNED BUSINESSES AND PARTNERSHIPS IN PINE BLUFF 1880s TO 1925

The 1880s was the fastest growing decade in the history of Pine Bluff. The city grew from having thirty-two hundred residents to nearly ten thousand in the 1890 census. Business and community infrastructure increased as a result of the growth, and both White and Black national publications noted the quality of life that existed for Pine Bluffians.[52] Between 1880 and 1925, the victory of the Battle of Pine Bluff [1863] and numerous business, civic, and social interactions garnered Pine Bluff the designation "The African American Paradise of the South." In her book *Caste and Class*: *The Black Experience in Arkansas, 1880–1920*, Fon Gordon lists entrepreneurial opportunities at the turn of the twentieth century in Pine Bluff:

> Pine Bluff, located in black-majority Jefferson County, had the second largest urban black population in the state and maintained a sizable black business community that included in 1903 sixteen grocers, four blacksmiths, seven restaurants, five saloons, two dry goods stores, including the Southern Mercantile Company on Main Street, and four of the five barbers in town. By 1908, the number of black-owned businesses had increased. Blacks in the city owned nine of the eleven cleaning and pressing shops. The number of restaurants and groceries had increased to twenty-two and thirty-five respectively. One of the more successful groceries was the Freeman-Patillo Grocery Company, which advertised as a grocery, restaurant, and meat market and also carried notions. Several services crossed the color line in Pine Bluff. Moses Offord began the only taxi service in the city in 1905, with a horse-drawn carriage. Nettie Hollis Johnson, the black owner of the first beauty shop, opened in the city in 1906, and her staff catered exclusively to white women, but it also functioned as a beauty school to train black women to become certified by the state cosmetology board.[53]

Little Rock had the largest Black population in the state and the largest number of Black-owned businesses during this period. Business communities promoted and supported events such as the Colored State Fair, an annual event in Pine Bluff that became a showcase for Black talent from around the state. Founded by an African American dentist, inventor, and author in Little Rock, Dr. J. H. Smith, the annual affair attracted crowds from both races.[54]

**The Masonic Temple**

Built in stages during 1902, 1903, and 1904 by the Sovereign Grand Lodge of Free and Accepted Masons of the State of Arkansas, the state's Black Masonic order, the Masonic Temple was the tallest building in Pine Bluff when it was completed. Built by and for African Americans, the Masonic Temple was designed by Little Rock architects Frank Gibb, W. S. Hetton, and Theo Sanders in the Romanesque Revival style with arched window openings on the top floor and stone columns at the storefront. It was completely paid for exactly fourteen years after the cornerstone of the building was laid. The period of greatest significance for the Masonic Temple was 1900–1924. Privately owned, the Masonic Temple was/is a professional, historic structure that functioned as a social clubhouse, a commercial and trade facility, and a venue for specialty stores.

The first floor housed a variety of retail shops. The second floor was used as office space for the Grand Lodge as well as doctors, dentists, and other professionals. The third and fourth floors were the lodge rooms/lodge hall. The Masonic Temple is listed on the National Register of Historic Places, 1978.

*The Masonic Temple*

## Streetcar

In August 1886, Wiley Jones became one of the first African Americans in the nation to receive a franchise to operate a mule-drawn streetcar system. The business was named Wiley Jones Street Car Lines and was nearly six miles long. The railway was laid with twenty-pound steel rails, manufactured by Paddock Hawley Iron Company of St. Louis, expressly for the Wiley Jones railway. His cars were all new and the very best built by the John Stephenson Company of New York City and the St. Louis Car Company. Jones used the best equipment for his railway. Records show that his car stables and barns were fine and were suited to the service. The business was located on the periphery of his belt-line, at his beautiful park of fifty-five acres, south of the city, in which is a half-mile racing track, said to be second to none in the South.[55] Operating on its own about four years, the Wiley Jones Street Car Lines merged with the Citizens Street Railway in 1890. This latter venture became the electric railway, which the city purchased. Adjoining the park was the octagon-shaped Colored People's Fair Grounds. The structure included a large and well-constructed amphitheater, stock stables, and stalls.

## Merchant and Cotton Broker

E. E. Fluker was a merchant and cotton broker.

## Lucey Memorial Hospital

Lucey Memorial Hospital was one of the city's historic African American hospitals. Monsignor John Michael "J. M." Lucey, pastor of St. Joseph Church in Pine Bluff, helped to establish the hospital.[56] Ferdinand Havis was one of the city's first African American aldermen. He was elected in 1871. Havis later served as President of Lucey Memorial Hospital.

## Barber and Beauty Shops

Ferdinand Havis owned a profitable barbershop on West Court Street in Pine Bluff. The shop later moved to Barraque Street.

Opened in 1906, the Nettie Hollis Johnson Beauty Shop was African American owned and staffed but served only White customers. The first location of the beauty shop was across from the Saenger Theater on Second Avenue in Pine Bluff. Nellie Johnson owned and operated the shop for forty years.

## Taverns

The Ferd Havis Building, which was a popular meeting place for the Black society of Pine Bluff, was located on Third and Main streets. Havis told the *Pine Bluff Press Eagle*:

> While he was in the tavern business, he never allowed his saloon to be opened on Sunday. Technically, this was true, as he opened the tavern on Saturday night. It closed at some time in the wee hours of Sunday morning, not to open again the rest of the day on Sunday. On the police court docket of Pine Bluff in 1882, every Monday from July 4 until November, a certain F. Havis pleaded guilty to "Sabbath breaking" and paid a weekly fine of five dollars.[57]

Ferd Havis formed a partnership with Essex Bellamy. They bought Lot 4, Block 33, Old Town, on the northeast corner of Main Street and Third Avenue. The business was called Wiley Jones' Wine, Liquor, and Tobacco Store, located at 207 Main Street, Pine Bluff. It was a wholesale and whisky business. An advertisement in *The Press-Eagle* of December 16, 1884, reads

> Havis and Bellamy, wholesale and retail whisky dealers, beg leave to inform the public that they are now in their elegant new brick. Corner of Main and Lake (Pine) Street

## Hotel

P. K. Miller started the Miller Hotel.

## Resorts

Jefferson County once had a resort that was the center of summer activity for many years. Located seven miles southwest of Pine Bluff on Highway 54, White Sulphur Springs was settled as early as 1845. The medicinal properties of the springs had gained a reputation and were visited by many seeking to cure their health problems. On June 14, 1889, Wiley

Jones made investments of forty acres with Edward B. Houston of White Sulphur Springs. The location is now called Sulphur Springs, which is located in the Watson Chapel area[58] of Jefferson County. The partnership sold lots to Pine Bluff residents for summer homes. World War I stopped development of the area, although Pine Bluff continued to use the area. After the war, people visited Sulphur Springs for picnics and dances, but it declined in popularity.[59]

## Retail Business

Formed in 1898, the Southern Mercantile Company was a successful Pine Bluff business owned by Marion Perry Sr., Ferdinand Havis, and Wiley Jones. With assets of $50,000, this company remained in business until the death of Wiley Jones in 1904.

## Pharmacy

Around 1900, Dr. D. W. Young's drugstore started. It became a successful business.

## Movie

The Vester Movie was started by P. K. Miller. The movie's name honored his wife, Vester Miller.

## Undertaking and Insurance Company

Marion Perry Jr. owned a half-interest in the family undertaking business in Pine Bluff and was president of the Olympic Life Insurance Company of Pine Bluff.

## Taxicab Service

In the 1940s, Wiley Austin Branton [1923–1988] worked in the taxicab business started by his father and grandfather. The latter two family members came to Arkansas from Mississippi in 1915 and began the first taxicab business in town. Branton's 98 (the original telephone number) was for many years the only taxi business in town. It made the family prominent. A man reared in Pine Bluff in the 1950s recounted how a "party" was held each time Branton's 98 brought in new taxicabs. It always occurred on a Saturday, when people were in town shopping, and the cabs—shiny black—would be unloaded from the truck ceremoniously and with great fanfare.[60] Wiley A. Branton was a Pine Bluff civil rights attorney who later moved to Washington, DC. In 1977, he was named dean of Howard University School of Law, where he remained until 1983.

## Street Names

Located in the neighborhood along University Drive (formerly Cedar Street), Havis Street honors Ferdinand Havis, an alderman, Republican Party delegate, and founder of the first Black hospital in Pine Bluff. Another street along University Drive is named Fluker, in honor of E. E. Fluker, a local merchant and cotton broker.

## P. K. Miller Funeral Home

## Newspapers

Jesse C. Duke was publisher and editor of the *Pine Bluff Weekly Echo*, the *Hornet*, and the *Republican*—three of many African American newspapers in Pine Bluff. Before coming to the city in the late 1880s, Duke was editor in 1887 of the *Montgomery Herald*, a Black newspaper in Alabama. He represented Booker T. Washington's interests in discouraging the removal of William B. Patterson's Marion School to a new location, which was Montgomery, Alabama. In midcourse, Duke shifted his position and became active to a committee of African American citizens favoring removal to Montgomery.[61]

## African American Businesses in Pine Bluff Before 1950s
### Courtesy of the *1941 Lion Yearbook* and the *1950 Yearbook*

Bettye J. Williams

## African American Businesses in Pine Bluff before the 1950s
Courtesy of the *1941 Lion Yearbook* and the *1950 Yearbook*

**The Great Protective Association**

The Largest Association in the South
$20,000 Deposited With State of Ark.

"INSURE TODAY—Tomorrow may Be too Late"

P. K. MILLER, President
3rd & Alabama Sts.        Phones 1762-229

COMPLEMENTS OF BRANTON'S 98 TAXI

Ph. 5-2198

Pine Bluff, Arkansas

COLLEGIATE BARBER SHOP
WILLIAMS BROS, Props.        610 N. Cedar

**Medical & Dental Clinic**

DR. F. P. LYTES
Dentist

DR. H. P. M. BROWN
Physician and Surgeon

Masonic Temple, Pine Bluff
PHONES:
Office 1263        Residence 1331, 1399

Office Phone 1074        Res. Phone 4273

### DR. R. T. JOHNSON
Dentist

12 Masonic Temple        Pine Bluff, Ark.

Congratulations From

MR. McKINDRA and CLEON FLOWERS

COMPLIMENTS

### THE LION'S DEN
Good Meals—Short Orders
Sandwiches
"On the Edge of the Campus"
PHONE 1329

Complements
Of
THE GREAT PROTECTIVE BURIAL ASSC.
AND THE
P.K. MILLER FUNERAL HOME ESTAB.
PINE BLUFF, ARKANSAS
301 E. 3rd. Ave.
Pho. JE 5-1012 & 5-1013

Mrs. P. K. Miller, President

### The Vester Theatre

"Always Has Good Movies"

Merchants and Businesses in the 1950s
*From The 1967 Lion Yearbook*

U. S. Brown, Owner
General Manager

Mrs. Manzilla D. Brown
President

## Brown Funeral Home
## Progressive Burial Association
## Crown Casket Co.

Home Office: 215 E. 2nd St.    Phones 765 — 6576

BRANCH OFFICES: DUMAS, ARK.... STUTTGART, ARK.

## Interviews of Arkansas Ex-Slaves

Works Progress Administration (WPA) in the 1930s[62]

The information for this segment was gathered from ex-slaves who gave their testimonies during the 1930s to interviewers employed by the Works Progress Administration (WPA) of the Federal Writers' Project (FWP) during the presidency of Franklin Roosevelt.[63]The FWP was a branch of the New Deal, which provided jobs for out-of-work writers, historians, and other researchers. Ex-slaves shared statements on work life, hard labor, squalor, flogging and torture, the pain of separation from family members, indignity of being sold, acts of resistance directed against their master and mistress, humiliations, superstition, education, food, and family life.

### Slave Births

Many slaves did not know the date of their birth. They would say, "I was born in the cotton patch, at springtime, harvest time, or at Christmas time." Those born on Christmas Day did not consider themselves Christmas gifts.

## Cabin

Their cabins were made of logs with dirt between logs. The cabins were one room, one door, and one window or plenty of windows. The windows had shutters. There were cracks between the logs that let in more air than the windows would. The cabin had dirt floors or planks for the floor. Most had little or no furniture. The bed extended from a side wide of logs. No springs were used. The mattress was made of corn shucks, cotton, or hay. Field slaves lived in the quarters. For heat in the cabin, a fire burned in an iron bucket. Paper and trash were used for fuel. There was a fireplace. Cooking was done on the fireplace with a skillet and lid.

## Clothes

Clothes for girls and women were woven on a loom. The cotton came from the field, and it was spun on the spinning wheel on rainy days. The women spun the thread and wove the cloth. For the boys (ages 5–15), women made long shirts out of the cloth. The shirts had deep scallops. Slave women would dye the cloth with indigo to make pants. Boys never wore indigo pants to the field. No young man wore pants until he began to court. Slave women combed their hair on Sundays. Slave men cut their hair on Sundays.

## Education

Slaves had no chance to get an education. They were not allowed to have books or learn to read.

## Emotions

After their freedom in 1865, many ex-slaves suffered from amnesia: (1) the memory was gone; (2) some remembered practically nothing; (3) many could not tell others where he/she lived; (4) the emotions surged at the mention of slavery time; (5) only emotions remained; (6) such details as names, times, places, or happenings were gone; (7) many did not remember the names of mother, father, relatives, masters, or old-time friends; (8) nothing would rise out of the mind; and (9) a constant refrain was " I want to go back home," and "I would not be in this condition if I was back home." Interviewers noted that *back home* meant Africa.

## Entertainment

Slaves would play with an old fiddle. Some could "ring up" and play in the yard. They knew a few songs, such as "Go Down, Moses," "Steal Away," "Didn't My Lord Deliver Daniel from the Lion's Den."

## Expressions

Almost all of the ex-slave narrators were in their seventies when they were interviewed. An expression shared with many WPA recorders was, "I wish my recollection was like it used to be." Other sayings suggest a conversant language:

"I reckon."
"I been down sick."
"I been right low, and they didn't speck me to live."
"You is free."
"My mother birthed me in the world."
"I done tole you all I know."
"I seed him."
"Them questions been called over to me so long most forgot 'em."
"Then was when my father was killed."
"I never seed him no more. I was a orphan."
"I never born children. I help raise some."
"I can't see 'bout getting 'round no more."
"Don't ask me about the young nigers. They too fast for me. If I see 'em, they talking a passel of foolish talk. What I knows is times is hard wid me shows you born."
"You come back to see me. If you don't, I wanter meet you all in heaben."
"I don't vote. I don't know who to vote for."
"My estimony [for opinion]."

## Folk Customs

Making a bedspread of tobacco sacks was a common custom. When slaves left a location, the women would leave a plait of hair to be remembered by. Many Whites shared that thinking would give the slaves a headache.

## Folk Magic

Hoodoo, or folk magic, has been at work in the South for generations. Hoodoo and root work are very southern things. Unlike voodoo, which is considered a religion, hoodoo incorporates the reading of scriptures and using spices and charms. Hoodoo has been preserved by using compounds, herbs, and pharmacies. Herbal remedies perfume the air. Ingredients could include Chinese "business powder," devil's club root, coffin nails, African mojo wishing beans, coyote skin, teeth, and private body parts. Practitioners strike matches at their door to entice the devil out with sulfur. They boil bayberry to cleanse their homes at New Year's. For protection against evil, they keep a bowl of lemons near the door and hang bottles in trees. People look for control in an uncertain world—over court cases, jobs, and relationships. Women seek relief from abusive husbands and unfaithful men—or seek protection from being cursed by the wife of the man with whom she has been cheating.

People use mojo bags and lucky candles as in "get a man candles" or "steady work candles." Enemies can leave evil work in the form of occult, candles, and dead animals. One can do the worst evil against someone in his or her bedroom and bathroom. There are recipes for "making evil-removing bath salts," "African powers spray," and "law-stay-away" candles. For love, read Psalm 23 and the Song of Solomon nine times a day. For the "stay away" spell, recite Psalms 100 and 59 ("Deliver me from my enemies, O God ..."). Two candles are needed, one for "love," one for "stay away." Oils used are narcissus, black tulip, and myrrh. If money is needed, it is violet, orange blossom, and bayberry. Snakes can be used for good or evil. The skins can be filled with nutmeg and other lucky items, and then sealed with bayberry wax to make mojo bags. The mojo bag is the charm blues singers lament losing or having used against them. A Mercury dime works well in a mojo bag.

## Food

Food was prepared for the master's family in huge kettles and ovens in the common kitchen presided over by a well-trained and competent cook and supervised by the mistress of the Big House. Young children were fed a gruel composed of whole milk and bread, which was set before them in a kind of trough, from which they ate with their fingers. Food was sometimes put in wooden trays. They put fat meat, pot-liquor, hominy, or cornbread in the trays. Biscuits came only on Sundays. After the crops were harvested, owners gave their slaves a barbecue, where huge quantities of beef and pork were served, and the evening was given over to dancing. Owners played the fiddle. They loved to see their slaves dance. Weekly food allotment per slave family was two and a half bushels of corn, three bushels of wheat, and three pounds of meat for each adult in the family. On most plantations, slaves had to cook for themselves in the quarters after coming home from the field.

Only the house slaves were given a measuring cup of coffee—no sugar. Field slaves did not get coffee. House slaves were given two pieces of bread with butter and fruit spread between. Rabbits were a staple in the Big House and the slave quarters. Boys would track six or eight rabbits at a time. Slaves had rabbits for breakfast, rabbits for dinner, rabbits for suppertime, fried rabbits, stewed rabbits, and boiled rabbits. In the quarters, slaves went fishing for the evening meat.

Many slaves were starved out until they were grown. Men ate together. Women ate together. Slaves were not supposed to have food in their cabins unless they went fishing or hunting. They stole sweet potatoes from the master and roasted them in their cabins. Slaves stole hogs and killed them for meat in the cabins.

## Gifts

Slaves were given as gifts to newly married white couples. The purpose was to give them a "start"—six to eight grown slaves and the same number of children from two to four years of age.

## Illness

The slave nurse took care of the Colored people. Medicine was calomel, castor oil, and grub.

## Intelligent and Apt Slaves

Slaves were singled out and given special training for those places most useful in the life of the plantation. Girls were taught in housework, cooking, and in the care of children. Boys were trained in blacksmithing, carpentry, and being personal servants around the home. Some were even taught to read and write when it was thought that their later position would require this learning.

## Jail

Jails were found on most plantations. They were made of wood but close built. A slave could not get out because the building was padlocked and the slave tied to the pen. Owners kept a male hog in the pen to tramp and walk over the slave. Male hogs in the pen were used as a blind. Light punishment was five hundred lashes. Some were shot. Richmond and New Orleans were the big selling blocks for slaves.

## Marriage

Owners matched couples from separate plantations. When a boy child was born, they reserved him for breeding purposes. If the boy child was puny or sickly by the time he was thirteen years old, he was placed on the auction block. People would bid on him. The couple jumped a broomstick and were married. Or one could court a woman and just go on and marry her. No license, no nothing was needed. Sometimes slaves would *take up* with a woman and go on with her—no ceremony necessary.

## Master

The will of the master was the law of the plantation, and prompt punishment was administered for any violation of established rules. Owners were firm in the execution of the law. Respect and obedience were steadfastly required and sternly demanded. Laziness and disrespect were not tolerated or permitted. A healthy, grown male slave sold for $1,000 to $1,500. The smaller the plantation, the better they were to their slaves.

## Pass

A pass was needed if a slave wanted to see a girl on a nearby plantation. Without a pass, the neighboring planter or the patrollers would whip him and send him back to his plantation. Patrollers or jayhawkers were out all the time. There was no movement without a pass.

## Religion

On most plantations, the same White minister spoke to the family in the Big House and the slaves in the quarters at the same time. The slaves stood in the back of the room. On some plantations, slave services were held on Sunday afternoons. The plantation minister insisted that slaves be righteous, obedient, respectful, and dutiful to both their heavenly and earthly masters. On some plantations, there were no church, no church school—no nothing going on on Sundays. Slaves could not move about. Slaves had no church building. They had to hide around to worship God any way they could. Many slaves would dig a big hole in the ground in order to pray.

## Songs

Many ex-slaves did not remember slave songs. One well-known song was "Am I Born to Die." Another song was "Amazing Grace, How Sweet the Sound That Saves a Race like Me." Another song was "I Want to Be Free."

## Superstitions

Avoid stepping on sidewalk cracks, walking under ladders, or crossing paths with black cats.

To wear a dime (Mercury one) around your ankle will ward off witchcraft.

To dream of dancing is a sign of happiness.

To dream of silver money is a sign of bad luck; bills—good luck.

Catnip tea is good for measles or hives.

If it rains while the sun is shining, the devil is beating his wife.

To bite your tongue while talking is a sign that you have told a lie.

Persons with gaps between their teeth are big liars.

It is bad luck for a black cat to cross you to the left, but good luck if he crosses you to the right.

To dream of a woman's death is a sign of some man's death.

To dream of a man's death is a sign of some woman's death.

If a cat takes up at your house, it's a sign of good luck; a dog—bad luck.

If a spark of fire pops on you, it is a sign that you will receive some money or a letter.

To dream of fish is a sign of motherhood.
To dream of blood is a sign of trouble.
To dream of eggs is a sign of trouble unless the eggs are
    broken. If the eggs are broken, your trouble is ended.
To dream of snakes is a sign of enemies. If you kill the snake,
    you have conquered your enemies.
To dream of a funeral is a sign of a wedding.
To dream of a wedding is a sign of a funeral.
To dream of dead folk is a sign of rain.

## Whipping

Many reasons were given for whipping a slave: (1) a slave would not obey, (2) a slave would sass the master or overseer, (3) a slave would not work, (4) the slave did not perform work well, and (5) arguing back to the master or the overseer. On large plantations, slaves were whipped by an overseer. Straps were made of harness leather.

Forms of whippings were: (1) slaves were tied down; (2) whipped with a leather strap up to five hundred times before stopping; (3) after whipping, the overseer put their *rags* on and went about his business; (4) after beatings, slaves were given no medical attention; (5) women were whipped like the men; (6) women were stripped down to the waist—her *rags* hanging down around her hip; (7) women were whipped until the blood ran down their *rags*; (8) men removed their pants and were whipped like a dog; (9) on large plantations of nine hundred or more, slaves were whipped from Saturday night to Monday morning; (10) some slaves would run away; (11) owners would put the dogs on the runaways; (12) dogs treated the slaves like a coon or a possum; and (13) sometimes overseers would make the dogs bite the slaves. If slaves were out without a pass, they received twenty-five licks. If they outran the patrollers and arrived at the home plantation, slaves saved themselves a whipping.

## Work—House Slaves, Women

House slaves were reared in the master's house. The mistress called her, "My Little Nigger," and did not allow her to be whipped or driven around. They never did field work. Born in the slave quarters, female slaves were separated from the biological slave mother and reared by the mistress of the plantation. They did all the housework for the mistress.

## Work—House Slaves, Men

Men house slaves did blacksmithing and repaired wagons and plows. They worked from Monday morning until Saturday night. When the horn blew, slaves left the quarters for the fields. The overseer would come "down the line" (road in the quarters). Slaves started working at six years old cleaning off new "ground." They (the younger ones) thinned corn on their knees with their hands.

## Work—Women

Women worked in the fields from the time they could see to the time they could not see. They worked from sunrise to after dark. They worked in the field or were house slaves. A midwife nursed babies to both slaves and the Big House. Cooks prepared meals for the Big House but in a separate building. Other slaves washed dishes and ironed clothes in the Big House. Weavers wove for the master's family and special pieces of clothes for outsiders. They wove woolen cloth too. Women made quilts at night, chopped cotton, picked cotton, pulled fodder, plowed the land, cleared the land, split rails, and cut logs and rolled them like a man.

*Row of Shotgun Houses*

Bettye J. Williams

# HOME

The Big House, Cabins, the Quarters, Shotgun Houses

Most house slaves lived in better condition than field slaves. They did not get Sundays off and usually attended church with the master and mistress. They cleaned, cooked, served meals, and took care of the children. They did other chores too such as waiting on tables, washing clothes, ironed, took up and put down carpets, hauled the large steaming pots for the preservation of fruits, lifted barrels with cucumbers soaking in brine, opened up barrels of flour, swept floors, dusted furniture, hoed and weeded gardens, and collected chicken eggs. Serving as wet nurses, female house slaves took care of infants, allowing the wife to do whatever she wanted. They also weaved, quilted, and spun linens. Having more privileges, the house slave worked all day—basically standing rather than bending. Some house slaves lived in attics, closets, or corners in the Big House, even if their families lived in the quarters. A cook's day was long and hard. She rose early in the morning to cook breakfast, and the day ended with cleaning up after dinner and gathering firewood for the next day. A house slave had a better chance to learn how to read and write. House slaves often listened in on the conversations of their owners so they were able to warn field slaves of the owner auctioning certain slaves and other important plantation business.[64]

Working from sunrise to sunset, field slaves worked an eighteen-hour day during harvest time. From the first sign of light and then until it was too dark to see, men and women worked the same hours. After a day on a cotton plantation, slaves formed a line to have their cotton weighed and received their daily food. The minimum amount of cotton to be picked in one day was two hundred pounds. At the age of twelve, a child's work became almost the same as an adult. On Sundays, slaves fed the stock, after which they did whatever they wanted. Field slaves were given Sundays off and maybe a part of Saturday unless it was during harvest time. On very hot days, they were given one to two hours off at midday. During their free time, slaves sometimes hunted and fished. Expectant mothers worked until the child was born, and after the child's birth, she worked in the field with the child on her back. In the late 1860s, Black women, seeking to devote more time to their families, withdrew from field work.

Every year each slave would receive two linen shirts, two pairs of trousers, one jacket, one pair of socks, one pair of brogan shoes with brass tips, an overcoat, and a woolen hat. After *Emancipation*, men wore three-piece suits—preachers wore tuxedos delivering sermons. Slave houses were usually shacks with dirt floors; sometimes these cabins were made of boards nailed up, and the cracks were stuffed with rags. Beds were straw and grass, old rags, and one blanket for covering. In the quarters, one single room could have as many as a dozen people in it—men, women, and children. Each month, one slave family would receive cornmeal, salt herring, and eight pounds of pork or fish. Over 32 percent of marriages were canceled by owners as a result of slaves being sold away from their families. A slave husband could be separated from his wife and the children from the mother.

Living "down home" meant being in the South. The old house place, which was a cabin, a shanty, or a *shotgun* structure, included a garden and outbuildings full of implements. Families had little access to the inside of each other's house. It was rare to walk beyond the front door. People visited in the other's yard. Children in large families usually slept and lived shoulder- to-shoulder, with just enough space between beds to roll out. Two, three, or sometimes four slept to a bed or a pallet on the floor. Poor people borrowed cedar tubs or tin tubs that they bathed in from neighbors. A few White neighbors borrowed tin tubs from Black families.[65] Hog farmers would collect everybody's table scraps as food for their farm animals. Slaves worked their small garden patches by moonlight. Trash was burned in the backyard.

When a slave became ill, a plantation doctor or the mistress was called. On the other hand, slaves had herbs of their own and made their own salves. It was in the slave quarters that children watched adults create potions for healing or select plants to produce dye for clothing. The only charms that were worn were made out of bones. There were slave funerals with no service. A graveyard on the plantation served as the burial site for slaves. A wooden post showed where the slave was buried.

Known as a backhouse, privy, or necessary, the outhouse was the toilet. They were made of wood. Many had multiple holes cut for seats. A moon was carved on the door of the women's backhouse and the sun for the men's. Lime was used to eliminate waste. Toilet paper was available as early as the late 1800s, but the JC Penney catalog, discarded newspapers, old clothes, and corn cobs served the purpose of toilet paper. In Arkansas, eventually indoor plumbing, septic systems, and municipal sewage systems replaced the outhouses but not completely.[66]

Every farm or plantation had a barn or several. They came in many shapes and sizes and included lots of stuff, such as a hay hole, plows, rollover rakes, wagons, sleighs, and livestock. The barn was built around a threshing floor. Before 1800, they were built entirely of logs. The Dutch barn is one of the oldest styles. Its architecture has close ties to the church—as in the barn's end structure and the floor plan; the nave and aisles in the church translate to the threshing floor and cattle stalls in the barn. Distinct features of the Dutch barn are the end doors and clapboard sheathing used for the walls. Many had hip-gabled roofs, with the rafters widely spaced. Some barns included living quarters—located at the end opposite the main doors. In the nineteenth century, Dutch barns included doors at both ends to provide more room for wagons. English barns had doors centered on the long sides of the structure as opposed to its ends. The English barn was built for grain farming.

Cabin in a Cotton Field, near Pine Bluff, Arkansas

*Cabin in a Cotton Field*

## *Dwellings of Slaves*

*Above:* This picture shows the Red Brick House with Slave Quarters in Biloxi, Mississippi. The house dates back to 1845. It is of antebellum architecture with French influence. House slaves lived in the smaller structure to the left of the Big House. *Below:* Old slave huts at the Hermitage in Savannah, Georgia. Postcard.

## *Dwellings of Slaves*

*Above:* A store with live fish for sale near Natchitoches, Louisiana, July 1940. Postcard  *Below*: Slave quarters downstairs at the Lee Mansion

## Barn-Raising and Barn Frame

A barn was a necessary structure for a farmer. It was large and costly and used for the storage of food grains, hay, and the keeping of animals. A barn-raising, also called a raising bee or rearing, is a collective action of a community, in which a barn for one of the members is built or rebuilt collectively by members of the community. Barn-raising was a common practice in 18th –and 19th –century rural North America. Participants are not paid. One or more persons with prior experience are chosen to lead the project. Most barn-raising were accomplished in June or July, over a one—or two—day time period.

## Early Barns

*Top:* With chickens scraping for worms and seeds around the barn, a farmer sits on a hayloft ledge of his barn. *Second row:* The first two barns are Dutch, the oldest style in the United States. Its end doors are the distinct feature of this style. Many had high-gabled roofs, with the rafters widely spaced—more so than other barns, This style did include living quarters. Walls were made of clapboard sheathing. The third barn has the English style.

*Bottom row:* Every farm had a barn which was built behind the house (in the yard). Most were filled with hay, tools, and livestock. People loved to bail hay: cut it, let it dry, and then bailed it. Hay came in many forms: loose hay, square bails, and round bails. There were hoedowns in the barns. Hobos slept in barns. Near the entrance of the barn, slaves were given their weekly allotment of food, seasonal clothes, whipped, and auctioned out.

## THE BLACK CHURCH

To Educate the Newly Freed

Churches and schools were essential institutions for preserving cultural ties.[67] Dated January 15, 1868, from Little Rock, an American Missionary Association (AMA) representative traveling to Pine Bluff scripted his observations to AMA administrators:

> It is very difficult for those residing in States provided with all the modern facilities for travel to realize the difficulties of a missionary in this state [Arkansas]. There are but forty miles of railroad and though we have many streams, traveling by boat is impossible and we have to adopt either the stage or horseback mode of transportation. I choose the saddle . . . . Taking a tour, you meet the intelligent educated men who dwell for the most part on the rivers, and own large plantations. You meet the unlettered, yet industrious poor white men who work small farms on the hills, and you also find the poor "white trash," who stay anywhere and everywhere, and eke out a miserable existence by fishing, hunting, and stealing . . . . The churches are far apart. Many of the ministers are too ignorant to accomplish much for the cause of Christ, even were they in every other respect qualified.[68]

In *The Historical and Biographical Memoirs of Central Arkansas* (1889), the editor pens the ensuing article about the African American church from 1865 to the 1880s:

> The "Colored" churches have sprung up since the Civil War with a rapidity almost tropical in its luxuriance. The denominations represented are the Missionary Baptists, Primitive Baptists, African Methodist Episcopal Church, Methodist Episcopal Church, and Colored Methodist Episcopal Church in America. The Baptists are offshoots of the white Churches.
>
> The Missionary Baptist churches (Colored) of the county have sprung up from time to time, ever since the first independent organization in 1869, and even before the war, services were held regularly, though unorganized. What was known as McGuire's church, at Pine Bluff, has been in existence since before the Civil War. The churches of the county belong to the St. Marion Baptist Association, which was organized in 1868, and of which

Rev. George Robinson of Pine Bluff is an aged and well-known moderator. They have over fifteen churches in the county with a membership of probably 2,700. The largest churches are St. Paul, Taylor Chapel, Auburn, Cherry Hill, Hurricane, and Lake Side. Their property is valued at $11,000. The first church organization was St. Paul, at Pine Bluff in 1869, now the largest in the city.

The African Methodist Episcopal Churches of Jefferson County were first begun at the time that body organized and is now a part of the South Arkansas Conference, which was organized in 1875. The Pine Bluff district embraces 12 circuits with a membership of over 1,000 and property valued at $15,000. The largest circuits are Swan Lake, Round Lake, and Bartholomew, while the Pine Bluff station is the most extensive.[69]

As late as 1800, most slaves in the United States had not been converted to Christianity. In the years that followed, widespread Protestant Evangelicalism brought about the first large-scale conversion of enslaved men and women. At first, itinerant ministers reached only a small percentage of the slave and free Black populations, preaching a plain-styled message of hope and redemption, while also catering to manners of worship that African men and women carried with them to America, including spirit possession, call-and-response singing, shouting, and dancing. With limited rights and separate seating, the pre-Civil War church was a biracial congregation. After some time, it became necessary for the congregation to divide, whereupon African Americans evolved as distinct churches, but still under the oversight, if not the exclusive control, of Whites. While some planters became convinced of Christianity as a type of social control, others welcomed ministers to the slave quarters and built plantation chapels out of genuine Christian impulses. Yet there were regulations on Black meetings and Black preaching without White supervision. Some Black preachers were termed "best Colored preachers." White landowners gave money and clout to these *preachers*. They could keep their "people together." No one was taught to read. Slaves were taught the Lord's Prayer and catechism. Church evening services were filled with summer mosquitoes and ligh'nin' bugs (fireflies).

After the Civil War, Black churches offered African Americans refuge from oppression and focused on the spiritual, secular, and political concerns of the Black community. With freedom, African Americans rejected the second-class status they had experienced and withdrew in large numbers from biracial congregations. Slaves sang spirituals filled with lyrics about salvation and references to biblical figures like Moses, who led his people to freedom. On occasion, these songs functioned even more explicitly as expressions of resistance, encoding messages about secret gatherings or carrying directions for escape.

Founded in 1894 by Monsignor John Michael "J.M." Lucey, pastor of St. Joseph Catholic Church in Pine Bluff, and Wiley Jones is the Colored Industrial Institute, the first African American Catholic Church and school in Pine Bluff. The school was later named St. Peter Catholic School.

*The Colored Industrial Institute*

## HISTORY OF THE BLACK CHURCH IN AMERICA

Historians tell that the first Black congregation in America was organized at Silver Bluff, South Carolina (Aiken County), in 1773. During the Revolutionary War, when the battles came to Aiken County, the Silver Bluff Church went into exile, with part of the church members going to Savannah, Georgia, and organizing First African Baptist Church, and others going to Augusta, Georgia, and organizing Springfield Baptist Church. Other Baptist churches were organized in the early 1800s. The African Methodist Episcopal Church was organized in Philadelphia, Pennsylvania, in 1794, when Richard Allen and others were pulled from their knees at the St. George Methodist Episcopal Church. The African Methodist Episcopal

Zion Church was organized in New York in 1804. By 1870, the Christian (Colored) Methodist Episcopal Church had been organized in Tennessee. When freedom came in 1865, many White congregations had baptized Black persons, and these persons were allowed to sit in the balconies of the White churches. Little by little these Blacks separated themselves from the White congregations and organized churches where they were free to sing in the choir and offer their own type leadership. Blacks asked for their dismissal so they could organize a new church. The request for letters was granted, and the separation was cordial. Generally, Blacks were allowed to use the basement of the White Church on Friday nights and Sunday afternoons—or a new structure was built for the new congregation.[70]

From the beginning, Black congregations took an interest in education. Some of the early Black ministers and other Black leaders had received an education as the result of the efforts of northern White missionaries. Local Black Baptist associations organized academies and other schools for Blacks in parts of the South. In the area of higher education, the Black Baptists of South Carolina organized Bettis Academy and Morris College; Baptists in North Carolina organized Shaw University; in Virginia, Virginia Union University; in Georgia, Morehouse College; in Alabama, Selma University; in Florida, Florida Memorial College; in Mississippi, Jackson College (now Jackson State University); in Louisiana, Leland College; in Texas, Bishop College; in Arkansas, Southeast Baptist Academy (a precursor to Morris Booker Memorial College) and Arkansas Baptist College; and in Tennessee, Roger Williams University. The AME Church organized Wilberforce University in Ohio; Allen in South Carolina; Morris Brown in Georgia; Payne in Alabama; Paul Quinn in Texas; and Shorter in Arkansas. The CME Church organized Paine in Georgia; Lane in Tennessee; Miles in Alabama; and Texas College in Texas. Many other colleges were organized by predominately White denominations whose missions were to educate Black youth.[71]

The end of slavery brought about a new era for the education of Blacks. Northern missionary societies were eager to provide learning opportunities for the newly freed Blacks. White missionaries, teachers, and preachers came South during Reconstruction. They were protected by the Union armies. Whites kept in touch with the Freedmen's Bureau, an agency that had been created by Congress for the purpose of helping the newly freed Blacks adjust to their new surroundings and situations. This period after the Civil War was probably the first time that African Americans were educated on a mass scale in the South. Many of the students who attended college after the Civil War were the offspring of White slave masters. They were called mulattoes. They were light-skinned and had worked in the slave master's house rather than in the cotton fields. Mulattoes were not accepted in the White community. Some of the White fathers secretly supported schools for Blacks so that their Black children and grandchildren could get an education. In some cases, White former slave masters gave land to their Black offspring. Many of the early Black leaders had White ancestors. These mulattoes became the first Black middle class—doctors, lawyers, teachers, and preachers.

## *St. Paul Baptist Church and St. John AME Church*

*Top*: St. Paul Missionary Baptist Church, founded in 1892. Rev. George Robinson was the first pastor. Rev. Robinson and other organizers were once members of the First Baptist Church located on Cherry Street. The church was called a Mission Church. *Bottom:* St. John African Methodist Episcopal Church, founded in 1868.

## *Churches Founded at the Turn of the Twentieth Century*

*Top left*: First building of First Baptist Church, built in 1854 and used until 1863. *Top right*: An early St. Peter Catholic Church. *Bottom left*; the second Temple Anshe Emeth, completed in 1902. Later the structure housed the First Missionary Baptist Church; at present, the True Vine Church. *Bottom right*: St. Peter Catholic Church.

## *Churches Founded at the Turn of the Twentieth Century*

*Left:* Highland Baptist Church, founded in September 1916. Church built in 1952.

*Bottom left*: St. Peter Catholic Church, founded in 1894, by Monsignor John M. Lucey and Wiley Jones.

*Bottom right*: New Town Baptist Church. First structure was wooden, built in 1903. The edifice pictured here was in place from 1951-1972.

Morris-Booker Memorial College

Dermott, Arkansas dates back to 1832, when it was founded. As travelers went West, after they had crossed the Mississippi River at Gaines' Landing, they often stopped off at the home of Charles McDermott. Slaves in the area brought water in cedar tubs for the guests at the McDermott home. A lumber company industry in the area caused the Iron Mountain Railway, which later became the Missouri Pacific Railway, to be established in the town. As the lumber industry grew, and cotton made it a permanent settlement, the town took on the name Dermott. In 1899, Dermott became the home of the Southeast Baptist Academy, which served as a predecessor to Morris Booker High School and Memorial College. The academy grew out of a passion for education. Dermott was a likely place to locate this new school. The town grew to be known for the prominent Blacks who lived there. A number of Black medical doctors held their practices in Dermott. They were graduates of Meharry Medical College, a medical institution founded in Nashville, Tennessee, in 1876. Many of the businesses in the downtown section of Dermott were owned and operated by Blacks. Sawmills, farming, and a growing cotton industry made Dermott the target of a growing population in southeast Arkansas.

Southeast Baptist Academy grew to be a school of prominence. It was like a boarding school. Students came from all over the state to attend. Because the school required tuition, students who attended were considered children of parents who were well-to-do. Students attended the school from as far away as Helena, Fort Smith, and Little Rock. The curriculum offered to students in the early part of the twentieth century was Hebrew, Greek, Latin, science, biology, chemistry, physics, algebra, English, geometry, history, and economics. The curriculum cited above prevailed for at least the first fifty years of the twentieth century. The faculty was well-prepared and capable of teaching the curricular offerings. Teaching Hebrew and Greek, Rev. S. M. Taylor was a classic example of the instructors at Southeast Baptist Academy. Another teacher was Mrs. Evangeline Brown who taught Latin. Until 1933, Arkansas Baptists were all under the rubric of one state convention, the Arkansas Baptist State Convention. In that year, an ecclesiastical rupture occurred, rendering Black Baptists in twain. In 1934, the Regular Arkansas State Convention was formed and assumed responsibility for the Southeast Baptist Academy. The other group formed the Consolidated Baptist State Convention of Arkansas and assumed the responsibility of the other school, Arkansas Baptist College, located in Little Rock. Upon the formation of the Regular Convention, the name of the school in Dermott was changed to Morris-Booker Memorial College.[72]

*Below: The main building on the campus of Morris-Booker Memorial College, formerly the 1899 Southeast Baptist Academy.*

## Leadership at Morris-Booker Memorial College

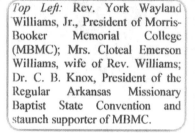

*Top Left:* Rev. York Wayland Williams, Jr., President of Morris-Booker Memorial College (MBMC); Mrs. Cloteal Emerson Williams, wife of Rev. Williams; Dr. C. B. Knox, President of the Regular Arkansas Missionary Baptist State Convention and staunch supporter of MBMC.

*Second Row:* Rev. S. M. Taylor, professor of Hebrew and Greek at MBMC; Mrs. Lois Enoch Taylor, wife of Rev. Taylor; S. W. Dawson, teacher of Ushers and Laymen in the Regular Arkansas Missionary Baptist State Convention and supporter of MBMC.

*Third Row;* Mrs. L. V. Hayes, Director of Young People in the Regular Arkansas Missionary Baptist State Convention and MBMC supporter; Mrs. Georgia McCain, Recording Secretary to the Regular Arkansas Missionary Baptist State Convention; and George Howard, III, *Esq.*, attorney to the Regular Arkansas Missionary Baptist State Convention.

## *Arkansas Baptist College*

Arkansas Baptist College was founded as the Minister's Institute in August 1884, at the annual convention of the Colored Baptists of the State of Arkansas. It opened three months later at the Mount Zion Baptist Church in Little Rock, Arkansas. In 1885, the school was renamed Arkansas Baptist College. It is the only Baptist HBCU [Historically Black College/University] west of the Mississippi River. In 1884, the Executive Board of the Convention of Colored Baptists hired Rev. J. P. Lawson, a White Baptist minister from Joplin, Missouri, to serve as the principal and teacher. At the same time, a block of land was purchased at Sixteenth and High Streets within the Little Rock city limits, where several buildings were erected. Completed in 1893, Old Main, the college's administration building, is the oldest structure in the state of Arkansas established for the purpose of educating African Americans. The first president, Dr. Joseph A. Booker, served from 1887 until his death in 1926. He was succeeded by Rev. S. P. Nelson, Rev. R. C. Woods, and Rev. S. R. Tillinghast. Dr. Tandy Washington Coggs Sr., the fifth president, served from 1937 to 1955. It was during the tenure of Dr. Coggs, in 1947, that the college received its initial two-year accreditation from the Arkansas State Department of Education. [73]

*Top left*: Dr. Joseph Albert Baxter Booker, 1859-1926; first president of Arkansas Baptist College; *Top right*: Dr. Tandy Washington Coggs, Sr., the fifth president of Arkansas Baptist College. *Bottom left*: The family of Dr. Coggs who had five children. Dr. Coggs holds Granville. Mrs. Coggs is seated. *Bottom right:* His daughter, Nanette Coggs, worked at Arkansas Baptist College before moving to California. The photo was taken in 1929.

## Haygood Seminary

The church provided families help in rearing children. Sometimes elementary education was located in a church, which served as a school and a center for all community activities. Haygood Seminary in Hempstead County (Washington) was established in 1883, as one of the first schools for African Americans funded by the Colored Methodist Episcopal Church (CME) in Arkansas. Its mission was to prepare preachers and teachers for their vocation so that they could help with the education and development of other African Americans. Haygood Seminary was one of the first five educational institutions in the South supported by the CME Church in the late nineteenth century. Also known as Haygood Academy, the institution was organized by former slave John Williamson in Washington, Arkansas. His former master was the Reverend Samuel Williamson of the Presbyterian Church in Washington. The seminary was named after Bishop Atticus Green Haygood, a supporter of Black education; president of Emory College in Atlanta, Georgia; and leader in the CME, South. By the 1890s, the seminary expanded its outreach to include students within the elementary grades. To reinforce the vocational education, a laundry, a blacksmith shop, and an industrial hall were built to train students in millinery, carpentry, brick masonry, and sewing.

Fire destroyed two buildings at Haygood Seminary in 1915. The church felt the need to establish an educational institution in another location in Arkansas. It found such a spot in Moten (Jefferson County), five miles south of Pine Bluff and bought three hundred acres of land. The school was named the Arkansas-Haygood Industrial College and was founded in 1915. The first session was held in the fall of 1922. The Arkansas-Haygood Industrial College continued promoting vocational and educational training for African Americans across Arkansas. It was officially closed by World War II.

## Early African American Churches in Pine Bluff and Princeton Pike 1840s-1930

| Name of Church | Information about Church | Date of Founding |
|---|---|---|
| First Baptist Church, organized as a White congregation; the original location near Fifth and Cherry Streets | First Baptist church in Pine Bluff. Mixed congregation. In the 1860s; George Robinson, a freed man, was a member and later ordained a minister. | A structure built in 1854 |
| Woodstock Baptist Church | Rev. George Robinson and the African American members left First Baptist Church to worship separately. | Founded in 1869 |
| St. Paul Missionary Baptist Church | Building an edifice on Georgia Street, members of Woodstock Baptist Church and Pastor George Robinson started a new church, naming the new church St. Paul Missionary Baptist Church. | Founded in 1892 |
| St. John African Methodist Episcopal Church | | 1868 |
| St. Hurricane Baptist Church, now New St. Hurricane Baptist Church | Plantation church and pre-Civil-War life | 1856 |
| Eighth Avenue Baptist Church | Rev. J. C. Rodgers, Pastor | 1898 |
| St. Peter Catholic Church; first named the Colored Industrial Institute | Monsignor John M. Lucey and Wiley Jones | 1894 |
| Mt. Pleasant African Methodist Episcopal Church | Rev. A. H. Hill, pastor | 1895; rebuilt 1941, 1960, 1974, 2004 |
| | | |
| New Town Baptist Church | Prayer band started in 1900 | First edifice built in 1903, rebuilt in the 1950s, 1972 |
| First Missionary Baptist Church | First African American Baptist church in Pine Bluff | 1853 |
| Temple Hill, now Greater Mount Calvary Baptist Church | | 1900 |

| New Jerusalem Baptist Church | Rev. A. D. Rowan, pastor | 1900, rebuilt 1954, 1968 |
|---|---|---|
| Sentennial Missionary Baptist Church, later spelled Centennial, now named Indiana Street Missionary Baptist Church | Rev. Asy Reed, pastor Centennial MBC, built by Rev. S. B. Scott, pastor, July 15, 1946 | Established in 1899, built in 1921 Second edifice built in 1946 |
| Mt. Olive Missionary Baptist Church | Princeton Pike Baptist church, meeting two Sundays a month with St. Luke AME Church | Late 1800s |
| St. Luke African Methodist Episcopal Church | Princeton Pike AME church meeting two Sundays a month with Mt. Olive Missionary Baptist Church | Late 1800s |
| Mt. Nebo Missionary Baptist Church | | 1889 |
| Elm Grove Baptist Church Cottondale and Noble Lake areas | Plantation Church and pre-Civil-War life | 1843 |
| St. James United Methodist Church | Rev. William Wallace Andrews, pastor | 1866 |
| Morris Chapel Missionary Baptist Church, Sherrill, Arkansas | | 1869 |
| New Salem Missionary Baptist Church, Sherrill, Arkansas | | |
| Antioch Missionary Baptist Church, Sherrill, Arkansas. Antioch Church Cemetery on the National Register of Historic Places | | 1885 |
| Grace Temple Missionary Baptist Church, formerly Stranger Rest and Grace Temple Church | Rev. Samuel A. Mosley, pastor | 1904 |
| First Baptist Church Humphrey | | |
| Barraque Street Baptist Church | A group of African American Christians living in Battleville Township | 1885, rebuilt in 1970 |

| | | |
|---|---|---|
| Damascus Missionary Baptist Church | Rev. R. W. Rose, pastor | 1900 |
| Rose Hill Baptist Church | | |
| Pine Hill Baptist Church | Rev. H. S. Spikes, pastor<br>Bill Brown<br>Mary Congo<br>Emma Clark | 1905, rebuilt in 1943, 1970 |
| Liberty Hill Missionary Baptist Church, Watson Chapel | | 1907, rebuilt in 1981, 2016 |
| Mt. Zion Baptist Church | Princeton Pike Road | 1920? |
| St. Paul African Methodist Episcopal Church | Princeton Pike Road<br>Rev. N. W. Coleman, pastor | 1920, rebuilt in 1982; Rev. W. C. Burks, pastor, 1994 |
| St. Peter's Rock Baptist Church | Rev. I. Harris, pastor | Rebuilt in 1912 |
| Trinity Temple Church of God in Christ, now First Trinity Church of God in Christ | | August 1912 |
| Highland Baptist Church | Rev. V. C. Jones, pastor | Congregation met in September 1916; edifice built in 1952 |
| King's Highway Baptist Church | Rev. J. J. Butcher, pastor | November 20, 1927, rebuilt September 26, 1943 |

African American churches founded after 1925 will be listed in another book.

Bettye J. Williams

# The Black School

Education Is a Form of Liberation

I pledge allegiance to the Flag of the
United States of America, and to the
Republic for which it stands, one Nation under
God, indivisible, with liberty and justice for all.

Pine Bluff's first public school building was constructed on West Sixth Avenue between Laurel and Beech Streets in 1870 by Bell and Bocage, contractors. The building was sixty-four feet by sixty-eight feet, sixty-four feet high with an eighty-eight-foot tower. It had a seating capacity for thirty-seven students. It was called "City High School." All grades were taught to its White students. [74] African American students attended a school at West Second Avenue and Linden Street, which was started by the American Missionary Association in 1867 to educate the children of the newly freed slaves. The Pine Bluff School Board bought the property on Second Avenue in 1870, and employed M. W. Martin of Worthington, Minnesota, the White teacher of the missionary school, as principal of the city's Black school.[75] In this book, read more about the first African American school in Pine Bluff in the school section, entitled "Martin School."

Education and land were two of the most desired goals among the freedmen. In 1865, there was opposition to educating African Americans. Most towns refused to sign a document proposing that "the freedmen should have a school."[76] Southeast Arkansas contained some of the most fertile farmland in Arkansas. The region was controlled by large plantation owners whose first priority was not the education of the African American population, most of whom were poor. Blacks were forced by the White planters to keep their children out of school in order to work the cotton fields. The majority of Arkansas' African Americans population was located in the Delta, and a few of the children attended school. Fewer than 5 percent attended high school and less than one-half of 1 percent graduated.[77]

Early September was the beginning of the school year. The school building was usually located by itself at the corner of two country roads or on a small piece of land at the edge of a farmer's field. Schools varied from one room to several levels. Made of wood or sometimes brick, schoolhouses contributed to the community and acted as the center for meetings, dances, social events, and voting. Special programs for Thanksgiving and Christmas were planned. Teachers were expected to instill morals and etiquette in their students (and maintain themselves). Black children attended school when they could—usually three or four months a year, when crops were planted or harvested.

The schoolteacher walked to school from a farm where she was living or drove from a nearby town with a horse and buggy. Teachers were primarily women and were required to follow strict rules in the care of their classrooms and careers. They were not allowed to marry during the term of their contract. All were given curfews and limitations on what they could do or on what they must do: (1) not smoke cigarettes, (2) not loiter in public places, (3) not dress in bright colors, (4) not dye their hair, (5) not travel beyond the city limits without permission from the school board, (6) be at home between the hours of 8:00 p.m. and 6:00 a.m. unless attending a school function, (7) not loiter downtown in ice cream stores, (8) not ride in a carriage or automobile with any man unless he is your father or brother, (9) wear at least two petticoats; and (10) dresses must not be shorter than two inches above the ankles. Female teachers were separated by gender and could not keep company with men. If the female broke any of the preceding rules, she was fired immediately.[78] Women wore long skirts with petticoats and blouses. Men wore suits with ties and dark socks and dress shoes. Wearing simple and modest fashion, children dressed in similar style as adults.

In rural settlements, morning farm chores were done first, and then the children would get ready for school. They left before dawn. Many walked miles from their homes each day. For longer distances, some rode ponies, keeping them in a little shed or a fenced-in area near the school throughout the day. In smaller schoolhouses, entire families of children might be in the same classroom—all at different grade levels. Teachers were responsible for teaching all students in the class. The teacher's desk was larger and near the front, with all the desks in a row facing the teacher. Students brought their own lunches [sandwiches, cornbread, biscuits, apples, cookies] from home, usually carried in a lunch pail. They stored their lunch pails on the floor of the cloakroom. They ate at their desks. Those who lived near the schoolhouse walked home to eat with their families.

The school day began with the *Pledge of Allegiance* to the flag. Black children acquired their first knowledge of the alphabet from a Sunday school speller; the Protestant, Anglican, and Catholic Bibles; and William Shakespeare's poetry. African American adults and children were taught during the early years of freedom; however, children were taught separately. School subjects included spelling, arithmetic, reading, history, geography, and physiology. There was always a homework assignment. Students used pencils and lined paper. They used individual slates (with chalk) for arithmetic problems. For penmanship practice, they used glass bottles of ink with a fountain pen.

There was no electricity, running water, or telephone. Water for drinking and washing came from an outside well, and students took turns pumping to raise the water. There was usually a bucket of drinking water with a dipper inside the classroom. Everyone studied by the light coming in through the windows. Oil lamps along the walls were used for night meetings. Restrooms were out of doors at the back of the school yard— one large toilet for girls and another large one for boys with a tall fence between the structures.

Rules for teachers around 1827 were as follows: (1) fill lamps and clean chimneys; (2) bring a bucket of water and a scuttle of coal for the day's session; (3) make your pens carefully, by whittling nibs to the individual taste of the pupils; (4) men teachers may take one evening each week for courting purposes, or two evenings a week if they go to church regularly; (5) after ten hours in school, spend the remaining time reading the Bible or other good books; (6) lay aside from each pay a goodly sum for the declining years; (7) and do not smoke, use liquor in any form, frequent pool and public halls, or get shaved in a barber shop, which will give good reason to suspect his worth, intention, integrity, and honesty. The teacher who performs his labor faithfully and without fault for five years will be given an increase of twenty-five cents per week in his pay, providing the Board of Education approves.[79]

After 1850 and before the 1900s, teachers fulfilled many tasks during the school day. Some of the responsibilities were as follows: (1) keep the school room neat and clean; (2) sweep the floor at least once daily; (3) scrub the floor at least once a week with hot, soapy water; (4) start the fire at 7:00 a.m. so the room will be warm at 8:00 a.m.; (5) set a broken leg in a crisis; (6) patch the shingles on the school roof; (7) cook lunch on an open fire; (8) wallpaper the residence with newspapers to keep out the winter winds and snakes; (9) stay fresh all day from a weekly swim in the dam; (10) teach a class of children aged five to fifteen; (11) ride a horse sidesaddle four miles (or more) to school and maybe carry a couple of pupils; (12) keep the school property free of goats and cattle; and (13) study at night for the examination at the end of the year.[80]

Around 1915, some teachers taught a grade level in the morning and another grade level in the afternoon. Students did not ride buses to school—there were none. Teachers and students walked to and from school daily. There was little need for physical education classes in those days. Girls played on one side of the playground, and boys played on the other side. They played baseball, tag, hide-and-seek, crack-the-whip, and marbles. A fence enclosed the school. Many schools did not have running water. They used well water. The school board dug a well and put a house around it with a door that could be locked. The custodian filled up the filter, which was a large stone jar, several times a day. Faculty and students had dippers for drinking the water. The heat was wood and/or natural gas stoves. Parents asked the school board for gas lights, so that plays, ice cream suppers, and box suppers could be enjoyed at night. End-of-the-year school plays were performed, delighting parents who were anxious for their children to get an education and fine character—both were accomplished. For fund-raising projects, enough money was made to purchase a piano, a Victrola, and records for music appreciation.

White students and African American students did not attend the same school. There were not as many public schools available for African American children or teachers. Most African Americans lived in rural areas, where schools were not readily available due to lower funding. If an African American child lived and worked on a farm, the owner of the farm could pull him/her out of school at any time to work alongside the parents. Many African American children left school after the fourth grade. African American teachers did not receive as much training as their White peers, and the salaries of Blacks were very low, making it difficult for schools to find good teachers.

*Learning to Read*

## Branch Normal College
### Presently the University of Arkansas at Pine Bluff

The University of Arkansas at Pine Bluff is a historically African American institution. Located on an oak and pine grove on the mighty Arkansas River, UAPB was created in 1873, as a branch of the University of Arkansas in Fayetteville. The name of the school at its opening was Branch Normal College. It was opened on September 27, 1875, with an enrollment of seven students: three from Jefferson County and four from Drew County. Professor Joseph Carter Corbin recommended an institution for the "education for the poor classes" during the early 1870s. His recommendation moved toward the establishment of a school for Blacks: Branch Normal College, 1873–1928; renamed Agricultural Mechanical and Normal College (AM&N) 1928–1972; later named the University of Arkansas at Pine Bluff (UAPB), 1972 to present. Administrators have been men and one woman who were educators, visionaries, and civic leaders:

Founder and Principal Professor J. C. Corbin     1875–1902
Principal Isaac Fisher     1902–1911
William Stephen Harris-Frederick Venegar Years     1911–1915

| | |
|---|---|
| Superintendent Jefferson Ish | 1915–1921 |
| Principal Charles Smith | 1921–1922 |
| Headmaster Robert Malone | 1922–1928 |
| President Dr. John Brown Watson | 1928–1942 |
| Dr. Lawrence A. Davis Sr. | 1943–1972 |
| Interim Chancellor Dr. Johnny B. Johnson Sr. | 1973–1974 |
| Chancellor Dr. Herman B. Smith Jr. | 1974–1981 |
| Chancellor Dr. Lloyd Hackley | 1981–1985 |
| Interim Chancellor Dr. Johnny B. Johnson Sr. | 1985–1986 |
| Chancellor Dr. Charles A. Walker | 1986–1992 |
| Interim Chancellor Dr. Carolyn F. Blakely | 1992–1992 |
| Chancellor Dr. Lawrence A. Davis Jr. | 1992–2012 |
| Interim Chancellor Dr. Calvin Johnson | 2012–2013 |
| Chancellor Dr. Laurence B. Alexander | 2013–present |

The leaders were the thinkers, scholars, intellectuals, theoreticians, and academicians for a brand new educational enterprise for the "convenience and well-being of the poorer classes" in Pine Bluff. The school was designated as a land-grant college under the 1890 federal amendments to the Morrill Land Grant Colleges Act. UAPB is now a multicultural institution with a diverse faculty, teaching more than seven hundred courses in fifteen-plus departments. UAPB students are taught as folows:

> To Think Only of the Best.
> To Expect Only the Best.
> To Work Only for the Best.

UAPB is the second-oldest public institution in Arkansas and is popularly known as the "Flagship of the Delta," a phrase first used during the leadership of Chancellor Lawrence A. Davis Jr. Since 1988, UAPB has gained recognition as a leading research institution in aquaculture studies, offering Arkansas' only comprehensive program in aquaculture. UAPB and the Aquaculture/Fisheries area support a growing regional industry through the Mid-South, and UAPB has the only PhD program in Aquaculture/Fisheries in Arkansas. In 2009, the UAPB band, known as the "Marching Musical Machine of the Mid-South" (M4) was selected to participate in the United States Presidential Inaugural Parade when

Senator Barack H. Obama from Illinois became the first African American president of the United States.

## PHOTO

*Branch Normal College of the University of Arkansas at Fayetteville. This picture was taken about 1895 by R. E. Henchey, a photographer for the Cotton Belt Railway. Courtesy of the Lites-Wallis Collection at Pine Bluff. See James W. Leslie, Saracen's County, Chapter XIII, p. 205.*

# Leadership
## Branch Normal College; Agricultural, Mechanical and Normal College; and the University of Arkansas at Pine Bluff

J. C. Corbin, 1875-1902

Isaac Fisher, 1902-1911

F. T. Venegar, 1911-1917

Jefferson Ish, 1917-1921

Charles Smith, 1921-1922

Robert Malone, 1922-1928

John Watson, 1928-1942

L.A. Davis, Sr. 1943-1972

Earl Evans, 1959-1960

Herman Smith, Jr., 1974-1981

Lloyd Hackley 1981-1985

Johnny B. Johnson 1973-1974/1985-1986

Charles Walker
1986-1991

Carolyn F. Blakely
Summer 1991- Nov. 1991

Lawrence Davis, Jr.
1991-2012

Calvin Johnson
2012-2013

Laurence B. Alexander
2013-

**BRANCH NORMAL/AM&N**

Branch Normal School was created April 25, 1873, as a branch of what is now the U. of A. Instruction began in 1875 in a house at Sevier and Lindsay Streets (2nd & Oak)- seven students enrolled. In 1882 the school was located west of Pine Bluff. The institution became Agricultural, Mechanical and Normal College in 1932. In 1972 AM&N was merged with the U. of A. and designated the University of Arkansas at Pine Bluff. This merger re-joined the two oldest public higher educational institutions in the state.

DONATED BY: GRADUATE & UNDERGRADUATE GREEK ORGANIZATIONS

This marker was erected by the Jefferson County History Commission as part of the Bicentennial Celebration in Pine Bluff, to identify the original location of Branch Normal College on the southeast corner of West Second and Oak Streets. The old building, leased from M. L. Bell, was razed soon after the school moved from the location. Fraternities and sororities at UAPB donated the funds for the marker. One date is incorrect on the marker. The name of the institution was changed to Arkansas Agricultural, Mechanical and Normal College by an act of Arkansas General Assembly in 1927. Photograph by James Leslie.

# Homes of the Presidents

Above: President John Brown Watson was the first administrator to live in the president's house which was constructed in 1929. Dr. Lawrence A. Davis, Sr. was the last president to live in this first residence, located to the left of Caldwell Hall. Around 1966, the university upgraded the campus. Other 1929 landmarks removed were the old home economics building, the Arts and Sciences building, and the Joseph C. Corbin Laboratory School. *Below*: The new home of the president was constructed in 1966. It was demolished in May 2013.

Bettye J. Williams

## *Martin School*
American Missionary Association Pine Bluff Private School

Prior to the creation of the Freedmen's Bureau, the efforts of the American Missionary Association (AMA) in Arkansas consisted of individual teachers attempting to establish schools under the protection of the Federal army. In December 1863, twelve teachers from Chicago, Illinois, were commissioned by the AMA to teach in Pine Bluff (Jefferson County), Little Rock (Pulaski County), and Helena (Phillips County). In 1864, the AMA was left focusing solely on Pine Bluff, where the schools lacked sufficient funds and staff to remain consistently open. Other difficulties were mixed reactions from the Whites in the area, the instability of racial relations, and financial wants. Despite the preceding hardships, AMA teachers reported high attendance figures and a willingness in their pupils to learn. [81]

### 1871–1877 Martin School Record

| Type of School | Location | Staff | Students |
|---|---|---|---|
| Normal (teaching) | Pine Bluff, Arkansas | Principal M. W. Martin of Ripon, Wisconsin | 90 students enrolled 30 normal students 50 Sabbath students |
| | | Asst. Principal, Mrs. M. W. Martin | |
| | | In 1871, Martin School Superintendent Prof. Marion R. Perry Sr. | |

Principal Martin's note from Pine Bluff:

> The religious interest here during the past few months has taken some of our pupils into churches, where I think they will do good, yet they are regarded with suspicion by the old people, unless they follow all the extravagancies so common among them. Our Sabbath-school is smaller, but very interesting. I give a half-hour Bible lesson each day, and thus, reach many who do not attend any Sabbath-school.

> —1876 meeting of the American Missionary Association

In March 1868 and lasting for several years, there was a shaky period of transition as AMA schools came under governmental control. Some AMA teachers were successfully integrated into the new state system, while others were forced out due to tensions from competing schools. A well-recognized private school in Pine Bluff in 1871, Martin School was the first Negro public school. It was located at Second and Linden Streets. From Worthington, Minnesota, Professor M. W. Martin was the principal from 1871 to 1877. The assistant principal was his wife. In 1878, Martin School fell victim to a defeated mill tax that cut school funding. Martin left the state, ending the work of the AMA in Pine Bluff and Arkansas. AMA schools were absorbed into the public school system.[82]

In 1878, the Pine Bluff School Board purchased the Martin School building to be used as the new Black public school. Marion R. Perry Sr. was the superintendent of the new school. After Professor Martin returned to Minnesota in 1878, Perry was both principal and superintendent. Perry won the hearts and minds of Pine Bluff school patrons and most of the students—many of whom, inspired by him, entered the school system as teachers upon their own graduation.

## Negro Boys Industrial School
Work Farm for Juveniles

Dr. Tandy Washington Coggs Sr. was the first Superintendent of the Negro Boys Industrial Schools (NBIS) located in Pine Bluff and Wrightsville, Arkansas. Founded in 1923, NBIS was a juvenile correctional facility for African American male youth in the state. For most of its existence, it was a juvenile work farm. There were two locations in 1936, one in Jefferson County and one in Pulaski County. The first location was in Pine Bluff, and then, in the mid-1930s, in Wrightsville. Prior to 1923, Black youths who were convicted of crimes were sent to the Adult Black Penitentiary to serve their sentences. Black male orphans were also sent to the Adult Black Penitentiary for maintenance. From 1923 to 1937, Dr. Tandy was the superintendent.

The facility became a symbol for the disparities that prevailed in Arkansas during segregation. In a 1940 report to the governor summarizing programs at vocational trades schools, a white boys' school taught "carpentry and joining, cabinet work, glazing, painting cement work, brick laying, wood and metal lathe operation, blacksmithing, acetylene welding, plastering, tailoring, and shoe mending. NBIS is mentioned only once—as the recipient of 156 mattresses made by the white boys' trade school. At the time the decision was made to move NBIS to Wrightsville, the Arkansas General Assembly formally decided that the best treatment for Black boys sentenced to the institution was farming. In a 1956 report and his master's thesis on NBIS, sociologist Gordon Morgan, the first tenured African American professor at the University of Arkansas at Fayetteville, documented the horrific conditions at Wrightsville:

> The squalor was mind bogging. Many boys go for days with only rags for clothes. More than half of them wear neither socks nor underwear during [winter of] 1955–1956. It is not uncommon to see youths going for weeks without bathing or changing clothes. At times, the number of boys at the school was over 100. There was no laundry equipment. A single thirty-gallon hot water tank served the bathing needs of the entire population. The water was deemed undrinkable. Employees brought their own drinking water to work . . . . In an earlier era, armed guard had overseen the boys in the fields. Boys were whipped with a leather strap for infractions.[83]

In March 1959, the Wrightsville School had sixty-nine boys aged fourteen to seventeen. Most of them were convicted of minor and petty crimes. Some boys with no criminal record lived at the school solely because they had nowhere else to reside. They lived in a 1936 Works Progress Administration building described by *Time Magazine* as "rickety."[84] In the pre-dawn morning of March 5, 1959, a fire started in the dormitory. The fire mysteriously ignited around 4:00 a.m., on a cold, wet morning, following earlier thunderstorms in the same area of rural Pulaski County. The doors in the dormitory were locked. Forty-eight boys managed to escape, while twenty-one died. Governor Orval E. Faubus asked a committee to investigate the fire. The committee concluded that the correctional facility, the State of Arkansas, and the local community be held responsibility for the incident, but recommended no course of action. A KTHV report said that "somehow the story faded into the backdrop of the Civil Rights Movement."[85] The land once occupied by the unit now houses the Arkansas Department of Correction Wrightsville Unit. There are no markers there that indicate that the boys' school existed or that the fire occurred.

## Colored Industrial Institute
St. Peter Catholic School

After 123 years of serving the Pine Bluff community except when it was closed from 1975 to 1985, St. Peter's School closed its doors May 25, 2012. Serving African American students, St. Peter's School opened in 1889 as the Colored Industrial Institute. Monsignor John Michael "J.M." Lucey, pastor of St. Joseph Church in Pine Bluff, opened the first Black Catholic elementary school to provide opportunities for students that did not have any. The school was renamed St. Peter's Academy in 1897 and was relocated to St. Peter's Church.

The Colored Industrial Institute was called St. Peter's Catholic School after 1916. Monsignor Lucey was the driving force behind the establishment of St. Peter's School. It was located near Jones' Park on State Street between Fifteenth and Sixteenth Avenues. The school was staffed by the Sisters of Charity from Nazareth, Kentucky, from 1889 to 1901; then the Sisters of the Holy Family from New Orleans, Louisiana, from 1901 to 1909; the Sisters of the Holy Ghost and Mary Immaculate from San Antonio, Texas, from 1913 to 1927; and the Sisters of the Holy Ghost from Techny, Illinois, from 1927 until the school closed in 1975. St. Peter's Catholic School reopened as an elementary school staffed by the School Sisters of Notre Dame from Dallas, Texas, in 1984. The 1889 building was the first two-story wooden academy building. The next structure was the three-story brick and cut-stone academy building of 1889. The first St. Peter's Church was established in 1894.

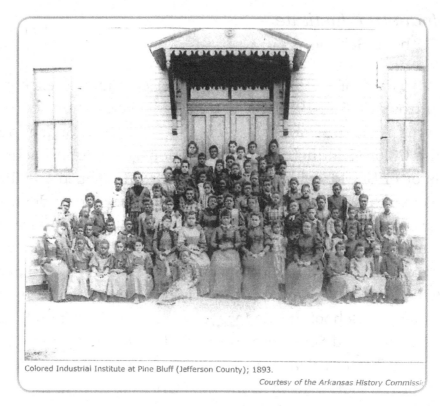

Colored Industrial Institute at Pine Bluff (Jefferson County); 1893.

*Courtesy of the Arkansas History Commission*

*Colored Industrial College*

## Merrill School
1215 West Pullen Street

The history of Merrill School began in 1886, when the city purchased from Joseph Merrill for $4,000 the site between Pullen, Scull, Linden, and Mulberry Streets.[86] On the block was his own property—a two-story frame dwelling that was converted into a five-room school building. This structure was to be used as the Black high school. The school was first called Greenwood School, but after the death of Joseph Merrill in 1890, as a tribute to his money, it was named Merrill School. Located at 1215 Pullen Street, the men selected as principals were well-qualified, and the growth of the school reflected their strong leadership. According to a history of the school by the late J. W. Wiley, the school was first opened by Rev. Lewis Johnson, who served as principal for one year and is remembered as a fine teacher. Marion R. Perry Sr. was the next principal of Merrill School. A very capable man, he worked very hard in the interest of public education, and his physical and mental qualities enabled him to endear the school to the community after quite a struggle. During his administration, crucial

128

problems arose that challenged his ability as an administrator. The *Pine Bluff Weekly Press Eagle* related the burning of the school three times within a short period of time. According to the newspaper account, the fires were the result of arson.

The first graduates of Merrill School, in 1894, were James H. Marshall, Malachi M. Lee, Minnie B. Fulton, James Moore, Henry D. Hewlit, and Isaac Moon. Professor William J. Townsend served as principal from 1901 to 1903. He was transferred to Missouri Street School, which became the high school, leaving Merrill School an elementary school for a number of years. According to Ella Brandon McPherson Wade, who taught at Merrill School thirty-plus years and retired as Assistant Principal in 1971, some strong teachers at Merrill School during its early years were Professor Joseph C. Corbin, from 1902 to 1911, after twenty-seven years at Branch Normal College as the first principal; Isaac Hathaway gained national and international fame for his work in art; and Mrs. Willie E. Clark, a strong and brilliant teacher who was an inspiration to all whose lives she touched, served for several decades. Alma Ferguson Crockett of California, a former student of Willie E. Clark, pays this tribute: "Mrs. Clark taught by precept and example the three M's—mathematics, manners, and morals."[87]

In 1913, the high school was transferred from Missouri Street School back to Merrill School with Professor William J. Townsend as the principal. Under his administration, the school expanded, the curriculum was enriched, enrollment increased, and several teachers were added. Professor Townsend was retained until his death in 1941. Reuben Napoleon Chanay, who served as assistant principal under Professor Townsend, then became principal. During Chanay's leadership of Merrill School, several long-range goals were achieved: (1) the first six grades were separated from the high school; (2) Merrill School became a junior-senior high school, with nine teachers transferred to Carver Elementary School; (3) the purchase and lighting of an athletic field became a reality; (4) Merrill School earned accreditation in the North Central Association of Secondary Schools and Colleges; (5) the faculty was upgraded by the principal, and more than twenty teachers earned Master's Degrees; (6) a well-equipped library (with a librarian with a degree in Library Science) was established, the preceding met the requirements of the North Central Association; (7) a part-time guidance program was set up based on the needs of students; and (8) a testing program began.

## Principals of Merrill High School

| | |
|---|---|
| 1887–1997 | Professor Marion Rowland Perry Sr. |
| 1897–1900 | Professor T. M. Makin |
| 1900–1901 | Professor A. N. Freeman |
| 1901–1903 | Professor William J. Townsend |
| 1903–1904 | Professor B. Y. Head |
| 1904–1909 | Professor Joseph C. Corbin |
| 1909–1910 | Professor B. Y. Head |
| 1910–1913 | Professor J. B. Short |
| 1913–1941 | Professor William J. Townsend |

| **Names of Elementary Schools** | **Opening Dates** |
|---|---|
| Missouri Street Elementary School | 1889 |
| Indiana Street Elementary School | 1949 |
| Carver Elementary School | 1953 |
| Southeast Junior-Senior High School | Early 1960s |

*Merrill High School*

## Missouri Street School
619 Missouri Street

Missouri Street School is the only one of Pine Bluff's larger schools of the nineteenth century that has disappeared completely.[88] Many old-timers are even uncertain about its original location. The school's first structure—at 619 Missouri Street—was a four-room frame building erected in

1889. This building was replaced in 1901 by a brick structure. Having lived for many years not far from the site of the original school, Professor Marion R. Perry Sr. [1855–1914] recalled that the school was housed temporarily in a building known as "Vining Hall" at Eleventh and State Streets while the new school building was under construction. Although Missouri Street School was built as an elementary school and used chiefly for that purpose, during the first decade of the twentieth century, it was the Negro high school in Pine Bluff. According to Professor Marion R. Perry Sr., Missouri Street School and Merrill School were—at no time—both high schools simultaneously.

Missouri Street School was served by a number of principals who were prominent in early Negro education. The first principal was S. W. Crump, who was a strict disciplinarian. Remembered principally for his long service at Merrill School, Professor William J. Townsend was principal of Missouri Street School for a decade—from 1903 to 1913. The longest-serving principal was O. L. Douglass, who served from 1918 to 1942. The last principal of Missouri Street School [1942–1949], W. T. Cheney recalled that Mrs. Bessie Pearson, who was one of the early presidents of the Parents Teachers Association, began a hot lunch program before such programs were sponsored by the federal government. Lunches were sold at a nominal price, which meant better nutrition for the students from the many low-income families in the district.

The faculty of the Missouri Street School was always fairly stable and with little pupil turnover. Although they lived in Pine Bluff, many residents worked on farms to which they were transported daily. As Pine Bluff grew, the school population of Missouri Street School moved southward. By the late 1940s, the 1901 building had become uninhabitable. Sources say that numerous bats made raucous noise, which made teaching difficult. A site was located at 1519 Indiana Street with space for a playground. The land was purchased. In 1949, Missouri Street School gave way to Indiana Street School. Principal W. T. Cheney and many of the faculty members moved to the new school, which carried on in the same tradition as the old one.

Principals of Missouri Street School

| | |
|---|---|
| 1891–1901 | Principal S. W. Crump |
| 1901–1903 | Principal A. W. Freeman |
| 1903–1913 | Professor William J. Townsend |
| 1913–1918 | Principal J. B. Short |
| 1918–1942 | Principal O. L. Douglass |
| 1942–1949 | Principal W. T. Cheney |

*Indiana Street School*

*Greenville School*
2501 West Tenth Street

> *In the morning when we entered*
> *And each child was in array,*
> *Ere our lessons we had started*
> *We would stand and sing and pray.*
>
> ...
>
> *In the little russet school house*
> *Where the bench sits 'round the tree.*
> —Lanier Callion Stevens

Available records show that the first year of Greenville School's existence was the school year 1894–95.[89] It was started as a school for primary pupils in areas south of Sixth Street and west of Cherry Street. At its beginning, there were only two grades, known as the "first primary and the "second primary." It was located at Tenth and Spruce Streets, or just across the railroad tracks (east of St. Louis Southwestern Railroad) and adjacent to the property owned by lawyer N. W. Shelton, at 2115 West Tenth Street. The first principal was Pine Bluff citizen A. S. Moon. Mrs. A. T. Strickland was the first assistant teacher. The enrollment for the first year was 112. Outstanding among later assistant teachers was Mrs. Bettie Shaw, who served capably with A. S. Noon and during much of the tenure of J. J. Nunn. During this period, the third grade was added. Greenville School pupils began entering Merrill School in the fourth grade. When she was a first-grade teacher in 1927, Mrs. Blanche W. Douglass recounted that there were four grades and four teachers when she arrived at Greenville School.

In 1942, Greenville School was moved directly across Tenth Avenue into the pine grove, where students spent recesses "making straw beds—playing ball." The building, a frame structure, was renovated, and additions were made sufficient to house the fifth and sixth grades. Mrs. Blanche W. Douglass later became a principal. Her administration was marked by considerable growth in the curriculum, faculty, and pupil enrollment.

Principals of Greenville School

| | |
|---|---|
| 1895–1922 | Principal A. S. Moon |
| 1922–1937 | Principal J. J. Nunn Sr. |
| 1937–1941 | Principal J. J. Nunn Jr. |
| 1941–1943 | Principal J. C. Freeman |
| 1943–1951 | Principal Mrs. Blanche Douglass |

*Greenville Elementary School*

# Colleges/Universities Attended by African American Leaders in Pine Bluff

| Name of College/University | Name of College/University |
| --- | --- |
| Chicago Theological Seminary (leading Congregational school in the Middle West) | Atlanta University |
| Hampton Institute | Tuskegee Institute |
| Fisk University | Branch Normal College (Pine Bluff) |
| Wilberforce University | Lincoln University (Pennsylvania) |
| Harvard College | Oberlin College |
| University of Pennsylvania | Columbia University School of Law |
| University of Chicago | The Ohio University |
| Southland College (a Quaker institution in Phillips County, Arkansas) | Newton Theological Seminary in Boston |
| University of Pittsburgh | Alcorn A&M. College |
| Chicago Musical College | Burnham School of Beauty (Chicago) |
| Paris, France Beauty Doctor | Chandler College (Lexington, Kentucky) |
| New England Conservatory of Music and Art (Boston, Massachusetts) | Cincinnati Art Academy |
| Pittsburg College | New York State College (Alfred, New York) |
| Alabama State University | Natchez College (Mississippi) |
| Moody Bible Institute (Chicago) | Teachers College of Emporia (Kansas) |
| University of California at Los Angeles | Colgate University at Hamilton, New York. |

| Brown University, Providence, Rhode Island, | Maryville Normal College in Tennessee |
|---|---|
| Spelman Seminary | |

## THE BLACK COMMUNITY

Farm structures included a shop, the barn, smokehouse, chicken coop, an outhouse, and other outbuildings. In the 1880s or thereabout, residents in Arkansas received land grants of 160 acres. Some families received as many as two grants. Cotton was a sharecropped product in Arkansas and the South. Other crops were sweet potatoes, corn, and sorghum. Living at a time when folks protected their own, farmers spent considerable time tending a truck patch, mending fences on the place, and caring for farm tools. Southern crops were garden truck, rice, tobacco, cotton, wheat, corn, hemp, wheat, and oats. People lived off the land by tending their truck patch. Mending fences on the place was a frequent spring activity. Hand-drawn wells served as a community-wide water source, never having been known to run dry, and always produced cool water.

During the nineteenth century and early 1900s, mules were essential to the agricultural economy of the South. By 1925, there were 4.5 million mules in the South. At the highest point of mule use during the 1920s and 1930s, over 360,000 animals were thought to have been in Arkansas performing agricultural work such as pulling up stumps, breaking ground, tilling soil, hauling lumber and firewood, and serving as transportation, including their use in pulling streetcars across the state. Used for storage and as a location for sales more than a century ago, mule barns were structures where farmers came to buy horses or mules—or not. Produce, livestock, chickens, ducks, and quilts were sold in these barns. Livestock stayed outside.[90] With a metal roof and metal sheeting on the outside painted read, mule barns were made of wood.

In the 1800s, saws were used to clear the forest/woods. They were replaced by chain saws. Farmers cut the wood, hauled it, and then trucked it to someone's yard or to the mills that would turn the wood into lumber or process it into paper. The sawdust was in their veins. It was a dangerous business and very much physical. Logging entailed a number of jobs, including fallers, who cut down trees by hand; lumberjacks, operators of axes or chain saws used to fell the trees; and graders and scalers, who checked the amount and quality of the wood. Fathers passed on to their sons their love and knowledge of wood and the independence that came from working for oneself.

Enslaved children would often imitate their reality as a form of play. When they were not engaged in light tasks, children ate, talked, played with their companions, roamed the plantation, waded streams, fished, hunted, and gathered food (nuts, berries, and fruits) with other children.

## Games of Children

| Hide the Switch | Auction Games | Goose and Gander |
|---|---|---|
| No Bogeyman Tonight | Stick Horse | Tops |
| Drums | Looking at Stars at Night | Ring Dances |
| Snail Away Rauley | Ball Games | Skinny |
| Rolly Hole | Anti Over | Blind Man's Bluff |
| Stilts | Marbles | Dancing |
| Fox and Hound | Pig in the Pin | Base Games |
| Ole Hundred (Hide-and-Seek) | Jump Rope | Chase Games |
| Jumping Poles | Smut (like cards using corn) | Throwing Horseshoes |
| I Spy | Potato Sack Race | |

## BLACK SETTLEMENTS

Lumber Markets Opened in Jefferson County

Following Reconstruction [1866–1877], many African Americans left the Deep South for land in the West, North, and East. They were fleeing economic exploitation, political repression, educational handicaps, and social humiliation. However, the flood of Black emigrants created cracks in the thin crust of local tolerance. Yet freedmen were able to become independent farmers through the Homestead Act, which made it possible for a person to stake a claim to 160 acres at a federal land office and to acquire the land for a nominal filing fee after five years of residence. Most families divided the homestead into three plots—eighty acres for cultivation, forty for hay, and forty for pasture.[91]

Together with the church, family and kinship ties remained the foundation of the African American community. During the 1800s and early 1900s, settlements developed around natural springs, crossroads, churches, post offices, and early churches. Most of the settlements had no definite boundaries and usually consisted of widely scattered dwellings and outbuildings. Originally, they had only a small number of families. When a prominent building such as a school was removed, the identity of a small settlement soon diminished. The relocation of churches and post offices often resulted in the gradual movement of a settlement's designated center and changed the boundaries of a community from one generation to another.

Migrating to Pine Bluff from settlements such as Bookman, Sheridan, Prattsville, and Malvern, African Americans from the preceding settlements inhabited homes on the West End of Pine Bluff. They arrived in the 1880s. Located west of Pine Bluff, the Bookman community is located along the old Princeton Pike Road, east of the junction of Highways 35 and 190 in Darysaw Township. Having more than one name, Bookman was also known as Okay and Goolsby,[92] This community was originally populated by former slaves from South Carolina—Willingham, Haltiwanger, Tobias, Drayer, Burkett, Waddell, Ainsworth, Ruth, Counts, Dorn, Cannady, Mathious, Coogler, Stoudamire, Ghee, Litzsey, Ussery, Mays, Boyd, James, Bishop, and Cooper—and their descendants after the Civil War. These families resided in Bookman, Stoudamire Camp, Sheridan, Grapevine, and other points along Princeton Pike. Many of the families were from the same areas of South Carolina, and most were acquainted.[93] The Bookman community had its own schoolhouses—Number 48 School and St. Paul Elementary School—and a United States post office. Most of the people were farmers who had fruit orchards, and raised hogs, beef, and cattle. Bookman also had a gristmill and a general store.

With the coming of the railroads in the 1870s and 1880s, Pine Bluff grew from 2,081 in 1870 to almost 10,000 residents in 1890. An agrarian boom developed. Planters could transport their cotton to markets in New Orleans and St. Louis. The Cotton Belt Railway played an important role in the growth of the city with the building of maintenance and car building facilities.[94] The year 1900 brought the flourishing lumber industry to two Pine Bluff lumber companies—Sawyer-Austin Lumber Company and Bluff City Lumber Company. They opened lumber markets nationwide.

Located near railroad tracks, houses for African Americans grew up around sawmills. Many of these houses were constructed of split poles called slabs. They were built during the 1920s and 1930s, using wood from a sawmill set up in that area.[95] Many other settlements grew up around a Masonic Lodge, logging camps, logging railroads, and railroad tracks—the Rock Island Railroad and the Missouri Pacific Railroad. Horse-drawn buggies clopped in the streets, but open-topped jalopies crowded the curb. Many farmers had ox wagons. Monthly wages for African Americans were only $10 for men and $5 for women in 1866.

*A Cotton Picker in Arkansas and Rural Post Office Boxes*

Cotton picker near Arkansas City (Desha County).
*Courtesy of the Arkansas History Commission*

## Transportation: Wagons and Carts

Postcard: A hay wagon.

Postcard: Workers bailing cotton.

# Transportation: Wagons and Carts

Postcard: A racing cart.

Postcard: Horses and wagons traveling West.

Postcard: Horse-drawn hay cart.

## Transportation: Wagons and Carts

Postcard: A horse and carriage.

Postcard: Horse and steer harnessed to a cart.

Postcard: A bridge and a speedway.

# Transportation Vehicles

Postcard: A 108-year old former slave who died in 1938. He is driving a steer.

Postcard: An old slave market.

# African American Pioneers
## [1833—1892]

## Mr. Walter "Wiley" Jones
### Entrepreneur

Mr. Walter "Wiley" Jones
*Entrepreneur*

Personal Data:

    Birth: July 14, 1848.

    Death: December 7, 1904, from a heart attack and Bright's disease in his home on Nineteenth Avenue and Georgia Street.

    Parents: George Jones (a white planter, one of six children); Ann (slave); Wiley was Ann's fourth child

    Birthplace: Madison County, Georgia; in 1853 moved to Arkansas, settled on the Richard's Plantation in Jefferson County, twelve miles north of Pine Bluff.

    Siblings: Matthew, Thomas, Julia, Taylor, James.

    Spouse: Unmarried.

Educational Data:

    No schooling.

Professional Experience:

    Instructed by his father (George Jones) and the Yell family, which purchased him following his father's death, Jones learned about business through hard work and meeting people. As an unmarried man, he worked from sunrise to sunset.

A Republican, Walter "Wiley" Jones became one of the first wealthy African Americans in the South. His mother named him "Walter" after his doctor, but he was given the nickname "Wiley" for being untamed and playful. Jones's siblings were Matthew, the eldest, who was the superintendent of the construction of the Wiley Jones Street Car Lines of Pine Bluff; Thomas, who worked for Wiley; Julia, who became the wife of Ben Reed, a prominent African American at the time; Taylor, who was murdered in Johnson County, Arkansas, for the money on his person; and James, who was the manager of Wiley Jones's mercantile business. [96]

When Wiley Jones was five years old [1853], George Jones moved, by wagon, from Georgia to Jefferson County, taking with him over forty slaves, his slave wife, and her children. They settled on Governor Byrd's plantation, twelve miles above Pine Bluff, on the Arkansas River, where George Jones died in 1858. Wiley was ten years old.

No freedom papers were found. Ann and her children were sold to the family of Peter Finerty, and then to General James Yell, an attorney and planter in Pine Bluff. Wiley Jones was given to Yell's son, Fountain Pitts Yell, as a wedding gift. Jones was a carriage driver for his master's wife. Promoted to Colonel, Yell enlisted in the Confederate army in 1861. Jones became a camp servant for Colonel Yell. After the death of the colonel, the family sought refuge in Waco, Texas. Jones worked as a caretaker in a mercantile store and drove a cotton wagon from Waco to San Antonio.

When the war ended in 1865, the Yell family returned to Arkansas, settling in Drew County. Wiley Jones worked as a mule driver in Lincoln County, then later was promoted to manager of the cotton plantation. He made $20 a month. By 1868, he is in Pine Bluff working at a local saloon, a barbershop, and a nearby hotel as a waiter. He invested his money in real estate, opened a successful saloon at 207 South Main, and owned several other businesses, including the well-known Southern Mercantile Company, where he rode his horses to check on his businesses. His hobbies were horses and horse racing. He built a park on fifty-five acres near Seventeenth and Main Street. It was a city recreational park with a harness-racing track.

Known for wearing a top hat at his stables, Wiley Jones owned twenty-four race horses and stallions. His favorite horse was "Excalibur."[97] In August 1886, he became one of the first African Americans in the nation to receive a franchise to operate a mule-drawn streetcar system. The business was named Wiley Jones Street Car lines. It merged with the Citizens Street

Railway in 1890. This venture later became the electric railway, which the city purchased. It is now known as Pine Bluff Transit.

In the 1880s and 1890, Wiley Jones was one of Jefferson County's most political citizens; however, he never ran for office. From 1892 to 1894, he served as a circuit clerk of Jefferson County and became a delegate to several national Republican conventions. In particular, Jones and Ferd Havis were the delegates from Arkansas at the 1892 Republican National Convention. Not attached to any church, he supported the Colored Industrial Institute (which became St. Peter's Catholic Church) on Sixteenth Avenue and State Street and donated land on Popular and West Fourth Avenue for the Black St. James Methodist Church (which moved to University Avenue under the leadership of Rev./Dr. Henry "Hank" Wilkins during the first decade of the twenty-first century). His guide through life was, "Do right." His motto was, "Owe no man."

On June 14, 1889, Wiley Jones made investments with Edward B. Houston of White Sulphur Springs (Watson Chapel). The location is now called Sulphur Springs. The partnership sold lots to Pine Bluff residents for summer homes. Wiley Jones was the richest African American in the state at the time of his death in 1904. He had an estimated worth of $300,000. He is buried in his own cemetery, now known as Miller Cemetery.[98]

Alert Attention is the Mother of Intelligence. Intelligence is the Door to Freedom.

The streetcar stables of Wiley Jones, an ex-slave and a leading businessman, in Pine Bluff (Jefferson County); circa 1890.

*Courtesy of the Butler Center for Arkansas Studies, Central Arkansas Library System*

*Stables of Walter "Wiley" Jones*

# Mr. Ferdinand (Ferd) Havis

## Politician, Wealthy Businessman, Republican Party Delegate

Mr. Ferdinand (Ferd) Havis
*Politician, Wealthy Businessman, Republican Party Delegate*

Personal Data:

　Birth: November 15, 1846.

　Death: August 25, 1918. Died at his home at 920 West Barraque Street, probably of a heart attack.[99]

　Parents: John Havis, a White farmer, and a slave mother.

　Birthplace: Desha County, Arkansas.

　Siblings: only son of slave mother.

　Spouse: Married three times: Miss Dilsa, died childless in 1870; Miss Geneva, mother of one [Ferda], died of consumption on August 12, 1886; and Miss Ella Cooper on November 2, 1887. Ferdinand and Miss Ella (age twenty when married; he was forty) had three children: Viessy, Alma, and Felton.

　Children: Four children: Ferda, Viessy, Alma, and Felton.

Burial: Bellwood Cemetery.

Educational Data: Little common school education.

Professional Experience: Learned the barbering trade. Professional Affiliations:

　　　　Elected city and county officer.

　　　　Elected officer and delegate to the Republican Party.

Honors and Awards:

　Governor Elisha Baxter commissioned him a Colonel in the Arkansas Militia [Brooks-Baxter War] in April 1874. He was a member of the Masonic fraternity, the G.U.O.O.F. Lodge, and United Brothers of Friendship organizer.

Funeral: He was survived by his wife, Ella, and three children: Ferda P. Havis Donnelly, Viessy E. Havis, and Alma L. Havis.

Ferdinand Havis was born a slave in Desha County, Arkansas, on November 15, 1846. He was the son of John Havis, his White master, and a slave woman whose name is unknown. John Havis moved to Jefferson County in 1859, taking Ferdinand and his mother with him. Ferdinand Havis began his political career in the 1870s. From slave to freedman, from barber to wealthy businessman and large landholder, from ward hand to city alderman and pre-eminent leader, Havis was a central figure in Pine Bluff politics from 1872 to 1906. Charismatic, he was a lover of political conflict.[100] After the Civil War, he learned the barbering trade and opened a shop in Pine Bluff. His major means of livelihood continued to be his barber shop:

> Fred Havis has rented rooms on Barraque Street next to Murphy's saloon and removed to them. The rooms are nicely papered and neatly furnished. A bath house has been attached and a competent number of barbers engaged.[101] On November 7, 1871, he won his first elective office when he was successful as alderman of the Third Ward in Pine Bluff.

His elected positions were numerous and varied. Among them were Third Ward alderman in 1872, serving five terms total. He served in the Arkansas State House of Representatives in 1873 and was Jefferson County Assessor in 1873, after resigning as state representative. In 1882, he was elected Jefferson County Circuit Clerk and held the position for five terms. For twenty years, he served as chairman of the Jefferson County Republican Party. In 1880, he served as a delegate to the National Republican Convention, which met in Chicago. During that convention, he was one of the 306 delegates who supported Ulysses S. Grant in his bid for the presidential nomination. Havis became the vice president of the Arkansas Republican Party in 1888. In 1889, he was the Republican nominee for the U.S. Senate but did not win the election. One ambition Havis did not realize was the desire to become postmaster of Pine Bluff. In 1898, President William McKinley nominated him for the position of Pine Bluff postmaster, but the Senate refused to confirm his appointment. Senators James K. Jones and James A. Berry of Arkansas successfully blocked his nomination. Pine Bluff White citizens, along with the local newspaper, had opposed his nomination. Because he was an African American, he never became postmaster. Within two years, African Americans were eliminated from nearly all public offices in Arkansas. [102] Relationships between the races changed for the worst after Reconstruction, yet Havis had some influence with both racial groups, along with their support.[103] Other Black politicians serving in elected positions were: Major Minor, alderman; William Murphy, state representative; D. A. Robinson, First Ward alderman; Captain A. Montaque, service in the Brooks-Baxter War; and Dan Nevels, alderman.

The *Pine Bluff Weekly Press Eagle* made remarks on Havis's personal appearance:

> Mr. Havis is a handsome, well-proportioned man and owes much of his success as a politician to his ability as an orator. He is a good parliamentarian and has a memory so retentive, and is so logical a speaker that he rarely fails to carry his point in debate. He is a member of the Masonic fraternity, the Grand United Order of Odd Fellows, and the United Brothers of Friendship. He owns 2,000 acres of land in addition to valuable city property.[104]

Havis used his power to defeat those candidates for whom he had a personal dislike, and this almost led to his demise. David A. Parks had run for constable in Vaugine Township during the 1888 campaign and was defeated. He blamed his defeat on Havis and boasted Havis "would never be in his way again." In an elaborate plot, Parks, who was a saloon keeper on East Third Avenue, negotiated with an undercover man to shoot Havis.[105] In 1890, Havis was said to own a fine house at 920 West Barraque Street, two thousand acres of land, an office on Main Street, and other valuable city property.[106] His obituary reads:

> Ferd Havis was a born leader and forged his way into public life by methods that were conservative and looking toward the greater good for his race. He was loyal to the South and especially the state of Arkansas and as opportunities opened for a possible broader career in public life, he refused to be tempted to leave the state to whose interest he was anxious to give his service.
>
> During the Brooks-Baxter War and at other times when tense situations tended to mar the harmony of the races, he cooperated with the leading white citizens of Pine Bluff to quell any feeling that would bring strife. He was a politician that

kept abreast of the times and his pride in the advancement of his race was ample reward for the labor he contributed to the cause.

Ferd Havis had acquired ample means to be called a man of wealth and with increasing fortune, he gave an increase to charities. The educational advantages that had of late been offered the young Negroes of Arkansas gave him a hope that there would be many leaders for his race to take the place of the faithful ones that had risen by their own efforts to positions of trust.[107]

Ferd Havis Building on the northeast corner of 3rd and Main streets in Pine Bluff (Jefferson County); 1893.
*Courtesy of the Butler Center for Arkansas Studies, Central Arkansas Library System*

# Mr. A. David Parks
## Jefferson County Politician

Personal Data:
 Birth: February 14, 1852.
 Death: August 30, 1896.
 Spouse: On March 21, 1885, married Laura E. Graves; twenty-two years
   old—eleven years younger than husband.
 Children: No children.
Professional Experience:
 Elected First Ward alderman in 1880, 1881, 1883.
Burial: Bellwood Cemetery in Pine Bluff.[108]

Mr. David A. Parks's desire to become the ruling member of the Jefferson County Republican Committee nearly cost Ferdinand Havis his life.[109] According to James W. Leslie, he apparently arrived in Pine Bluff during the 1870s and became active in the Republican Party. Jefferson County and Pine Bluff were noted for the number of African American voters who were loyal to the Republican Party. The Democratic Party was composed of Whites who were involved in the Civil War as Confederates. By 1880, Parks had gained enough political strength to run for city alderman in the First Ward. With John M. McCain, who had the largest number for the position of alderman, Parks and McCain were declared winners from the First Ward. Major C. G. Newman wrote in the *Pine Bluff Weekly Press* on April 22, 1881: "Alderman David Parks is a colored man of more than ordinary ability, of good character and enjoying the confidence of all who know him." Mayor W. H. Holland, as customary, appointed the new committees. Parks was selected as a member of the Cemetery Committee and was appointed chair of the Pauper Committee with C. R. Breckinridge and Sam H. Hilzheim as the other members. The Cemetery Committee was chaired by African American member Waterhouse of the Third Ward. The council had three African American members, Ferdinand Havis, Waterhouse, and Parks. Out of office in 1885, Parks was issued a liquor license and prospered as a saloon keeper.

Politically, Parks's great ambition was to become chair of the county Republican Committee to replace Ferdinand Havis, who had served as circuit clerk of Jefferson County since 1880 as well as alderman from the Third Ward. S. J. Hollensworth, a prominent and influential attorney who had moved to the city from Washington, DC, was second to Havis in the hierarchy of the committee. Parks conceived a plan to rid himself of his political enemy (Havis). John A. Williams, a detective and former city marshal of Texarkana, agreed to work with Parks on plans for the Havis assassination. On April 29, 1890, the schemers went to Cochran's shooting gallery, where Williams, who was an excellent marksman, exhibited his proficiency with pistol and rifle. On Friday, May 2, 1890, Parks agreed to give his fine stallion worth $450 and provide the assassin with his Smith & Wesson .38 caliber pistol to be used in the killing. Williams had met with Police Chief Levy before he met Parks and arranged for their movements to be observed. Parks took Williams to the Havis residence at 920 West Barraque Street to show him the best spot to stand and accomplish the bloody deed. A. S. Moon, an intimate friend of Havis, was hidden in a work shed near the spot where Parks was giving Williams advice on how to shoot Havis on the following Monday night after the alderman returned from the city council meeting. Moon relayed to Chief Levy, Judge Elliott, and Prosecutor Taylor the information he had obtained by listening to Parks's information. Levy sent for Constable Louis E. Cheek as backup, and together the officers went to Cochran's shooting gallery and arrested Parks. The local newspapers, all staunch Democratic supporters who had chafed for years under the Republican rule by African Americans, had "a media feeding frenzy" over Parks's arrest. Surprised by his own arrest, Parks employed Colonel William Porter Grace, noted White criminal lawyer who was considered the best in his profession in Pine Bluff at the time. After a series of hearings, the case never reached the trial stage, and charges were dropped. Parks lost his political power, and Havis remained head of the Jefferson County Republican Committee.

Parks built a substantial and attractive residence at 907 East Sixth Avenue in the early 1890s and continued his saloon business until his death in 1896. He died without a will. The total value of his personal property was $279.10. Since the total value was less than $300, Laura Parks did not have to go through probate proceedings. She left a considerable amount of real estate upon her death on February 18, 1921. In 1901, she rented—or leased—the Parks home at 970 East Sixth Avenue to Dr. George W. Bell, prominent African American physician, who opened the first African American infirmary in the city. She left four houses to her nieces and nephews in the area of East Sixth and Virginia Street and "several houses" in the vicinity of East Fifth and Virginia, according to her will.

Pine Bluff (Jefferson County) early in the twentieth century. The Jefferson County courthouse can be seen to the right.

# Mr. Jesse C. Duke
Newspaper Editor and Republican National Convention delegate

Personal Data:
    Birth: 1853; born a slave in Montgomery, Alabama.
Professional Experience: Grocer and postal clerk in Selma, Alabama.
    Journalist in Selma and Montgomery, Alabama.
    Pine Bluff newspaper publisher and editor.
Professional Affiliations:
    Founder and editor of the *Montgomery Herald* in the 1880s.
    Delegate to the Republican National Convention from Alabama in 1884.
    Arkansas alternate delegate to the Republican National Convention in 1892.
    Member of the Afro-American Press Association.
    Founder of the Southern Afro-American Press Association.

Jesse C. Duke was the principal organizer of the "Southern Afro-American Press Association," and editor of the *Pine Bluff Weekly Echo*, the *Hornet,* and the *Republican*—all African American newspapers established in Pine Bluff. In 1873, Duke, of Selma, Alabama, was hired as a railway postal clerk. An outspoken local Republican and Baptist church leader, he was removed from the post office in 1886 for his political activism, at which time he began his crusading journalism career.[110] In 1884, he was a Republican delegate from Selma, Alabama, to the National Republican Convention. He had been the editor of the *Montgomery Herald* and president of the Alabama Black Press Association until he published an editorial against lynching, which commented upon "the partiality of White *Juliets* for colored *Romeos*." Montgomery's Whites soon drove Duke out of town. He maintained that the "howling, bloodthirsty mob" used the article as a pretext to terrorize all the city's educated African Americans, primarily because of opposition to locating a Black state university there.[111] In 1892, Duke was a Republican alternate delegate from Arkansas to the national meeting, held at Minneapolis, Minnesota, June 7–10. 1892. At the same national meeting previously mentioned, Ferd Havis was the delegate from Arkansas.

Ida B. Wells and Jesse Duke were both praised and criticized for their roles in forming the Southern Afro-American Press Association. On the subject of lynching, Duke opened the appeal with, "There should be some way to oppress mob law [lynching] in the South … There is no dodging the issue, we have got to take care of this problem ourselves, and make so much noise that all the world shall know the wrongs we suffer and our determination to right those wrongs." As it turned out, the Southern Afro-American Press Association, had little impact either positively or negatively. Only seven people attended the January 1892 meeting, including two from Memphis; a dozen more sent letters and telegrams of support. In her account of the first meeting of the Southern Afro-American Press Association, Ida B. Wells declared, "Editor Duke had no cause to feel ashamed." She blamed the low attendance on bad weather and late trains. The National Afro-American League, in which Ida B. Wells also played a role, had little early success either. The *Indianapolis Freeman* wished the new group well, noting that "we of the cold and frigid North, are dependent upon the Southern Negro press for much of the reliable information touching matters and questions affecting the surrounding of our people in the race's fatherland." The *Cleveland Gazette* speculated that the Southern Afro-American Press Association, "will work in harmony with the 'National Afro-American League' and be of additional service not only to the profession, but also to the race."[112]

Many Black editors had espoused the need for an organization of Black unity when in May 1887, T. Thomas Fortune [New York] issued a call: "Let the thousand and one organizations we now have unite into one grand body for the uplifting and up building of the fortunes and rights of the race."[113]

## THE HONORABLE JOHN GRAY LUCAS
### Republican Delegate

The Honorable John Gray Lucas
*Republican Delegate*

Personal Data:
    Birth: March 11, 1864.
    Death: In 1944.
    Birthplace: Marshall, Texas, or Arkansas.
    Spouse: Miss Olive Gulliver.
    Children: One daughter, Elaine Louise Lucas.
Educational Data: Pine Bluff (Jefferson County) public school—grammar course.
        Branch Normal College, where he remained up to a few months of graduation, earning the AB degree in 1884.
        Entered Boston University School of Law in October 1884, graduated in 1887.
Professional Experience:
        Practiced law in Pine Bluff.
        Merchandising business for two years following years at Branch Normal College.
Professional Affiliations:

An active Republican, John Gray Lucas, an African American officeholder, served as state representative and commissioner of the U.S. Circuit Court, while other Blacks routinely won election as county coroner and common council representatives. When he was a student at Boston

University School of Law, he was quoted in a local newspaper as saying, "Pine Bluff was a 'land of opportunity' for Blacks." He graduated from the law school with high honors in 1887, earning the degree of *L.L.B.* He was the only African American in a class of fifty-two and was one of seven students who received "honorable mention." He was admitted to practice law in Arkansas in 1887, after a rigorous bar examination in which he earned a perfect score. At the urging of friends in 1886, he was induced to make the contest for the gold medal by the Arkansas Colored Fair Association for the best poem on the subject "The First Colored Fair." His poem was printed and was well-received, earning him high praise. In personal appearance and deportment, he weighed about 175 pounds, well-built, tall, erect, broad shoulders, with a large and well-shaped head.

In the course of three years of practice, he handled several very important cases. The case of Jordan Foushee, sentenced to the penitentiary for twenty-one years, is one of the notable and important cases. He was appointed Assistant Prosecuting Attorney by Judge J. M. Elliott, in Pine Bluff, shortly thereafter. He was appointed to that position by the next Prosecuting Attorney, S. M. Taylor. An active Republican, Lucas served in state, county, and federal central committees, including the committee for the Eleventh Judicial District. On the death of United States Commissioner D. Ascheburg, he was appointed Commissioner (today's federal magistrate) for the U.S. District Court in the Eastern District of Arkansas by Judge H. C. Caldwell about 1890. In 1891, Lucas was elected to the state House of Representatives, where he was instrumental in opposition to the segregationist "separate car" bill. Although one of the youngest legislators at that time, he was selected to make the primary speech against the bill. Despite all efforts, the bill passed. Possibly as a consequence of this defeat for Black Arkansas, Lucas left the state soon thereafter, moving to Chicago.

In Chicago, he practiced criminal defense law and appeared before the US Supreme Court four times. During the 1930s, he left the Republican Party to join the Democrats. In 1934, he was appointed assistant US attorney of Cook County (Illinois) by President Franklin Roosevelt. He also held the positions of assistant corporation counsel of the City of Chicago and assistant recorder of deeds in Cook County, the first African American to do so. [114]

## REVEREND GEORGE ROBINSON
### Freedman, Member of First Baptist Church and First Pastor of St. Paul Baptist Church

Personal Data:
   Birth:
   Death: 1895.
Professional Experience: Ordained as a minister at First Baptist Church.
Professional Affiliations: Member of First Baptist Church at Sixth Avenue and Cherry Street until 1866.
   With others from First Baptist Church, he started First Missionary Baptist Church. After policy discontent, the latter church split. Woodstock Baptist Church emerged as St. Paul Baptist Church. .

All local Baptists, both Black and White, belonged to the same church (First Baptist Church at Sixth Avenue and Cherry Street) prior to the Civil War.[115] In 1854, fifty-seven members were African Americans.[116] On September 25, 1866, with the church's blessings and prayer, Rev. George Robinson and the Black members withdrew and organized what is currently called First Missionary Baptist Church. In 1869, part of that congregation became dissatisfied with policies and organized the Woodstock Baptist Church. Having been ordained as a minister at First Baptist Church, Rev. Robinson helped to found the new Baptist church. This new congregation bought the old Catholic Church building on Pullen and German (Georgia) Streets and decided to adopt the name St. Paul Baptist Church. Under Rev. Robinson's leadership, the church saw steady growth. On August 19, 1894, a new building was constructed—after a fire—to accommodate a larger congregation. In 1895, Rev. Robinson died, and the congregation called the Reverend E. C. Morris as pastor. Rev. Robinson was pastor of St. Paul Baptist Church for twenty-six years.

*First Baptist Church*

## The Honorable S. W. Dawson
### Teacher, Farmer, Businessman

Personal Data:
  Birth: 1857.
  Birthplace: Baker County, Georgia. In 1859, the family moved to Macon (Bibb County), Georgia.
  Spouse: Miss Rebecca Battle, married in 1879.
Educational Data: Attended a private school one year and then the public schools until he was able to attend Lewis High School
Professional Experience: Teacher, farmer, businessman
Professional Affiliations: Arkansas state legislator and Republican Party delegate
Board Membership: Masonic Temple Board Member

S. W. Dawson arrived at New Gascony (Jefferson County), Arkansas, on February 13, 1873, when he was sixteen years old. In 1874, he moved to Fairfield (Jefferson County), Arkansas. Besides being a teacher in Fairfield and Noble Lake in 1884, he owned his own business, which was a plantation of about 150 acres. In 1880, he was elected a delegate to the Republican County Convention of Arkansas and was re-elected in 1882. He served as secretary of the Republican County Central Committee for twenty-two years, from 1886 to 1908, and was elected to the legislature for two terms in 1882 and in 1890. He filled the latter office in Arkansas with great credit by introducing many bills; one became a law on March 6, 1889. He is the first African American member who had a law placed upon the statutes of Arkansas.

Bettye J. Williams

# WILLIAM GORDON
## Farmer and Entrepreneur

Personal Data:
  Birth: 1876 or 1878.
  Death: 1967.
  Birthplace: Camden in southern Ouachita County.
  Spouse: Armendia Doyle (1891–1934), called Minda.
  Children: Japhas Andrew Gordon, Rosamond B. Gordon, Ezekiel Gordon, Flossie Gordon, Ophelia Gordon
  Grandchild: Fon Louise Gordon.

A sharecropper, William Gordon migrated to Sherrill, Arkansas (Jefferson County), around 1901. While sharecropping, he was able to buy a pair of mules and a wagon. The acquisition of this collateral enabled him to become a renter. In 1916, he became a landowner with the purchase of over two hundred acres of land. William was forty-one years old when his son, Japhas Andrew (1917–1996) was born; his wife, Armendia Doyle, was twenty-six. At the age of twenty-two on April 1, 1940, Japhas was living in Plum Bayou Township with his father, mother, and two sisters. Situated on the Union Pacific Railway (UP) at that time, Plum Bayou is 15.5 miles northwest of Pine Bluff and was created between 1840 and 1850. The post office was created in 1843 and was discontinued in 1949. Communities near Plum Bayou are Allport, Altheimer, Bingham, Coy, Dickey, England, English Place, Gethsemane, Hensley, Jefferson, Keo, Orion, Plain View, Red Bluff, Red Bluff Ferry, Redfield, Samples, Scott, Sherrill, Tucker, Walnut Ridge, Woodson, Wright, and Wrightsville. A historic place, Plum Bayou had a population in 1895 of two hundred people.

William Gordon's granddaughter, Fon Louise Gordon, shares a glimpse of William's entrepreneurship in her book *Caste and Class, The Black Experience in Arkansas, 1880–1920*:

> His entrepreneurship is an example of the philosophy of Black solidarity and pride, economic development, and self-help that pervaded the Black middle-class community around the state during the late nineteenth- and early twentieth-century. Nevertheless, the nature of Arkansas agriculture linked land-owning Blacks to the White community and made them far

162

more vulnerable to the evils of racial radicalism. Gordon and other Black landowners had to gin and market cotton, purchase supplies, and even hire labor in the same market with Whites. Consequently, most Black farmers were loath to offend the White power structure.[117]

Bettye J. Williams

# Mr. Alex S. Moon
## Circuit Clerk, Recorder, Sheriff, Teacher and Principal

Personal Data:
- Birth: September 16, 1847.
- Death: 1922.
- Parents: Black farmers in Pine Bluff.
- Birthplace: Jefferson County.
- Spouse: First married to Miss Cornelia Henley in 1876. After having given birth to four children (Isaac A, Edward S, Emma L, and Sadie C.), his wife passed away in 1883. He then married Miss Lulu Wilson in 1890.
- Children: Four children.
- Educational Data: Reared by his father (a farmer) and educated at Martin School, remaining with his master, Robert W. Walker, until he was granted freedom.
- Professional Experience: Elected Circuit Clerk, recorder, and sheriff in Pine Bluff.
  Teacher and first principal of Greenville School in the Pine Bluff School District.
- Religious Affiliations: Member of the Presbyterian Church.

A one-time deputy Circuit Clerk and recorder, Alex S. Moon is conceded to be one of the most prominent Negro citizens of Jefferson County.[118] After graduating from Martin School, he farmed with his father for three years, after which he taught school in Pine Bluff and throughout Jefferson County with great success. In 1876, Alex S. Moon was elected county treasurer and served one term, afterward holding the office of deputy sheriff and collector until the year 1879, when he again resumed his farm work. In the fall of 1880, Alex S. Moon was elected circuit clerk and recorder, but turned that office over to Ferd Havis in 1882. He then secured a position in the United States Post Office, and for two and one-half years, he was a very efficient delivery clerk. In January 1883, he returned as deputy sheriff, a position in which he gave satisfaction even to the smallest details of his duties.

Alex S. Moon was a devoted member of the Presbyterian Church, which at that time operated the Richard Allen Institute, at Ninth and Hickory Streets. In early 1890, Miss Lulu Wilson, a registered nurse from

Pittsburgh, Pennsylvania, came to teach at Richard Allen Institute. Alex S. Moon soon met and married Miss Lulu Wilson, who gave enormous service and growth to the nursing profession in Pine Bluff. From 1895 to 1922, Alex S. Moon served as a teacher and first principal of Greenville School, located at Tenth and Spruce Streets, or just across the railroad tracks (east of St. Louis Southwestern Railroad) and adjacent to the property owned by Lawyer N. W. Shelton, at 2115 West Tenth Street. Lanier Callion Stevens said the following about Principal Moon: "As a teacher and principal, he was very positive and highly respected by all who came under his tutelage."[119]

## The Honorable Richard A. Dawson
### Lawyer, Republican Delegate to State and National Conventions

Personal Data:
  Birth: 1848.
  Death: 1906.
  Parents: Minister's son.
  Birthplace: Virginia; came to Arkansas from Illinois.
Educational Data: Oberlin College, Ohio.
Professional Experience: Lawyer.
                        Republican delegate to state and national conventions.
                        Clerk of the Jefferson County Court
Professional Affiliations: Arkansas State Bar
                        Residence at Death: 2939 Armour Avenue, Chicago,
Illinois.
Burial: Union Ridge Cemetery in Chicago.

Lawyer Richard A. Dawson was one of two African American men admitted to the newly created Law Department of the University of Chicago in 1869, and the second Black man admitted to practice in Illinois, on July 8, 1870. He is reputed to have been admitted to practice in Arkansas by the state Supreme Court on December 16, 1870, after arriving in Pine Bluff. Dawson attended an African American men's convention in South Carolina in 1871, as a representative of Arkansas. He was elected Senator from Jefferson County to the Arkansas General Assembly in 1873, and an extra session in 1874. He was described as about twenty-five years of age, "copper-colored man, low of stature, and a good talker …"[120] Also in 1873, Dawson was one of four plaintiffs in a successful lawsuit handled by Lloyd Wheeler and Mifflin Gibbs against a saloonkeeper for violating the Civil Rights Act of 1866 by refusing to serve them. He served as clerk of the Jefferson County Court during 1874–1876 and again represented Jefferson County in the Arkansas Assembly for the 1879 session.

He returned to Chicago to speak at a gathering celebrating the Emancipation Proclamation in 1891 and in 1892, when he represented Arkansas at a meeting of "Colored Republicans" from various states to protest lynchings and other discriminatory treatments of Blacks. In that meeting, a resolution was drafted to be presented at the Republican Convention in Minneapolis a short time later. By 1896, Dawson was back in Chicago full time and active in Republican politics. By 1900, disillusioned with that party, he had become an active Democrat.[121]

## The Honorable Alexander L. Burnett
### Lawyer and Commissioner for the Post Office

Personal Data:

    Birth: 1858.

    Death: May 26, 1928.

    Birthplace: Arkansas or Mississippi.

    Spouse: Married Laura G. Burnett about 1899; a public school teacher, born in Mississippi in February 1858. They lived in a rented house. By 1910, they resided with an aunt, Sarah J. Middlebrooks, in her home.

    Children: Sarah D. Burnett, born about 1903.

Educational Data: Branch Normal College.

        Legal training at Central Law School in Nashville, Tennessee.

        Professional Experience: Began law practice in Pine Bluff in 1886.

        Commissioner for the post office.

Professional Affiliations: In 1901, member of the Wonder State Bar Association, a Black lawyers group.

Place of Death: Pine Bluff.

Lawyer Alexander L. Burnett was appointed United States Commissioner for the Post Office in the Western Division of the Eastern District of Arkansas about 1894, and retained that post until his death in 1928.[122]

## THE HONORABLE JAPHETH F. JONES
### Lawyer

Personal Data:
    Birth: November 1863.
    Death: September 4, 1937.
    Spouse: Married about 1895 to Carrie, a Native American. A second spouse, Eliza, appeared in the 1922–1923 Pine Bluff City Directory, but is not listed in the 1925–1926 directory.
    Children: Farland J, Theodore X, and Alta (Carrie's children).
    Daughter-in-law: Versie Barnett, spouse of Theodore X. The couple married in 1945.
    Grandchildren: Gwendolyn, Janice, and Georgette (children of Theodore X and Versie).
Professional Experience: In 1891, he was practicing law in Pine Bluff.
    On June 4, 1917, he was admitted to practice by the state Supreme Court.
Professional Affiliations: In 1901, a member of the Wonder State Bar Association, an African American attorney's group.

Lawyer Japheth F. Jones came to Arkansas from either Alabama or Mississippi. In 1895, he owned his own home. In the 1920 census, Jones is recorded as divorced with three children residing with him. A widowed servant also lived in the house. He perhaps remarried. The second spouse is listed in the 1922–1923 Pine Bluff City Directory, but not in the 1925–1926 directory.[123] Jones appeared regularly as an attorney in city directories from 1910 to 1936. In 1936, he is listed as practicing as "Jones and Jones" when his son, Theodore X, joined the practice. Their law practice concentrated on real estate issues. Jones and Theodore X were active in civic affairs. Known for his skill as an electrician, Theodore X maintained the pipe organ of St. Paul Baptist Church in Pine Bluff.

## The Honorable Neely W. Shelton
### Lawyer and Businessman

Personal Data:
    Birth: 1875.
    Death: November 5, 1929, in Pine Bluff.
    Birthplace: Starkville, Mississippi.
    Spouse: Married about 1903 to Marian B. Shelton, who was born about 1871.
    Children: six children by 1910: Carlo, Irene, Della, Eugene, Marian E., and Ella C. By 1920, two more children: Wendell and Laurie Etta.
Educational Data:
    Agricultural and Mechanical College at Rodney, Mississippi.
Professional Experience:
    Taught school in Tennessee.

In April 1903, admitted to practice law by the Jefferson County Circuit Court. On April 12, 1917, admitted to practice before the state Supreme Court. From 1903 to 1929, practiced law in Pine Bluff.

Lawyer Neely W. Shelton came to Arkansas from Tennessee. In 1910, he owned his own home. In 1927 and 1929, Shelton and his wife owned and operated a radio sales and repair business.[124]

## FOUNDER/PRINCIPAL JOSEPH CARTER CORBIN
First Principal of Branch Normal College, 1875–1902
American Educator
Scholar
Linguist
Mathematician
Musician

Founder/Principal Joseph Carter Corbin
*First Principal of Branch Normal College, 1875-1902*
*American Educator*
*Scholar*
*Linguist*
*Mathematician*
*Musician*

Personal Data:

Birth: March 26, 1833.

Death: January 9, 1911, in Pine Bluff, interred January 14, 1911, at Waldheim German Cemetery, now Forest Home Cemetery in Forest Park (Chicago), Illinois. The cemetery was also a Native American burial ground and is the resting place for his wife (Mary Jane), two sons, the parents of Earnest Hemingway, the Haymarket Martyrs, and other local heroes.[125]

Parents: William and Susan Corbin; the eldest son of free Black parents.

Birthplace: Chillicothe, Ohio.

Siblings: John, Elizabeth, Lucy, Mary, Henry, and Isabella.

Spouse: Miss Mary Jane Ward, a native of Kentucky. They were married on September 11, 1866, in Cincinnati. His wife was a dressmaker.

Children: William W. Corbin, Fauolina Corbin, Pea Corbin, and Louisa Corbin. Two children lived to adulthood.

**Educational Data:**

Joseph C. Corbin attended subscription schools at Chillicothe, Ohio, during the winter months, which was a common practice at the time. In 1848, he traveled to Louisville, Kentucky, to assist Reverend Henry A. Adams as a teacher. He taught school for some time. In September 1850, at seventeen years old, Corbin matriculated at Ohio University, at Athens, Ohio, earning a BA degree (art) in 1853. While at Ohio University, he also studied Greek, Horace, Tacitus, geometry, calculus, political economy, logic, chemistry, international law, and philosophy. He earned two master's degrees from Ohio University (1856 and 1889). Corbin was a member of the Ohio Philomathean Society (a student literary and debating society), which facilitated his accomplishments as an orator.

**Professional Experience**

In 1870, Joseph C. Corbin was a clerk in the Bank of Ohio Valley in Cincinnati and edited and published a newspaper, the *Colored Citizen*, for eight years. He wrote articles on mathematics and mathematical puzzles in the *Barnes' Educational School Visitors, the Mathematical Visitor, the Mathematical Magazine, and the Mathematical Gazette*.

Joseph C. Corbin conducted teacher training institutes in Arkansas and Oklahoma. With R. C. Childress, a native of Little Rock, and a teacher at Branch Normal College, Corbin formed the Teachers of Negro Youth, the first state association for Black teachers. In 1898, Corbin was the first president of the Arkansas Teachers Association (the Black organization of the Arkansas Educational Association). With no Black members, this latter teachers' association was founded in 1868. Almost a century later, in 1969, the two groups merged.[126]

**Professional Affiliations:**

National Education Association.

State Teachers of Negro Youth (later the Arkansas Teachers Association).

**Board Memberships:**

1873–75, Arkansas superintendent of public instruction.

President of the University of Arkansas Board of Trustees.

**Awards and Honors:** An honorary doctoral degree conferred by an unknown Baptist institution in the South.

In 1872, Joseph C. Corbin migrated to Little Rock as a Republican who favored abolition of slavery, education and the establishment of schools for the Freedmen, and Reconstruction in the South. Corbin became well-connected with the Republican power structure. In Little Rock, he obtained a job as a reporter for the Republican newspaper—the *Daily Republican*. He ran and was elected in 1872 to the position of State Superintendent of Public Education, on the regular Republican ticket. As a result of this office, he became president of the Board of Trustees of the newly formed Arkansas Industrial University (now the University of Arkansas at Fayetteville) in 1871. This position of influence gave him the authority to sign the contract for the first building (University Hall, called "Old Main"). In 1873, a bill was introduced in the state senate to establish the Branch Normal College, mainly for the education of teachers, for the "convenience and well-being of the poorer classes," to be located south or east of Pulaski County. The school was established for the African American population of the state and was under the direction of the Board of Trustees of the Arkansas Industrial University.

In 1874, Reconstruction was overthrown with the Brooks-Baxter War of 1874. Republican state officials lost their jobs. Corbin did not sell his house in Little Rock but taught mathematics at Lincoln University in Jefferson City, Missouri, in the fall of 1874. While vacating in Little Rock, the US attorney general, Augustus H. Garland (later governor of Arkansas), encouraged Corbin to open Branch Normal College of the Arkansas Industrial University in Jefferson County. On August 18, 1875, at a salary of $1,000, Corbin was appointed principal, a position he held until 1902 (twenty-seven years). His job not only required teaching and administration, but also occasional tasks such as clearing land and building porches.

On the location of the college in Pine Bluff, Corbin spent a week in the city conferring with citizens privately—and in public meetings held in the courthouse. A house owned by Colonel M. L. Bell on the southwest corner of Lindsay (now West Second Avenue) and Sevier (Oak Street) was leased for $300 annually. The Bell house dogged Corbin from the beginning: house dilapidation; repairs not made for the school's opening; ill workmen; and the school furniture from Chicago sank on a steamboat in the Arkansas River.[127]

Being principal at Branch Normal was a daunting task. Corbin experienced conflict with the Board of Trustees of Branch Normal and the state legislature seemingly at every turn. False rumors circulated alleging that fees were excessive, and the school was a short-lived experiment. Seating the students was a problem, for the school had fewer seats than students enrolled. Both the Fayetteville campus and Branch Normal College had trouble with attendance due to farm work. At both institutions, students enrolled could not meet college standards and were placed in the Preparatory Department. From 1875 to 1882, Corbin concentrated on upgrading the students' skills needed in school, increasing the number of students and appointments, adjusting the curriculum, publishing a separate catalog, reducing fees, and securing a permanent location. The enrollment of Branch Normal College grew from seven students (four from Drew County and three from Jefferson County) in 1875 to 241 by 1894. In 1880, a two-story brick building with classrooms and an assembly hall was constructed at a price of $10,000. The preceding building was the first permanent one.

At first, Corbin was a one-man faculty at Branch Normal College. The first additions to the staff were former students who served as the principal's assistants. His wife taught art at the school. Corbin spoke and read Greek, Latin, German, French, Spanish, Italian, Hebrew, and Danish. He taught himself because he was very interested in languages. Until the curriculum was modified in 1889, he taught Greek and Latin. He played and taught students to play the piano, organ, and the flute and trained the Branch Normal College choir, which was featured at every commencement. For three years [1882–1885], a bachelor of arts degree was conferred by Branch Normal College. In 1887, a dormitory for girls was built. But in the period that followed, the school operated as a two-year junior college with a preparatory department until after it was separated from the Arkansas Industrial University (Fayetteville campus).

During the first sixteen years of its existence, Branch Normal College directed all its efforts to training teachers, but Joseph C. Corbin had become convinced that Blacks needed vocational training as well. His efforts were aided by the Morrill Act of 1890, which was the land-grant college act. Funds from land grants were given to colleges to finance industrial and agricultural educational activities. An Industrial Department was established with courses in sewing, typing, and printing. His daughter, Louisa Corbin, worked as the sewing and industrial teacher for women.

At the close of the 1899–1900 school year, the principal reported to the university board that due to overcrowding, the college sorely needed more funding. A $5,000 appropriation to erect an annex to the main building and $800 to improve and enlarge the vocational building were approved during the summer of 1891. The college continued to grow, and by the end of the century [1900], there were eight professors and more than two hundred students.

When the Board met in June 1902, it failed to re-elect Corbin as principal, with no explanation for its action. He had served as the principal for twenty-seven years. It is alleged that Corbin "challenged the behavior of the Treasurer, J. W. S. Harris (a white man), who was really the executive head of the school under Trustee W. H. Langford (of Pine Bluff)."[128] Following his departure from Branch Normal College, Corbin served as principal of Merrill Public School in the Pine Bluff school system for the next nine years; as secretary and third Grand Master of the Arkansas chapter of the Prince Hall Masons of Arkansas; and as vice president of the Colored Industrial Fair. He died suddenly at his home, at 1821 West Second Street, on January 9, 1911, at the age of seventy-seven.

Alumnae and historian Gladys Turner-Finney and noted genealogist Tony Burroughs found Corbin's resting place in Oak Park, Illinois. A headstone was placed on the site—102 years following his death. On May 27, 2013 (Memorial Day), Forest Park Mayor Anthony Calderone, together with an assembly of distinguished people, issued a resolution honoring Corbin's accomplishments. Having prepared a headstone for the occasion, the group unveiled the marker, whose inscription reads: *Founder of the University of Arkansas at Pine Bluff, Father of Higher Education for African Americans in Arkansas. Thanks for the gift of education to countless generations.*[129]

> The mediocre teacher tells,
> The good teacher explains,
> The superior teacher demonstrates,
> The great teacher inspires.
> —*William Arthur Ward*

# PRINCIPAL ISAAC FISHER
## Supporter of the Booker T. Washington Idea in Arkansas
## Second Head of Branch Normal College 1902–1911

Principal Isaac Fisher
*Supporter of the Booker T. Washington Idea in Arkansas*
*Second Head of Branch Normal College*
*1902-1911*

Personal Data:
   Birth: 1877.
   Parents: His mother died when he was eight years old, and he moved to Vicksburg, Mississippi to live with an older sister.
   Birthplace: Louisiana cotton farm.
   Siblings: The sixteenth and last child of slave parents.
Educational Data: A graduate of the Normal Program at Tuskegee Institute of Alabama.
   Study at Bloomsburg, Pennsylvania.
   Study at Farmington Teachers College in Trenton, New Jersey.
   Study at Albany, New York.
Professional Experience: Instructor in the Schofield Schools of Aiken, South Carolina.
   Organizer of the Negro Farmer's Conference of the Schofield Schools.
   Northern financial agent for Tuskegee Institute.
   Principal of Swayne Public School in Montgomery, Alabama.
   Head of Branch Normal College, 1902–11.

Growing up, Isaac Fisher was a newsboy, bootblack, houseboy, cake baker's assistant, and druggist-errand boy. At the age of sixteen, he entered the Normal Program of Tuskegee Institute in Alabama. A disciple of Booker T. Washington, Fisher headed Branch Normal College as principal from 1902 to 1911.[130] Booker T. Washington recommended him for the position. Fisher's tenure began on June 5, 1902, at a salary of $1,500. Branch Normal College owned twenty acres of land. Fisher began his duties on August 1, 1902, and his problems were immediate. The first predicament concerned vindicating the "Tuskegee idea" of education in Arkansas. The work that Professor Joseph Carter Corbin had done in the earlier twenty-seven years at Branch Normal College had been classical, not industrial—farming and trades. Another concern of Fisher was to establish his authority as principal, since he was challenged by James E. Smith, the first assistant. Finally, many African Americans and some of the White leaders in Pine Bluff were working on aiding Professor Corbin in his efforts for re-instatement as principal of Branch Normal College. The preceding were efforts Fisher believed to be in opposition to him and his education. Upon the letter submitted by Booker T. Washington, Fisher was considered by many as "no education," for he had only received a diploma at Tuskegee Institute, not a degree.

The Tuskegee idea was not accepted by many in Pine Bluff. Fisher was a Normal School graduate at Tuskegee Institute. He did not take a course in Greek or Latin. The previous two subjects had not been taught since Professor Joseph C. Corbin left Branch Normal College in 1902. An October 26, 1903, *Pine Bluff Commercial* article from the White press was sent:

> There are fifty Negroes in Pine Bluff and Jefferson County who have done more for their race than Booker T. Washington. Yet, they do not parade their good deeds like Booker T. Washington. Such men as Abram Collier, A. M. Middlebrooke, J. C. Corbin, J. C. Battles, Fred Havis, Phil Coleman, R. Y. Longley, Dave Robinson, S. A. Moseley, Wiley Jones, James Jones, et als., who do not wish to make a show of themselves.[131]

Fisher said that his most bitter enemies came from the list of men in the newspaper article. Everyone in the United States understood the Tuskegee idea of education at the time was "a return to the farm and farming." The preceding concept Fisher wanted instituted at the college. However, Branch Normal College was a teacher-training institution with a classical collegiate program. The June 3, 1903, graduates of Branch Normal College under Fisher's leadership were five students: William Harvey Triplet, David Benjamin Bolden, Nettie Bendelyne Hollis, Vienna Vermont Harris, and Beulah Earnestine Craig. The Corbin idea of education was the "good life," not the Tuskegee farmer "hewers of wood and drawers of water."[132] Booker T. Washington did visit Branch Normal College on November 16, 1905. A Branch Normal College student, Mercie White, recited a poem dedicated to Booker T. Washington:

> Booker T. Washington
> Thy place is fixed, when thou art gone,
> Kind friends will do their best,
> Thy noble work to carry on,
> And God will do the rest.
>
> Thy fame will live—it is secure,
> Go labor on for peace,
> So long as Love and Right endure
> Thy name shall never cease.
>
> Teach whites and blacks the Christian way,
> To live, and be thou bold,
> To plead for justice day by day
> As Abrah did of old.
> So living; thou shalt never pay
> Death's cruel price, nor see
> The twilight of eternal day—
> Thou shalt immortal be.[133]

On May 1, 1907, Fisher submitted his letter of resignation. But on July 1, 1907, the Board of Trustees re-elected him unanimously. He was in position two years, rather than the traditional one year. Yet, he was not allowed to hire teachers; nor was he successful in implementing the Tuskegee idea of education or establish his authority as principal of Branch Normal College in the next two years [1907–1909]. However, Thomas S. Childress, Licentiate of Instruction, was hired as an assistant teacher. He taught penmanship and typewriting for $600 a year. He also served as librarian without extra compensation.[134] Having very little or no authority at Branch Normal College, Fisher began to write essays in October 1907. On March 24, 1908, he was the third-prize winner in an essay contest sponsored by *Craftsman Magazine* on the subject "The Relation of Manual Training in the Public Schools to Industrial Education and Efficiency."[135]

By this time, Fisher was completely shorn of power at Branch Normal College. He had no authority in the selection or retention of teachers for quite some time. At the end of the 1908–1909 school year, the course of study had dropped to less than a standard normal school. None of the teachers held degrees. The authority figures were the White American treasurer, W. S. Harris, and the Superintendent of Public Instruction, George B. Cook.[136] On May 28, 1911, the *Pine Bluff Graphic* announced that Fisher had resigned. His resignation was accepted by the Board of Trustees on June 5, 1911. The board accepted W. S. Harris to head Branch Normal College. Frederick T. Venegar was named principal. Unlike Corbin and Fisher, Venegar was head or Principal of the Normal Department and not Supervisor of the entire college. The Supervisor of Branch Normal College was W. S. Harris. Both Harris and Venegar remained in these positions until the 1914–1915 school year. There had been no graduating classes in 1911 or 1912. In 1913, two students were graduated with the LI degree—the degree program (Normal) for teaching in the public schools of Arkansas. In 1914, ten students made up the graduating class. Under Corbin's administration, the Branch Normal College plan included (1) the Preparatory Program; (2) the Normal Program; (3) the Collegiate Program (earning the AB degree); and (4) the Mechanical Arts Program. The Collegiate Program was deleted under Fisher's tenure. Fisher himself did not have the AB degree. Branch Normal College during the 1914–1915 school year was a school of elementary and secondary grades with good industrial equipment, having no dormitories, and racked with administrative difficulties.[137]

# Principal Frederick T. Venegar
## with William Stephen Harris
### Third Leader of Branch Normal College 1911–1915

Principal Frederick T. Venegar
*with* William Stephen Harris
*Third Leader of Branch Normal College*
*1911-1915*

After Isaac Fisher's resignation, William Stephen Harris (a White man), who worked in the Mechanical Arts Department, and Frederick T. Venegar led Branch Normal College. Harris was named as Supervisor and Venegar as Principal. Harris really headed the total institution and administered the budget.[138] Their tenure was unpopular. The Board supported Harris and Venegar as heads, but community leaders in Pine Bluff called for their dismissal. During their leadership of 1914–1915, a student strike broke out on March 22, 1915, lasting for more than two weeks. The strike was provoked by student outrage at the behavior of Harris, who had recently given a package containing black silk stockings to a female student—part of a pattern of inappropriate behavior by Harris toward students for years. Venegar admonished the young lady to avoid Harris's presence while moving around on campus. His resolution raised the ire of the students. A strike ensured, which led to the closing of the college and ending the Harris-Venegar administration. Graduates during their tenure:

| | |
|---|---|
| 1911 | 0 |
| 1912 | 0 |
| 1913 | 2 |
| 1914 | 10 |

LI degree (Normal School degree)

## SUPERINTENDENT JEFFERSON GATHERFORD ISH JR.
### Educator and Fourth Leader of Branch Normal College 1915–1921

Superintendent Jefferson Gatherford Ish, Jr.
*Educator and Fourth Leader of Branch Normal College*
*1915-1921*

Personal Data:
    Birth: January 4, 1888.
    Parents: Slave father, Jefferson Gatherford Ish.
    Birthplace: Little Rock, Arkansas.
    Sibling: brother, G. W. Ish, a prominent physician in Little Rock.
Educational Data: Educated with his master's sons.
        Graduate of the Maryville Normal College in Tennessee.
        Earned his BS degree from Yale College in 1909.
Professional Experience: Served as principal of three Little Rock schools from 1887 to 1906.
        Principal of the Negro High School at Ninth and Hickory Streets in Argenta (North Little Rock) in 1913.
Awards and Honors: Gatherford Ish Elementary School in Little Rock was named in his honor in 1965. It ceased operation as a school in 1994. The structure now serves as the Little Rock School District Instructional Resource Center.

Jefferson Gatherford Ish came to Arkansas about 1881. He had been teaching mathematics at Branch Normal College since 1910.[139] He was the principal at Branch Normal College from 1915 to 1921. In 1915, he became the first Arkansan to be named head of the college. During his tenure, Branch Normal College was organized into departments, and intramural sports were initiated. He started a summer school for teachers. Under his administration, a standard high school program and a Home Economics Department were established. The faculty and curriculum were expanded, which laid the foundation for a multipurpose college. His most important achievement was in the direction of making the institution a land-grant college as contemplated by the 1890 Morrill Act. He established a strong Agriculture Department for the first time, along with training in allied trades. During his tenure as principal, the following classes graduated with degree:

| LI degrees | | No LI degrees | | Earned LI degrees | |
|---|---|---|---|---|---|
| 1916 | 10 | 1919 | 16 | 1922 | 32 |
| 1917 | 0 | 1920 | 16 | | |
| 1918 | 6 | 1921 | 18 | | |

The preceding graduates were finishing the elementary or secondary program.

The governance of Branch Normal College was still vested in the Board of Trustees of the University of Arkansas. A Prudential Committee was responsible for carrying out the policies and rules of Branch Normal College. Girls were now under the supervision of a preceptress. Young ladies were required to wear uniforms. At 9:00 a.m., students and faculty assembled for chapel devotions. Fees were $5.00 matriculation, $1.00 student activity, $1.00 tuition fee for each month, $1.50—$1.95 girls' uniforms, and $1.65 uniform cap. Superintendent Ish taught mathematics and chemistry. Former Superintendent Frederick T. Venegar was now director of the Normal Department and taught pedagogy, geometry, and physical science.

Most of the effort of Branch Normal College was in the direction of making the institution a land-grant college in practice as required by the Morrill Act. The expanded program included agriculture, home economics, auto mechanics, and carpentry. The previous courses complied with the Second Morrill Act. In 1921, the school's name changed to Agricultural, Mechanical, and Normal School (AM&N). After six years, Principal Ish resigned to become national director of the Adequate Rate Department of the Mosaic Templars of America.

## SUPERINTENDENT CHARLES SMITH
### Educator and Fifth Leader of Branch Normal College 1921–1922

Superintendent Charles Smith
*Educator and Fifth Leader of Branch Normal College*
*1921-1922*

Principal Charles W. Smith followed Principal Ish as head of the college and served for one year, 1921–1922. He had come as a teacher of mathematics in 1920–1921. He held the AB degree.

## Superintendent Robert E. Malone
### Educator and Sixth Leader of Branch Normal College 1922–1928

Superintendent Robert E. Malone
*Educator and Sixth Leader of Branch Normal College*
*1922-1928*

Personal Data:
  Birth: April 25, 1888
  Birthplace: Louisville, Kentucky
Educational Data: Central High School in Louisville, Kentucky.
                 Entered Hampton Institute in 1906.
                 Earned the AM degree from Cornell University in 1912.
Professional Experience: A teacher at Tuskegee Institute, 1915–18.
                 Supervisor with the State Board of Vocational Education in
                 North Carolina, 1918–20.
Professional Affiliations:

In 1922, Robert Malone was named superintendent of Branch Normal College. He developed the school as a multipurpose institution. On his induction into office, Superintendent Malone suggested that all buildings of the college be named. When he took office in 1922, there were twenty-two teachers, no college courses, and four hundred students. In 1925, there were twenty-five graduates. LI=Licentiate Instructions for Normal School. By 1926, 411 students were enrolled, with twenty-one in junior college courses. The school was granted junior college status. In 1927, Legislative Act 568 changed the name of the school to Agricultural, Mechanical, and Normal College (AM&N), signifying a new emphasis upon agricultural studies. The college was made independent of the University of Arkansas, with Governor John Martineau appointing an independent Board of Trustees for the college. For fifty-four years, the University of Arkansas had a responsibility for the growth and development of the institution. State appropriation for 1925 was $25,000 and the Morrill fund added $13,636. AM&N was advanced in 1925-1926 to junior college rating. The junior college period was 1925-1928. Graduates were also given a state certificate, which entitled them to teach six years without examination, and at the end of this period, their certificate was renewed.

## PRESIDENT JOHN BROWN WATSON
### Educator and First President of AM&N College 1928-1942

President John Brown Watson
*Educator and First President of A.M. & N. College*
*1928-1942*

Personal Data:
  Birth: December 28, 1869.
  Death: December 6, 1942, at his home on the AM&N College campus.
  Parents: Crystal and Frank Watson.
  Birthplace: Near Tyler, Texas.
  Spouse: Married Harriet (Hattie) Louise Rutherford on September 25, 1907.
  Children: one adopted daughter, Marian Anderson Watson, born in 1938.

Educational Data: Educated near his home in Tyler. Texas. Passed the county teacher examination in 1887 and taught for two years. Entered Bishop College at Marshall, Texas, in 1891, at the seventh-grade level and completed his high school diploma in 1898. Entered Colgate University at Hamilton, New York. Transferred to Brown University, at Providence, Rhode Island, and graduated with a Bachelor of Philosophy degree in the class of 1904.

Professional Experience: Served as professor of mathematics and science at Morehouse College from 1904 to 1908. From 1908 to 1920, served as secretary of the Colored Men's Department of the International Committee of the Young Men's Christian Association (YMCA). Served as liquidating agent for the Atlanta State Savings Bank. State agent for the Southern Fire Insurance

Company. In 1923, administrator of Leland College (American Baptist Mission Society) in Baker, Louisiana. On June 1, 1928, the State Board of Education elected Watson as president of Arkansas Agricultural, Mechanical, and Normal College.

Professional Affiliations: Association of Presidents of Negro Land-Grant Schools. Association for the Study of Negro Life and History. The National Association for the Advancement of Colored People (NAACP). Sigma Pi Phi. The Monday Club of Atlanta. The Brown University Alumni Association.

Awards and Honors: The WPA library, named Childress Hall, was completed in 1939. It was dedicated and renamed in Watson's honor in 1958. This structure now houses the University Museum and Cultural Center. Arriving at Branch Normal College in 1889 as an assistant instructor, Rufus C. Childress, was the first graduate of Philander Smith College. Completed in 1969, the current campus library is named the John Brown Watson Memorial Library.

Church Membership: St. Paul Baptist Church of Pine Bluff.

Funeral and Burial: A memorial ceremony was held at AM&N College, followed by funeral services at Sale Hall Chapel on the campus of Morehouse College. He is buried in Atlanta, Georgia.

Named for John Brown—the antebellum abolitionist—John Brown Watson was a member of the first generation of African Americans born after the Civil War and representative of that demographic of cohorts, identified by Professor Willard B. Gatewood Jr. as "aristocrats of color." Son of ex-slaves, born on a farm in Tyler, Texas, in 1869, and a graduate of Bishop College in Marshall, Texas, Watson was fifty-nine years of age when he became president.[140] From 1928 until his death in 1942, he was president of Agricultural, Mechanical, and Normal College (AM&N)—earlier Branch Normal College, now the University of Arkansas at Pine Bluff (UAPB). After Watson's election as president of AM&N on June 1, 1928, the Arkansas State Legislature and two philanthropic agencies appropriated funds and bought a thirty-five-acre site for the campus, two miles from the center of Pine Bluff. Construction began in early 1929, and students and faculty moved in before Christmas of the same year. The new physical plant consisted of eight new buildings valued at almost $600,000. Watson's inauguration as president in the spring of 1930—at which John Hope delivered the commemorative address—enabled simultaneous dedication of the new campus site as well. Watson was mentored by John Hope, an 1894 graduate of Brown University and the first African American president of Morehouse College and Atlanta University.

Watson founded and co-edited with his wife, Harriet (Hattie) Rutherford Watson, the college newspaper, the *Arkansawyer,* and christened the new college catalog. In 1929, he attended the annual conference of the Presidents of Negro Land-Grant Colleges, the state's first participation in more than a decade. His leadership initiatives included both intercollegiate athletics and an intramural sports program, debate and dramatic clubs, and free "night school" offering courses in cooking, sewing, woodworking, automobile mechanics, and arithmetic. The college became a standard four-year institution in 1929. It was reorganized with four divisions: (1) Arts and Sciences, (2) Agriculture, (3) Home Economics, and (4) Education, including a training or practical school with both elementary and secondary grades. By the end of the 1929-1930 school year, Watson awarded the first two bachelor degrees at the college since 1885. In 1933, residences for instructors and a gymnasium were built. In 1938, the WPA funded a new library, two new dormitories, and eight brick faculty cottages. Twenty-five huts and five prefabricated dormitories were added. Watson's leadership also coincided with the Roosevelt administration's *New Deal.* AM&N participated in the distribution of college and graduate student funds by the Negro Division of the National Youth Administration (NYA). AM&N was the site of NYA Camp Bethune for unemployed young Black women in 1937, and for unemployed young Black men in 1940.

The enrollment at AM&N College at the beginning of Watson's tenure was thirty-six; the number of faculty and staff was thirty-two. When Watson died in 1942, the student enrollment was 474; the faculty was sixty-six; and the physical plant was valued at nearly $2 million.[141]

*Top:* One of the oldest buildings at the University of Arkansas at Pine Bluff is Caldwell Hall. It was the office building of many administrators including the President/Chancellor thru the years. A New Administration Building was constructed in the 1980s. *Below:* Built during the administration of President John Brown Watson (1928-1942), this structure is the first official home of the campus President. It was built in the 1930s and torn down in the late 1960s.

*J. C. Corbin Elementary School and High
School* Courtesy *Lion Yearbook 1950*

Under the leadership of principals Isaac Fisher, F. T. Venegar, Jefferson Ish, Charles Smith, and Robert Malone, Branch Normal College and AM&N College followed a Normal (teaching) degree program for graduates of the institution. During the leadership of President John Brown Watson, the college became a standard four-year institution. It was reorganized with four divisions: Arts and Sciences, Agriculture, Home Economics, and Education, including a training or practical school with both elementary and secondary grades. The faculty and curriculum were expended, which laid the foundation for a multi-purpose college. Both elementary and high school programs were developed. The elementary school (*above*) was a part of the campus landscape and was built next to Caldwell Hall. Some few years later, the two-story high school (*below*) was constructed. Later, the high school was torn down. Elementary students continued to attend J. C. Corbin School—first grade thru the eighth grade. Graduates of J. C. Corbin Elementary School then transferred to Merrill High School or Townsend Park High School for diplomas.

## *The John Brown Watson Sunday School*
## Courtesy *Lion Yearbook 1950*

The John Brown Watson Sunday School is a living memorial to the late President of the college. This is a volunteer organization with the President selected from the student body. Classes are taught by students and faculty members elected by the Sunday School. The best non-sectarian literature available is secured for class use. The School meets on Sunday morning at 9:00 a. m. in the Caldwell Hall Auditorium.

STAFF AND TEACHERS OF JOHN B. WATSON SUNDAY SCHOOL

Front row, left to right: J. B. Johnson, Samuel Kountz, President, Victor Starlard, Ann Dodson, S. A. Haley.
Second row, left to right: J. L. Wilson, Leon Benson, Nzwni, Charles Watson.
Third row, left to right: Imogene Moore, Mallory Jones, Chaplain, Arvene Reed, Secretary.

Dr. J. B. Johnson was appointed Chancellor twice. Dr. Samuel Kountz helped to develop a prototype machine to preserve kidneys for 50 hours after removal from the donor and performed more than 500 kidney transplants during his medical career. Dr. Victor Starlard was the Director of Freshmen Studies. S. A. Haley (father of Alex Haley, <u>Roots</u>) was appointed Chair of the Agriculture Department.

## *Housing for Faculty and Staff at AM&N College* Courtesy *Lion Yearbook 1950*

*Above*: President John Brown Watson's leadership coincided with President Franklin D. Roosevelt's *New Deal*. The Works Progress Administration (WPA) funded a new library, two new dormitories, and eight brick faculty cottages. Pictured here are the cottages during the 1950s. John M. Howard (Professor/Chair of the Art Department); Oliver E. Jackson (Professor/Chair of Modern Foreign Languages); and Hattie Rutherford Watson (Assistant Librarian)—among others—lived in the cottages. These buildings were torn down to make space for the New Administration building of 1966. *Below*: Named "Watson Boulevard," the framed houses pictured here (some later bricked and owned by Pine Bluff residents) lined the roadway north of AM&N College

## Visiting the AM&N College Farm

*The AM&N farm*: The most important achievement of Principal Jefferson Gatherford Ish was in the direction of making the institution a land-grant college as contemplated by the 1890 Morrill Act. He established an exceptional Agriculture Department for the first time, along with training in allied trades. Farm life in the 1950s is glimpsed on this page.

## Mrs. Harriet (Hattie) Louise Rutherford Watson
### First Lady of AM&N College, Educator, and Librarian

Mrs. Harriet (Hattie) Louise Rutherford Watson
*First Lady of AM&N College, Educator, and Librarian*

Personal Data:

    Birth: November 23, 1885.

    Death: 1974.

    Parents: Eldest daughter of freedman Samuel W. Rutherford, founder of the National Benefit Life Insurance Company in 1898, and Mary Anne Lemon Rutherford.

    Birthplace: Rome, Georgia, as part of the Black elite in the postbellum era.

    Spouse: Married John Brown Watson on September 25, 1907.

    Children: In the spring of 1939, after more than thirty-two years of marriage to John Brown Watson, the couple adopted infant daughter, Marian Anderson Watson—naming her after the famous contralto.

Educational Data: Public elementary schools of Atlanta, Georgia.

    High school diploma at Spelman Seminary.

    Spelman College, of Rome, Georgia; the only graduate from the college in spring 1907.

    From 1952 to 1956, completed a Masters degree in Library Science at Atlanta University.

Professional Experience: Living in Atlanta, both husband and wife taught at Morehouse College.

In 1936, Mary McLeod Bethune selected her as administrator of one of five National Youth Administration-sponsored educational camps for African American women in the country.

The publication of a camp newspaper for the NYA-camp organization.

Founded the NYA-camp newspaper.

co-founder and co-editor of the *Arkansawyer*, the official college newspaper.

AM&N Lecture Series.

Hosting visiting officials.

Group excursions for AM&N College.

Professional Affiliations:

American Library Association.

Arkansas State Library Association.

Social and Arts Club (National Association of Colored Women's Clubs).

Delta Omega Omega Chapter of Alpha Kappa Alpha (AKA) Sorority Inc.

Jack and Jill Club of America.

Pine Hill Community Club.

Parent-Teacher Association of the J. C. Corbin High School at AM&N College.

St. Paul Baptist Church (more than forty years).

Established the John Brown Watson Sunday School at AM&N College.

Board Memberships:

In 1929, the Board of Trustees of Atlanta University (which included James Weldon Johnson).

In 1931, alumna member of the Spelman College Board.

Served on the Morehead College Board from 1933.

Burial: Atlanta, Georgia.

Educator, librarian, and prominent member of the social and educational shaping of Pine Bluff/Jefferson County, Harriet (Hattie) Louise Rutherford Watson and her husband, John Brown Watson, were activists for the African American community during the early twentieth century. Watson's family background, elite education, and good marriage situated her as a member of the African American middle class. Her position as the wife of the president of AM&N College enabled the participation of the college in the Civil Rights momentum of the *New Deal*.[142] In 1936, the AM&N

National Youth Administration NYA-sponsored educational campus provided academic and paid vocational training, health care, and adequate
material-living conditions for young women aged eighteen to twenty-five
whose families received relief.

The NYA Camp Bethune held two sessions at AM&N in 1937, and enrolled more than 120 campers.

The Works Progress Administration (WPA) funded a nursery school
on campus from 1934.The agency provided staff salaries for five full-time
employees and a monthly allotment for food and supplies. Watson established a Free Baby Clinic, one day each week, in 1939, and it became an
important addition to the nursery school. Serving as its president for three
years, she organized an Advisory Council to manage the nursery school
and clinic. In addition to her college activities, she maintained local social
and community-building relationships. Watson retired from the college
library in 1962. She remained in Pine Bluff until her death in 1974, and
is buried in Atlanta.[143]

## Principal Marion Rowland Perry Sr.
### Superintendent of Merrill School

Personal Data:
>    Birth: 1855.
>    Death: 1914.
>    Birthplace: Yalobusha County, Mississippi.
>    Spouse: Miss Ida Robinson, a student and graduate of Oberlin College whose father was a Reconstruction era Arkansas State legislator, Superintendent of prisons, and sheriff of Phillips County.
>    Children: Two sons—Henderson T. Perry and Marion Rowland Perry Jr.
>    Grandchildren: One granddaughter, A'Lelia Mae Perry, born on June 7, 1928. She died in 1976. A stepson, Walker Jackson Perry, born in 1926, whom Marion Perry Jr. adopted.
>    Great-granddaughter: A'Lelia Perry Bundles.

Educational Data:
>    Southland College, a Quaker institution in Phillips County Arkansas.
>    Lincoln University in Pennsylvania (valedictorian) in 1883.
>    Newton Theological Seminary in Boston, Massachusetts, in 1886.

Professional Experience:
>    Taught school in Douglass, Arkansas.
>    Principal of Merrill School from 1887 to 1897.

Professional Affiliations:
>    After leaving the principal's position at Merrill School in 1897, he went into business with Wiley Jones and Ferdinand Havis, forming the Southern Mercantile Company located at Fourth and Main Streets. This company remained in business until the death of Wiley Jones in 1904.

Board Memberships:

Awards and Honors:

In 1887, Marion Rowland Perry Sr. arrived in Pine Bluff. School Board members W. L. Dewoody and M. Hanf gave him an overview of the situation on Pine Bluff. Although Perry found the condition to be very challenging, he agreed to serve as principal of Merrill School from 1887 to 1897. During these years, the African American community was divided, and the buildings housing Merrill School were burned three times within a short period of time. Dissension among African

American patrons and African American teachers over teaching positions in the school, coupled with disappointments of applicants seeking teaching positions, were believed to be the cause of the fires. Records attest to the belief that there was a struggle among the powerbrokers of Blacks in the Pine Bluff community. [144] In spite of the preceding, Perry was able to successfully guide the school, and Merrill continued to increase in enrollment and activities. Efforts put forth by Perry as an administrator to upgrade the quality of African American education in Pine Bluff resulted in the hiring of such dynamic, well-trained teachers as William Townsend and Mrs. A. T. Strickland, graduates of Alcorn College in Mississippi; J. C. Duke, publisher of the *Weekly Echo,* a Black newspaper of Pine Bluff; and Alex Moon, Mrs. Catherine Cartwright, and Bettie Rayford from the Martin School, a well-recognized private school of Pine Bluff at the time.

Perry was popularly referred to as the superintendent of Negro schools. In 1897, he left the public schools to enter the business world. He founded the Southern Mercantile Company with Wiley Jones and a mortuary company in Pine Bluff.

## ATTORNEY MARION ROWLAND PERRY JR.
### Law, Funeral, and Insurance Businesses

Attorney Marion Rowland Perry, Jr.
*Law, Funeral, and Insurance Businesses*

Personal Data:
    Birth: July 11, 1892.
    Death: July 22, 1983 (age 91).
    Parents: Son of Marion Rowland Perry Sr. and Ida Robinson Perry of Pine Bluff.
    Birthplace: Pine Bluff, Arkansas.
    Spouse: Miss Mae Bryant Walker (the adopted granddaughter of Madam C. J. Walker who had made a fortune in the cosmetics industry). He married her in Port Chester, New York, on August 27, 1927, by a justice of the peace. They had eloped. She died in 1945. Marion was married a second time, to a Pine Bluff beautician.
    Children: one daughter, A'Lelia Mae Perry, born on June 7, 1928. She died in 1976. A stepson, Walker Jackson Perry, born in 1926, whom Marion Perry Jr. adopted.
    Grandchild: A'Lelia Perry Bundles.
Educational Data:
        Left Missouri Street High School in Pine Bluff as a junior.
        Tutored for one year by Professor J. C. Corbin.
        A.B. in 1912, from Lincoln University, in Pennsylvania.

Obtained an *LL.B* from the Law School of the University of Pittsburg in 1924. Attended classes at Columbia University School of Law for three months. Admitted to practice law before the Arkansas State Supreme Court on February 16, 1925.

Educational Experience: Principal of a rural school at Gethsemane (Jefferson County) in 1914-1915.

Teacher at Merrill High School 1915-1917 and 1941.

Volunteered for the Armed Services and was commissioned to Second Lieutenant in 1917.

Professional Experience:

During World War I, he was one of four Blacks to graduate in the Seventeenth Provisional Training Battalion as a Second Lieutenant. After two years, he was promoted to First Lieutenant. Afterward, he worked for the Mosaic Templars of America for ten years. He is identified as an attorney in the *Little Rock City Directories* from 1926 to 1931, where he engaged in and represented a number of Black-owned businesses, such as the Mosaic Templars of America, in some of its business matters; Liberty Finance Corporation (Helena); Century Life Insurance Company (Hot Springs); and Guaranty Security and Investment Company. When his mother-in-law [A'Lelia Walker] died, Perry moved with his wife to Indianapolis, Indiana, to work with the Madam C. J. Walker Company.

He owned a half-interest in the family undertaking business in Pine Bluff and was president of Olympic Life Insurance Company of Pine Bluff. He returned to Pine Bluff from Indianapolis in 1936, where he resumed his work in the law, funeral, and insurance businesses. He served during World War II as a business agent for carpenters and bricklayers at the Pine Bluff Arsenal.

Professional Affiliations: Passed the Arkansas Bar in 1925.

Member of Free and Accepted Masons.

United Brothers of Fellowship.

Charter member of Alpha Phi Alpha Fraternity of Arkansas.

Church Affiliation:

St. Paul Baptist Church.

## THE FAMILY TREE OF MADAME C. J. WALKER [1867–1919]

Sarah Breedlove was born in Delta, Mississippi. Madam Walker was or-phaned at seven, married at fourteen, was a mother at seventeen, and was widowed at twenty. While working as a washerwoman, she began to go bald. Miraculously, the formula for the scalp treatment that had restored her hair was revealed to her in a dream. When she died at fifty-one in 1919, she was one of America's wealthiest self-made businesswomen.

Called a "Tan Cinderella,' Mae Bryant Walker met Marion Rowland Perry Jr. at Madam C. J. Walker's Villa Lewaro, a lavish mansion on the Hudson River, across from the estate of John D. Rockefeller Sr. Mae Bryant Walker's thick, waist-length hair had helped sell thousands of tins of Madam C. J. Walker's "Wonderful Hair Grower."

Upon the death of Madam C. J. Walker in August 1919, Mae Bryant Walker worked as the vice president of the company her grandmother founded in 1906 and incorporated in 1911. In 1927, the block-long com-pany facility—the Walker Manufacturing Company, the Walker Beauty School, and the Walker Theater—was built. The original Madam C. J. Walker Manufacturing Company closed its doors in the mid-1980s. Marion Rowland Perry Jr. returned to his childhood home of Pine Bluff in the 1980s. He died in 1983.

Cabin on the Burney plantation in Delta, Louisiana, where Sarah Breedlove was born on December 23, 1867. (A'Lelia Bundles/Walker Family Collection)

## Madam C. J. Walker's Family

| | |
|---|---|
|  | A'Lelia Walker<br>Daughter of Madam C. J. Walker, who adopted Mae Bryant Walker (an orphan). |
|  | Mae Bryant Walker<br>Adopted daughter of A'Lelia Walker and granddaughter of Madam C. J. Walker. Mae Bryant Walker was the only legal heir of Madam C. J. Walker's estate. Mae Bryant Walker married Dr. Gordon Jackson in 1923.<br>In 1927, she married Marion Rowland Perry Jr. of Pine Bluff. She died in 1945. |

| | |
|---|---|
|  | A'Lelia Mae Perry<br>Daughter of Marion Rowland Perry Jr. and Mae Bryant Walker. She is the great-granddaughter of Madam C. J. Walker.<br>A'Lelia Mae Perry died in January 1976, from complications of chemotherapy. |
| <br>*All photos can be found in the A'Lelia*<br>*Bundles/Walker Family Collection* | A'Lelia Perry Bundles<br>Daughter of A'Lelia Mae Perry and great-great-granddaughter of Madam C. J. Walker.<br>She is the family historian and griot.<br><br>In the photo, she sits between her parents, A'Lelia Mae Perry Bundles and S. Henry Bundles. |

All photos can be found in the A'Lelia Bundles/Walker Family Collection.

## Professor William J. Townsend
### Educator

Professor William J. Townsend
*Educator*

Personal Data:
    Birth: 1864.
    Death: 1941.
    Parents: His father was a financially strapped minister of the gospel.
    Birthplace: Port Gipson, Mississippi. Another source acknowledges Natchez, Mississippi.
    Siblings: The eldest of five children—three boys and two girls.
    Spouse: Married Miss Josephine Young of Vidalia, Louisiana, in 1890, a classmate and graduate with him at Alcorn A&M College.
    Children: Father of ten children.
Residence at death: Ward 3, Pine Bluff; Vaugine Township, Jefferson, Arkansas.
Educational Data: He attended the public schools in Mississippi. His love for learning led him to Alcorn A&M College in Lorman, Mississippi. Because his parents could not afford to pay for his college training, Townsend worked his way through Alcorn A&M College, earning a B.S. degree in 1886.
Professional Experience: Following his graduation from Alcorn A&M College, he was given a position on the Alcorn faculty but soon relinquished it and came to Arkansas. Migrated to the "Read Settlement" in Drew County, outside Monticello, where he began work as a public school teacher on July 18, 1886. This job was the beginning of a lifetime career in Arkansas' public schools.

In 1893, he began his career as an administrator when he was named principal of the Main Pike School in Pine Bluff. He worked at Main Pike School one year.

In 1894, he was named principal of the Missouri Street School.

From 1901 to 1903, he became principal of Merrill High School.

From 1903 to 1913, he was principal of Missouri Street School.

From 1913 to 1941, he served as principal of Merrill High School until his death.

Professional Affiliations:

Member, 1913 Arkansas Negro Teachers Association of Pine Bluff.

Religious Affiliation:

St. John A.M.E. Church, where he served as a trustee for many years.

Awards and Honors: In recognition of William Townsend's long and outstanding years of service to the city's public schools, a city park [Townsend Park] and an elementary school [Townsend Park Elementary School] were named in his honor.[145] The park was laid out, and the school was built in 1952.

During the last decade of the nineteenth century, a teaching career was begun in Arkansas that was to have enormous impact on the education of Negro boys and girls in Pine Bluff. As late as the 1930s, William J. Townsend was one of the best-known and most highly respected citizens in Pine Bluff. He was known as Professor Townsend, a title he well-deserved. Although he taught more than fifty years in Arkansas, forty-seven years in Pine Bluff—forty years of which he served as principal of Missouri Street School and Merrill High School. Next to family and church, his all-encompassing love was Merrill High School. Becoming one of the early pioneer educators in Arkansas, Townsend was not only a successful administrator, he was also an effective teacher. He believed administrators and teachers were required to teach by example and precepts. And he led his staff in that direction. He was a true disciple of "law and order." A favorite quotation that he often repeated was, "Order is the first law of heaven." He strove to live by this dogma and to pass it on to others as a guide to every aspect of life. The William Townsend

Chapters—both junior and senior—of the National Honor Society of Merrill High School duly honored his name as a man who espoused high scholastic attainment and moral character. In the library at Merrill High School was a life-size bust of Professor Townsend that was created by Professor Isaac Scott Hathaway, a member of the faculty and a renowned sculptor.

One of the overriding goals of Townsend was to improve school facilities for African American students. To that end, he was able to persuade the local all-White school board, in the waning years of his tenure, to construct a new brick building on West Pullen Street for Merrill High School. During the same period, he laid the groundwork—at considerable expense—for the purchase of the nearby Longley Park as a playground and athletic field for the school. The project was completed by his successor, R. N. Chanay. Townsend was active in many other projects to bring improvement to the Pine Bluff community. One such project was the initial step taken in getting the Pullen Street Branch Library established.

His religious background, his strong desire for knowledge, and his work experiences at Alcorn A&M College characterized the remainder of his life. At his passing in 1941, a contemporary of his attempted to translate Professor Townsend's aspirations for Merrill High School into words. Paraphrasing Sidney Lanier's poem "Dear Land of All My Love" as "Dear Merrill of All My Love," the poet says,[146]

> *Long as thine art shall love pure love,*
> *Long as thy science truth shall seek,*
> *Long as punctuality falters not,*
> *Long as children's wrongs are redressed,*
> *Long as the school rules prevail,*
> *Long as God is feared and revered,*
> *So long as thy youth shall good citizenship know,*
> *Thy name shall shine, thy fame shall glow.*

## PROFESSOR ISAAC SCOTT HATHAWAY
### Educator, Artist, Merrill School Faculty

Professor Isaac Scott Hathaway
*Educator, Artist, Merrill School Faculty*

Personal Data:

Birth: April 4, 1872.

Death: March 12, 1967, in Montgomery, Alabama.

Parents: Elijah and Rachel Hathaway. Rachel died in 1874. Reared by his father and grandparents.

Birthplace: Lexington, Kentucky.

Siblings: Two sisters.

Spouse: Married Miss Etta Pamplin of Maryland in 1912. She died in childbirth. His second marriage ended in divorce. He met his third wife, Miss Umer Porter, in Pine Bluff in 1926. She was an artist too who created a bust of her husband that is displayed in the Hathaway/Howard Fine Arts Center at UAPB.

Children: Isaac, and Etta's son, Elsmer, who died in 1941.

Residence/Death: Tuskegee, Alabama.

Educational Data: In 1894, he graduated from Chandler College in Lexington, Kentucky.

Received his training in sculpture at the New England Conservatory of Music and Art at Boston.

Received fine arts training at the Cincinnati Art Academy.

Studied ceramics at Pittsburgh College.

Studied ceramics at New York State College of Ceramics in Alfred, New York.

Professional Experience: Beginning in 1891, taught English at Keene High School in Lexington.

Taught at AM&N College, Tuskegee Institute, Alabama State College, and Merrill High School.

In 1904, commissioned to cast a death mask of a former ambassador of Russia, Cassius Marcellus Clay. Living in Washington, DC, he completed likenesses of Monroe N. Work and historian Carter G. Woodson.

Awards and Honors: His contributions to the Pine Bluff community in education resulted in naming the fine arts building at AM&N College in his honor in the early 1970s. The Hathaway-Howard Fine Arts Building is located on the site of the former Lion's Den. This diner first served AM&N students in 1939.

Professor Isaac Scott Hathaway was an educator and artist most known for creating more than one hundred busts and masks of prominent African Americans. He taught at UAPB for more than twenty years [1915-1937]. Hathaway introduced ceramics at Branch Normal College in 1915. He also established the Ceramics Department at Tuskegee Institute in 1937 and the one at Alabama State College in 1947. He was the first person to yield translucence in Alabama while working at Tuskegee Institute.[147] His model was the largest plastic mold used in litigation in the United States. In 1943, while at Tuskegee Institute, he sculpted his first bust of George Washington Carver. The original bust stood twelve inches tall. His busts (Frederick Douglass, Booker T. Washington, and George Washington Carver) proved to be popular in African American homes throughout the South. Hathaway was the first African American to have coin models accepted by the United States Fine Arts Commission. He designed the Booker T. Washington memorial half dollar in 1947 and the George Washington Carver half dollar in 1951.

Merrill High School's faculty through the years has been made up of outstanding teachers, many of whom achieved national prominence. Hathaway was one of these faculty members. In a 1960s conversation with Mrs. Ella

Brandon McPherson Wade, who was a teacher and principal at Merrill High School, his widow shared that Hathaway became an instructor at Merrill Elementary School in 1926. He was assigned to teach the sixth grade. A year later, he was assigned to the high school department, where he taught English courses. He taught elocution and public speaking after school hours twice a week. It was in the latter classes that he endeared himself to many young people who remembered him decades later and spoke of him highly as a teacher. Because of his success in journalism and public speaking courses, he became known throughout Arkansas and was appointed drama coach and public speaking director for literary contests locally and state-wide. He presented many plays that won fame and recognition for Merrill High School.

While teaching, he produced heroic-sized busts of Pine Bluff's noted Republican Ferd Havis, the abolitionist Frederick Douglass, Branch Normal College Principal Professor Joseph Carter Corbin, and the educator Professor William Townsend. He also painted stage scenery and produced anatomical specimens for schools. During his tenure at Merrill High School, he received numerous invitations to be visiting professor at colleges during summer sessions. He worked on the faulty for eleven years and often said to his wife, "I worked harder at Merrill than I had worked before or have since, and I enjoyed it more."[148] And although painting, sculpturing, and ceramics were his real vocation, he loved his avocation— teaching—as much as he did the fine arts.

He retired from teaching in 1963 and returned to Tuskegee Institute. The Isaac Scott Hathaway Collection at the Mosaic Templars Cultural Center in Little Rock is the largest known collection of Hathaway art in the world. The Mosaic Templars Cultural Center also holds Hathaway's papers, including correspondence, sketches, and other textual documents.[149]

*Coins Designed by Professor Isaac Scott Hathaway*

Booker T. Washington Coin
1947 half-dollar

Obverse

George Washington Carver
&
Booker T. Washington
1951 half-dollar

Obverse

# Professor C. P. Coleman
## Founding Principal

Personal Data:
    Birth: 1864.
    Birthplace: Mississippi.
    Residence at death: Ward 3, Pine Bluff; Vaugine Township, Jefferson, Arkansas.
Educational Data:
    Rust College, Holly Springs, Mississippi.
    Branch Normal College.
Professional Experience:
    Hall School in the Watson Chapel District.
Professional Affiliations: Member, 1913 Arkansas Negro Teachers Association
                of Pine Bluff.

Taking note of information received from Principal Joseph Carter Corbin and Professor Rufus C. Childress at Branch Normal College, Professor C. P. Coleman provided the foundation for Hall School, a small, rural elementary school located on West Seventh Street. Described as a "very crude and rough building used for a cheap dance hall," Hall School was sold to School District No. 24 to be used as an elementary school. Beginning with fifty pupils, Professor Coleman moved the school into a noted high school for African Americans between 1915 and 1955. He was the first superintendent and principal. For years he was the administrator and faculty. Some years later, Mrs. Bessie Hale Barnett became his first assistant. Under his leadership, Hall School became the Jefferson County Training School, and near the end of his career, the school was named the C. P. Coleman High School. In 1950, the high school graduated its senior class. Professor Coleman stressed, "Hard work and a sincere desire to achieve a positive goal would always bring success." In 1970, the Watson Chapel School District completed the segregation process, and the C. P. Coleman High School became one of the several elementary schools in the Watson Chapel School District.[150]

The Office of the Superintendent. *Left*: Superintendent C. P. Coleman. *Right*: Secretary, Dolores W. Nolen        Courtesy of Coleman High School All School Reunion (1950)

The Office of the Superintendent. *Left:* Superintendent C. P. Coleman. *Right:* Secretary, Dolores W. Nolen. Courtesy of Coleman High School All School Reunion (1950)

# MR. POLK K. MILLER JR.
## Funeral Director and Entrepreneur

Mr. Polk K. Miller, Jr.
*Funeral Director & Entrepreneur*

Personal Data:

Birth: May 3, 1883.

Death: 1951.

Parents: Polk K. Miller Sr. and Syna Miller (an indigent farm couple). His father was a country Baptist preacher who gave the gospel to farmers and cotton pickers.

Birthplace: Evansville, Mississippi (a cabin in the woods); population of three hundred residents.

Siblings: the youngest (only son) of five children.

Spouse: Miss Vester Matthews.

Children: Jo Ann Miller and Judith Miller.

Grandson: One.

Educational Data: At an early age, both parents died and left four older other children and him at the mercies of relatives who did not interest themselves in sending the children to school. Miller started school at the age of thirteen. For ten months only, his first lesson of simple reading, writing, and arithmetic was held at the Moon's Chapel Grammar School and church combined. He was placed out as an adult at the age of fourteen. The cotton field demanded his presence.

Professional Affiliations: Founder of P. K. Miller Mortuary. Founder of The Great Protective Burial Association in 1926.

P. K. Miller was fond of geography, a course that he was never taught. He loved to read, but not many books were available to African American children at the time. He was twenty-five years old when he opened his first business—a country grocery store—in another Mississippi town. Later, he entered the timber, farming, and brokerage business, where he made some money. Leaving Mississippi, he selected Pine Bluff for his camping ground because the city was the second largest one in the state of Arkansas. It was located on the Arkansas River and had a population of thirty thousand, of which fourteen thousand were African Americans. As a mecca for Jefferson County, Pine Bluff was in the lumber belt of the South and was a fertile agricultural region where crop failures were almost unknown. Cotton was the principal crop. African American businesses succeeded largely because farmers throughout the state came to the city for trading, amusement, and to avail themselves of the services of professional men and women who had already been established. At this time, Miller had in his possession several large farms. He immediately went into the business of establishing funeral homes, a casket factory, and a theater.

Besides Arkansas State College during the early two decades of the twentieth century, the only other institutions in Pine Bluff were the Miller interests. He had an amazingly successful cluster of Black businesses. They were varied and unique but all successful. They included a coffin factory, a mortuary, a cemetery, a hotel (P. K. Miller Hotel), and a theater, all the offspring of a gigantic parent, a burial league known as the The Great Protective Association. He is said to be the first African American to conceive the idea of organizing Blacks into a league for the purpose of guaranteeing to them burial at death in consideration of a nominal weekly membership fee. His organization grew in leaps and bounds, and by 1939 was said to comprise 150,000 members. His only associate in business was his wife, Vester Miller, who had secretarial and commercial training and who acted as secretary and treasurer of his combined interests. He had around four hundred men and women—both African Americans and Whites—employed in his various interests.

At the time of Miller's death in 1951, besides church and family plots, Miller's cemetery was the only African American place of interment in Pine Bluff. Purchased in 1929 and renamed The P. K. Miller Cemetery, the cemetery was owned by Wiley Jones, whose body lays in rest on the property. Not a perpetual care cemetery (meaning not supported by endowments or tax dollars from the city or county), The P. K. Miller Cemetery is the oldest African-American-owned cemetery in Pine Bluff. People own the land their family member is buried on. In 1991, Roy Hearn, who owns Perry Funeral Home, purchased the property from Judith Miller, Miller's daughter, who took over the business when the parents died.[151]

Miller's Coffin and Casket Factory was the largest in the Southwest. He had the largest undertaking business in the city. His hotel was the second largest in the city, surpassed only by the leading White hotels in Pine Bluff. Then he opened the Vester Theatre on July 1, 1938. His theater, a beautiful modern motion picture facility, was situated in the heart of the downtown business section, adjacent to the leading White theater. In an interview with an Arkansas State College student, Miller said, "He wanted to do something for the Negro race. He wanted to give the Negro citizens of Pine Bluff and of Arkansas a place where they could sit as they pleased and see the first-class motion pictures."[152] By his financial power and strictly business personality, Miller gained a large degree of influence in Pine Bluff, the state, and throughout the United States. Many times, he used his influence in securing jobs for people other than his own employees. Several times he was asked to consider matters concerning his race to city officials. It was said by some that Miller was "the backbone of Pine Bluff Negroes."[153]

Spectator and outdoor sports dominated recreational activities during the early twentieth century. Horse racing and baseball had a special following. Hunting and fishing provided many hours of entertainment. Miller's pastime was attending movies, fishing, horse races, and prize fights.

## About P. K. Miller

*In Mr. P. K. Miller, the student may find an interesting study of a man who, on his own, has accomplished far more and is now doing much more effective work than most men with college training ... [He] is a shrewd, intelligent man with a mind that is naturally analytical and discriminating, and with that he has curiosity and industry. Anyone can succeed with this equipment.*[154]

216

President John Brown Watson
Arkansas State College
February 14, 1939

*P. K. Miller is gifted with the ability of recognizing and becoming interested in investments which bring him large returns in money value and in the satisfaction that his enterprises are assets to his community and to his race. He possesses an extraordinary degree of self-confidence and an abundance of energy which have been essential factors in his triumphs of acquiring both the esteem of his fellow citizens and a goodly portion of material wealth. What he lacks in what we speak of as "education" is compensated for by the abundance of common sense and his understanding of the people with whom he works and associates. He is a man of great imagination and creative ability.*[155]

Mr. Frank B. Adair Jr.
Accountant, Arkansas State College
February 14, 1939

*P.K. Miller has an enviable place in the economic life of Negroes in Arkansas. There are several traits which he possesses that have lifted him to the place he now occupies: (1) his faith in his own race; (2) his vision of the possibilities for the Negro in Arkansas; (3) his simplicity and his sincerity of purpose; (4) his unselfish devotion to unfortunate humanity, regardless of race, creed, or color; and (5) his magnanimous support of everything pertaining to his race.*[156]

Mr. G. W. Woodard
Supervisor of Smith-Hughes jobs forNegroes in Arkansas
Arkansas State College
February 14, 1939

## Mrs. Vester Matthews Miller
### Cofounder and President of P. K. Miller Mortuary

Mrs. Vester Matthews Miller
*Co-Founder & President of P. K. Miller Mortuary*

Personal Data:

    Birth: 1897.

    Death: Friday, September 11, 1986.

    Parents: Calloway and Annie Patton Matthews.

    Birthplace: Chattanooga, Tennessee.

    Siblings: Thirteen sisters and brothers; surviving were three brothers, Walter Matthews of Wabbaseka; Arnett Matthews and Theodore Matthews of Pine Bluff; and a sister, Myrtle Matthews of Pine Bluff.

    Spouse: Mr. P. K. Miller Jr.

    Children: Two daughters, Jo Ann Miller Bell and Judith A Miller.

    Grandchild: A grandson.

Educational Data: High school graduate.

Professional Experience: Founder with husband of P. K. Miller Mortuary in Pine Bluff.

Professional Affiliations: Arkansas State Funeral Directors Association. National Funeral Directors and Morticians' Association. Council of Negro Women. City Civic Club. Chapter 40 of the Order of Eastern Star. St. John A.M.E. church.

Awards and Honors: Lecture Series at UAPB.

Funeral: Services were held at P. K. Miller Mortuary, Monday, September 19, 1986, at 11:00 a.m. Rev. T. D. Alexander, pastor of St. John AME Church, officiated. Pallbearers were Burl Smith, Dr. Ishmael S. Reid, Clifford Weems, Dr. W. L. Molette, Dr. M. C. Dedrick Jr., Steve Cheatham, Rev. H. O. Gray Jr., Dr. Rufus Caine Sr., Harry L. Cross, Dr. Ulysses G. Dalton, Herman Mitchell, and Federal Judge George Howard Jr.

Burial: P. K. Miller Cemetery.

Mrs. Vester Matthews Miller and her husband, P. K. Miller Jr., began the first African American burial association in Pine Bluff. Passing at the age of eighty-nine years, Mrs. Miller was the president of P. K. Miller Mortuary after her husband's passing. The mortuary is located at 204 East Second Avenue. Her residence can be found at 2000 West Pullen Street. P. K. Miller began a mortuary business in Wabbaseka in 1926. The following year, the couple moved to Pine Bluff and began their business here. Mrs. Miller once said, "The business began with a desk, two chairs, and a fan. It is now a funeral association with more than fifty thousand members." P. K. Miller passed away in 1951. Several local African American funeral home owners began their careers at P. K. Miller Mortuary. U. S. Brown, owner of Brown Funeral Home, stated, "I began working for the Millers as a teenager. She [Mrs. Miller] gave me my beginning. She was a good businesswoman and a wonderful person." L. E. Henson, owner of Henson Mortuary, began working for the Millers in 1937. Henson said, "I worked for them fifteen years. She was the loveliest person that I've ever known and an outstanding businesswoman." Mrs. Miller once said in an interview, "I was raised in the country. It was a family of fourteen. We were not able to attend college. We could not even go to school, and I barely made it through high school."[157]

Located on Second Avenue during the 1930s, the Vester Theatre was named for Mrs. Miller. Located on Pullen Street several blocks from the site of their cemetery, named P. K. Miller Cemetery, the Millers also operated a casket-manufacturing plant. They ran a farming operation in Wabbaseka.

## Goodfellow Club Is Organized By P. K. Miller Here

It we revealed here yesterday that P. K. Miller, Negro leader, who is head of the Great Protective Association, the Hotel P. K., the Vester Theatre, and other Miller enterprises, has completed organization of Miller's Goodfellow Club here, an organization to provide aid for poor, aged, needy and unfortunate people. Articles of incorporation were filed here by Theodore X. Jones, attorney for the club.

P. K. Miller is president of the club, his wife, Vester Miller, is secretary-treasurer.

The club will maintain headquarters in the Great Protective Association offices here at Third and Alabama street, located in the Hotel P. K. or at such other places that may be designated.

For a number of years, Miller, one of the leaders of his race in Arkansas, has made large contributions toward relieving suffering in Pine Bluff through distributions of food and other items, etc., during the Christmas holidays.

The new association, it is understood, will continue the work started by Miller.

The association is authorized to raise funds for its operation and maintenance and to establish charitable institutions and carry on a general charity program.

The club was incorporated in circuit court here today.

The Pine Bluff Chamber of Commerce has given its full approval to the program of the Miller Good Fellow club in a written statement issued over the signature of T. R. Green, secretary-manager and Moore, assistant secretary.

O. W. Barnett, AAA administrative.

## PROGRAMME

OF THE OPENING OF THE

# New Vester Theatre

### Thursday Evening, July 14, 1938

LOCATED 114 E. 2ND AVE., PINE BLUFF

TICKET OFFICE BOX OPENS AT 5:00 P. M.
PROGRAM BEGINS 7:00 P. M.

Opening—Song.

Invocation___Dr. W. E. Watson

Introduction of Mayor___Dr. F. P. Lytes

Welcome Address___His Honor Mayor J. P. McGaughy

Short Talks___By Other White Friends

Response on behalf of the Management___Dr. J. F. Clark

Remarks   By Dr. J. W. Parker, Dr. W. E. O'Bryant and Others.

THE PICTURE WILL BEGIN PROMPTLY AT 8:30 P. M.

DEAN PARKER, A. M. & N. College,
Master of Ceremony

# Professor William H. Zachary
## Music Professor

Professor William H. Zachary
*Music Professor*

> Personal Data:
>   Birth: January 22, 1880.
>   Death: August 8, 1980, at his home at 1906 West Ninth Avenue, in Pine Bluff. He was one hundred years old.
>   Parents: The seventh son of Rev. Wyatt and Nancy Zachary.
>   Birthplace: Jefferson County.
> Educational Data: Attended the old Presbyterian Academy at Ninth Avenue and Hickory Street in Pine Bluff.
> Professional Experience: In 1916, he studied at the New England Conservatory of Music in Boston. In 1943, he returned to the New England Conservatory of Music in Boston to study organ. In 1956, he enrolled in the Eastman School of Music at the University of Rochester (New York) and returned for three summers to study piano, organ, and violin.
> Professional Affiliations: At the age of eighty-six, he joined the National Guild of Piano Teachers, traveling to Europe on a tour sponsored by the guild.
> Church Membership: First Missionary Baptist Church.

Professor William H. Zachary operated a full-time music school out of his house for nearly sixty-nine years, retiring from full-time teaching in 1975 at the age of ninety-five. He was found dead at his home by his cousin, Mrs. Josephine Foster. The white, five-room frame house was filled with scrapbooks, sheet music, and recital programs. Pictures of great musicians surrounded the piano. As a pupil, he practiced piano during recess at the old Presbyterian Academy because his family did not have a piano. He lived in Pine Bluff until the age of seventeen. Upon the death of his parents, he moved to St. Louis to live with an older brother and continue the music training he had started as a young boy. In 1906, at the age of twenty-six, he returned to Pine Bluff, married, and opened a piano studio.

He went on to become an educational institution of his own in Pine Bluff, charging twenty-five cents for a half-hour lesson in 1906. One of his first students remembers:

> The Professor sweetening the lesson with jelly beans. I went when I had 25 cents … and when I didn't, he would come and get me. He even had me playing the violin. Whatever he did, he taught me to do some of it too.[158]

Professor Zachary brought more than music to his students. He was also a builder and shaper of personalities, nurturing not only talent but dignity. The annual recitals of his music school at Merrill Auditorium were occasions: "I wouldn't swap anything for those recitals," a student recalled decades later, "because I got a new long dress and Shirley Temple curls and patent leather shoes. You were somebody at those recitals and it gave me a sense of being." There was a lot of hard work behind those performances and not just on the student's part.[159]

Professor Zachary's patience never seemed to run out. During his working years, he would go from eight o'clock in the morning until six in the evening, six days a week not counting the extra hours with students he thought needed overtime. On Sundays, he served as church organist for sixty-one years at First Missionary Baptist Church, where he had been a member since being baptized in the Arkansas River in 1895.

He did not neglect his own music education. At the age of sixty-three, he studied at Boston's New England Conservatory of Music. When he was seventy-six years old, he attended the Eastman School of Music in Rochester, New York, for three summers. He was touring Europe with the National Guild of Piano Teachers at the age of eighty-six.

In 1895, Professor Zachary was baptized in the first church structure of Barraque Street Baptist Church during the pastoral leadership of Rev. J. C. Battle [1894–1910], but he elected to join another congregation. At

Barraque Street Baptist Church, he was the leader of the Music Department and played the church's first organ, which was a pneumatic air organ where air was supplied to the bellows by pumping. The organ remained in the church for thirty years.

# REV. M. L. BRANTLEY
## Educator and Clergyman

Reverend M. L. Brantley
*Educator and Clergyman*

Personal Data:
    Birth: March 18, 1888.
    Birthplace: Jackson, Mississippi.
    Death: December 1966, in Pine Bluff.
    Funeral: Monday, December 5, 1966, Eighth Avenue Baptist Church.
    Parents: Mack Brantley and Isabella Dixon Brantley.
    Siblings: Whit Brantley, David Brantley, Myrtle R. Brantley Hancock, and
    Luvenia Brantley Correthers.
    Spouse: Miss Fannie R. Mallett.
    Children: one son, Joseph W. Brantley.
    Grandchild: Rev. Jerrold D. Brantley.
Educational Data: Public school in Birmingham, Alabama. AM&N College, BS,
                in Pine Bluff.
Professional Experience: Principal of New Town School. First Principal of
                Townsend Park Elementary School. Pastor of Eighth
                Avenue Baptist Church, Pine Bluff. Pastor of Shiloh
                Baptist Church, Little Rock, Arkansas.
Professional Affiliations: President of the Royal Arch Mason. Member of Lodge
                #407. Organizer of the Charter Patron of Adah
                Chapter #424, Order of Eastern Star. AM&N Alumni
                Association, treasurer. Jefferson County Teachers
                Association, president and treasurer.

Church Affiliation: Pine Bluff Ministerial Alliance. Eighth Avenue Baptist Church.
Funeral and Burial: Eulogy by Rev. L. K. Solomon at Eighth Avenue Baptist Church. National Cemetery, Little Rock, Arkansas.
P. K. Miller Mortuary in charge of arrangements.

Besides being a teacher, Rev. M. L. Brantley was an administrator in the public schools of Pine Bluff and southeast Arkansas for more than forty years. He was a part of the genesis of Townsend Park Elementary School. In 1952, Springhill School, Barnett Chapel School, New Town School, and Haygood School of Pine Bluff merged into Townsend Park Elementary School. These schools comprised what was known as the Dollarway School District of Jefferson County, Arkansas (Colored). At that time, the Superintendent was Mrs. Hazel Watson. With Rev. Brantley were other inaugural school officers: (1) Mr. C. N. Toney, Assistant Principal; and (2) Mrs. Evelyn Young Taylor Hatchett, secretary to both principals. The first basketball team for the school was organized under the supervision of Rev. Brantley.

A World War I veteran, Reverend Brantley was actively involved in Arkansas as an educator, clergyman, and active member of Lodge #407. His life connected with many of the African American leaders in Pine Bluff between the 1920s and 1960s:

Mr. L. W. Johnson
Mr. Earl Chanay
Mr. C. N. Toney
Mr. M. Jordan
Mr. H. L. Watkins
Mr. Fred Martin
Mr. C. P. Coleman
Mr. S. E. Ryan
Mr. S. W. Dawson
Dr. W. L. Molette
Dr. L. A. Davis Sr.
Mr. O. E. Jackson
Mr. W. H. Zachary

Mr. T. C. Pierce
Rev. Albert King
Rev. Robert Dickerson Sr.
Mr. W. R. Jones, G.M

# Dr. Tandy Washington Coggs Sr.
## Administrator at Branch Normal College and President of Arkansas Baptist College

Dr. Tandy Washington Coggs, Sr.
*Administrator at Branch Normal College & President of Arkansas Baptist College*

Personal Data:

    Birth: February 17, 1887.

    Death: July 10, 1992.

    Parents: Eliza Williams and Tandy Calvin Coggs, slave parents. Parents were born in Crawford County, near Van Buren.

    Birthplace: Catcher, Arkansas.

    Siblings: Tandy was the nineteenth of twenty-one children.

    Spouse: Married Miss Nannie Elma Hinkle in 1914. She died in January 1965.

    Children: Louis Hinkle Coggs, Tandy Washington Coggs Jr., Nanette Coggs, Eloise Coggs, and Granville C. Coggs.

    Grandchildren: Anne Coggs Smith, Alma Coggs Smith, Harriette Coggs Stuckey, Louise Hinkle Coggs II, Janet Coggs Echols, Tandy Washington Coggs III, Anita Coggs Rowell, and Carolyn Coggs.

    Residence at death: Los Angeles, California.

    Burial: P. K. Miller Cemetery of Pine Bluff.

Educational Data: Attended elementary school in Crawford County, Arkansas. Attended high school and college at Arkansas Baptist College. In 1910, he graduated as valedictorian of his class. Attended Hampton Institute for two years, receiving a certificate in carpentry in 1912. In 1931, attended Arkansas State College (now UAPB) and received a Bachelor of Arts degree in education.[160] Degree in medical technology from Meharry Medical School.

Professional Experience: From 1912 to 1915, served as Dean of Men at Arkansas Baptist College. From 1916 to 1923, served as professor of Trades and Industry at Branch Normal College, first African American to hold this position.

Professional Affiliations: From 1923 to 1937, he was the first Superintendent of the Negro Boys Industrial Schools at Pine Bluff and Wrightsville, Arkansas. From 1937 to 1955, president of Arkansas Baptist College.

Professional Memberships: Arkansas Teacher's Association, president from 1938 to 1940; treasurer from 1940 to 1956. National Association for the Advancement of Colored People (NAACP). Ardent supporter of attorneys Thurgood Marshall and Wiley Branton Sr., during the Civil Rights movement in Arkansas in the 1950s and early 1960s.

Awards and Honors: Honorary Doctor of Law degree from AM&N College in 1957. In 1984, given the keys to the City of Little Rock, at the celebration of the centennial year of Arkansas Baptist College. Coggs was the guest speaker, being the oldest former president of Arkansas Baptist College.

Dr. Tandy Washington Coggs Sr. raised farm animals to help finance his matriculation at Arkansas Baptist College in Little Rock, Arkansas.[161] At Hampton Institute, he was indoctrinated with the philosophy of skilled craftsmanship and service to the community in similar fashion as Booker T. Washington, who had also attended Hampton Institute. Dr. Coggs studied under Booker T. Washington. During World War I, in 1917-1918, he was deferred from military service in order to train African American soldiers in the building and construction trades at Branch Normal College. In November 1964, Dr. Coggs's children sponsored the celebration of their parents' fifty years of marriage, which was held in the Razorback Ballroom of the Marion Hotel in Little Rock. This occasion was the first time that the Marion Hotel had catered a celebration for African American guests.[162] Nannie Coggs (spouse) died in January 1965, and in 1966, Dr. Coggs moved to Los Angeles. He served for the remainder of his life as an

Bettye J. Williams

Associate Minister at Progressive Baptist Church in Los Angeles, where his son, Rev. Tandy W. Coggs Jr. was pastor.

From 1923 to 1937, Dr. Tandy was the Superintendent of the Negro Boys Industrial Schools (NBIS) located in Pine Bluff and Wrightsville, Arkansas.[163]

## Mrs. Nettie Hollis Matthais Johnson
### Beauty Consultant and Educator

Mrs. Nettie Hollis Matthais Johnson
*Beauty Consultant and Educator*

Personal Data:

Birth: January 22, 1884.

Death: Monday, June 26, 1995, at Arkansas Convalescent Center in Pine Bluff.

Parents: Dr. Nathaniel J. Hollis (father), who died in 1906; Martha Barksdale Hollis (mother).

Birthplace: Born in Altheimer, Arkansas, but reared in Pine Bluff.

Siblings: Oldest of ten siblings—two sons and eight daughters.

Spouse: Her first husband was Mr. Joseph Montague Matthais, an Episcopal priest. He was rector at the Church of the Redeemer at Pine Bluff, which was demolished years ago to build the North Highway 65 Expressway [now called the Martha Mitchell Expressway]. Her second husband, Dr. R. T. Johnson, was a dentist who practiced in Pine Bluff for sixty-one years. Throughout their marriage of thirty-four years, they helped a number of young people get college degrees. They traveled extensively, visiting every state as well as Canada and Mexico.

Church Affiliation: She attended Trinity Episcopal Church for many years until she was moved to the Arkansas Convalescent Center.

Educational Data: Graduate of Branch Normal College in 1903. After graduating from Branch Normal, she was awarded a music scholarship to attend Chicago Musical College. She taught school for two years. She later studied at Burnham School of Beauty in Chicago.

Professional Experience: Beauty consultant.

Professional Affiliations: Arkansas College of Cosmetology.

Called "Mrs. Nettie," Mrs. Nettie Hollis Johnson was the oldest living graduate of Branch Normal College at the time of her death in 1995. She was 111 years old. Dr. Lawrence A. Davis Jr., Chancellor of UAPB, said in 1995, "She was a grand lady and a special person. Anyone who lives to be 111 years old is a miracle. She had a great life. She represented Branch Normal College, AM&N College, and UAPB." She loved football games and horse racing. In remarks made about the arts at Branch Normal College, Johnson said, "Principal Corbin's instructional approach emphasized reading intelligently, writing legibly, and drawing correctly. Writing exercises involved freehand drawing, map drawing, and studying from the blackboard animal pictures and other class assignments."[164]

## Madame Martha "Mattie" Ella Danner Hockenhull
### Beauty Culturist—Beauty Parlor Proprietor

Personal Data:
   Birth: 1873.
   Death: 1937, in Chicago, Illinois.
   Parents: Edward Danner, Civil War soldier; Louisa Bobo Danner.
   Birthplace: Panola County (Como), Mississippi.
   Siblings: sisters.
   Spouse: First husband, Mr. Robert Gray; second husband, Mr. Robert Hockenhull.
   Children: Isaac Gray, adopted by his mother's second husband.
Educational Data: Paris, France, beauty doctor.
Professional Experience: Beauty culturist of her day. Manufacturer of personal care products.
Professional Affiliations: Member of the Negro Business League of Pine Bluff. (Negro Business League was founded by Booker T. Washington in the first decade of the twentieth century.)

Recalling the stylishness of the famed Madam C. J. Walker, Madame Martha Ella Danner Hockenhull owned her own beauty parlor and ran a correspondence school in the 1920s. Historian and collector Archie Lee Moore Jr. [1960–2015], accumulated one of the largest collections of African American memorabilia in the state of Arkansas. Among his collections is a series of books about beauty techniques published by Madam Hockenhull in 1917. The pamphlets are entitled (1) Improved Method in Beauty Culture, Manicuring, and Facial Massage; (2) Hair Dressing and Scalp Treatment, the Mme M. E. Hockenhull System; and (3) Beauty Culture Chiropody, Physical Culture, Bust Development. The location of her business was 200 East Barraque Street, Pine Bluff, Phone 2036. She was ahead of her time—having a telephone in 1917, when most families did not get telephones in Pine Bluff until the 1950s.

Madam Hockenhull's son, Isaac, married the great gospel singer Mahalia Jackson in Chicago, Illinois, thus making Madam Hockenhull the mother-in-law of America's noteworthy gospel legend. With Isaac Hockenhull, Mahalia Jackson was an early hair stylist.

A newspaper article entitled "Mme. Hockenhull's Corresponding School of Improved Method in Beauty Culture," appeared in the *Pine Bluff Daily*.[165] The article reads:

Mme. Hockenhull, Owner and demonstrator
Dr. R. S. Stoutt, General Superintendent
R. B. Hockenhull, President and manager

> Mme Hockenhull is touring the West and demonstrating the Eight courses in Beauty Culture and teaching same for the same money which you are now giving for washing and straightening the hair.
>
> Join this school and learn Beauty Culture for your own benefit. The terms are so reasonable until all who are interested in Beauty Culture can learn these Eight courses which prepare them to open parlors and do work for white and colored. Her face creams are guaranteed to keep back the sign of old age for a number of years.
>
> Full treatment, Three and Ten cents ($3.10) and her hair oils for falling Harish, Kinky, care than any oil for the growth of the hair. Full treatment, $2.95.
>
> Her Foot Ease Powders, cure all ailments of the Feet. Fourteen Treatments for one Dollar.
>
> Mme. Hockenhull's first stop will be with Rev. McClemon at his association held at Ft. Gibson, Okla, Oct. 2, 1917, of which she will demonstrate and solicit demonstrators for the school. Her gift as Beauty Doctor is a wonder to her people. She finished Beauty Culture under a Paris, France, Beauty Doctor, which makes her fully able to instruct her people as what to do to make themselves beautiful. Her goods are manufactured under the Pure Food and Drug Act. Her literature has been examined and copyrighted by the Department at Washington, D. C. and rated in Class A. All communications will be sent to Main Office and postage to cover parcel post. Mme. Hockenhull will be accompanied by her demonstrator, Mrs. Wilhight.
>
> Mme. Hockenhull
> Pine Bluff, Ark

1900–1920
PRICE LIST FOR GOODS AND SERVICES[166]
PROVIDED BY
MADAM M. E. OCKENHULL

Trusting you are well-pleased with the instructions given in hair dressing. Will give a price list of same.
The average price for hair dressers in first-class establishments range about as follows, and in making private calls, the prices are usually double.

PRICE LIST FOR GOODS

| | | |
|---|---|---|
| No. 1 | Cleansing Cream | .65 |
| No. 2 | Cleansing Cream | 1.00 |
| | Hockenhull's Beauty Special | .60 |

| | |
|---|---|
| Hair dressing, plain | .50 |
| Hair dressing, fancy | .75 to 1.00 |
| Trimming Bangs | .15 |
| Trimming and Curling Top Bangs | .25 |
| Shampooing, medium length | .50 |
| Shampooing, Heavy Hair | .75 to 1.00 |
| Shampooing, Short Hair | .25 |
| Singing Short Hair | .25 |
| Singing Long Hair | .50 |
| Bleaching, medium length, each application | .50 |
| Bleaching, long length, each application | 1.00 |
| Dying Short Hair, all over | 2.00 |
| Dying medium length, all over | 4.00 |
| Dying lengthy Hair, all over | 5.00 to 10.00 |
| Scalp Massage | .50 |
| Scalp Massage, electric | .75 |
| Straightening Kinky Hair, first treatment | 1.00 |
| Straightening Long Hair, first treatment | 1.50 |
| Straightening Very Short Hair | 1.00 |

Bettye J. Williams

## Mrs. Maggie Roselee Davis Stevens
### Teacher, Missouri Street School and Merrill School

Mrs. Maggie Roselee Davis Stevens
*Teacher, Missouri Street School and Merrill School*

Personal Data:

    Birth: March 13, 1874.

    Death: 1957.

    Parents: Henry and Margaret Davis.

    Birthplace: Natchez, Mississippi.

    Siblings: Fifteen children; Maggie was the seventh born.

    Spouse: Mr. Nathaniel R. Stevens, Stevensville, Mississippi (a community named for her husband's family).

    Children: A daughter (Maggie) and a son (Nathaniel), both born in Pine Bluff.

    Niece: Miss Josephine Davis, reared by Mrs. Stevens.

Educational Data: Natchez, Mississippi, local school. Natchez College in Natchez, Mississippi. Branch Normal College, in Pine Bluff. Moody Bible Institute, Chicago, Illinois.

Professional Experience:

    Started teaching career at Moscow, Arkansas. Missouri Street School (later Indiana Street School) after the death of her husband. Merrill School (taught third grade for years). Arkansas, AM&N College, Pine Bluff, Arkansas. The university presented a bronze plaque posthumously to her son in appreciation for Mrs. Stevens's outstanding work in education. Stevens Hall, a unit of the women's housing at AM&N College was so named to honor her. Alcorn A&M College, Lorman, Mississippi.

236

Professional Affiliations: Arkansas Teachers Association.
Religious Affiliation: Member of the St. John A.M.E. church. Served as superintendent of the Sunday School for years. Outstanding representative to the National Congress of the AME Church.
Civic Affiliation: National Republican Convention.

*You can't keep* a good man down. In order to keep him down, you must stay down with him. The moment you get up, he is up too.

Hold your head up and use your feet for walking,

If no one is going that way—*but you.*

*From Mrs. Maggie R. Davis Stevens*

The preceding words were a part of the practical philosophy by which Mrs. Maggie Roselee Davis Stevens lived and inspired others.[167] She was a religious and civic leader, and all who knew her were deeply impressed with her knowledge of the Bible. She inspired many young men to be clergymen and young women to become leaders in the work of the church. Her life revolved around the activities at Merrill School and St. John AME Church. Miss Josephine Davis, her niece and a teacher in the St. Louis Public School System, recounted an experience at St. John A.M.E. Church:

> Mrs. Maggie Stevens was addressing a convention of young people at the church when several members of the Ku Klux Klan came in. Retaining her usual composure, she continued to speak as if she did not see the addition to the congregation. When she finished and had taken her seat, the Klansmen came forward and gave a contribution to the convention. This incident was characteristic of the courage and determination of Mrs. Maggie R. Stevens.[168]

An organizational woman, she attended conferences on a regular basis. A 1901 high school graduate and friend, Mrs. Pearle S. Covington, accompanied Mrs. Stevens to many national meetings in which both were delegates. Of note is the National Congress of the AME Church, held in

Atlanta, Georgia. The last Republican National Convention that she attended was held in Chicago in 1952. Mrs. Covington recounts, "She [Mrs. Stevens] didn't have a ticket for admission to an event, so she sat at the door until her Congressman came along. He asked why she was not inside and her reply was, 'I don't have a ticket.' He became her 'ticket.'"[169]

Interested in all aspects of life to the end, Mrs. Steven died in 1957 in Chicago with her son, Nathaniel. This son and Miss Josephine Davis, a niece whom she reared, were her only immediate survivors. She was returned to Pine Bluff for burial. Mrs. Lanier Callion Stevens said, "She lived to a ripe age, but she never lived in the past."

## Mrs. Leona Cooper Cockerham Jones
### Teacher at Missouri Street and Merrill School

Mrs. Leona Cooper Cockerham Jones
*Teacher at Missouri Street and Merrill School*

Personal Data:
   Birth: 1881.
   Death: October 1968.
   Parents: Reared by a sister of affluence in Pine Bluff.
   Birthplace: Camden, Arkansas, but orphaned at an early age. As a child, she lived with an older sister in Pine Bluff, who was married to Ferdinand Havis, a businessman. The Havises lived on the southeast corner of Barraque and Popular Streets.
   Siblings: an older sister.
   Spouse: First husband, Claflin C. Cockerham, whom she married in 1905. He preceded her in death in 1927. Her second husband was Wilson S. Jones, whom she married in the mid-1940s. Jones passed away in June 1968.
   Children: One son, Claflin C. Cockerham Jr.
Educational Data: Her schooling was received at the Colored Industrial Institute (now St. Peter's Catholic School). It was living with the Havises and the Colored Industrial Institute where she gained much of her appreciation for the finer things in life. She was one of the first two graduates of the Colored Industrial Institute. She later attended Tuskegee Institute for several summers.
Professional Experience: In 1899, Missouri Street School (later Indiana Street School) where she taught the fourth grade. Dressed in a white shirt waist, black skirt, and often

a white apron, she taught the fifth grade at Merrill School, where she was just as fastidious about conduct and the general decorum of her room as she was about her dress. In 1942, she concluded her teaching career at Merrill School as one of the home economics teachers. She was most conscientious in her efforts to have every student develop the highest respect for authority.

Professional Affiliations: Arkansas Teachers Association.

Religious Affiliations: St John AME Church.

It was during a session of the Arkansas Teachers Association that Miss Leona Cooper met Claflin C. Cockerham, also a teacher, and married him in 1905. A son was born. In the mid-1940s, she married Wilson S. Jones, a schoolmate of many years before.

During the first decade of the 1900s, fractions [arithmetic] were studied in the fifth grade in Pine Bluff. Of all her effective teaching, "Mrs. Leona Cooper Cockerham Jones' teaching of fractions stands out most predominantly in my mind," said Mrs. Lanier Callion Stevens. "With the use of yardsticks, apples, oranges, or any other readily divisible object, she made the study of fractions a child's sheer delight and something never to be forgotten." [170] Later in her teaching career, Mrs. Jones became interested in the teaching of home economics. She had attended Tuskegee Institute in Alabama for several consecutive summers in order to prepare herself for this new field. Mrs. Stevens shares, "As an adult, I was in her home economics night class and found that she was just as methodical in her new field as in her fifth-grade teaching of fractions." She had an insatiable love for music. Mrs. Stevens further recalls:

> She possessed a melodic soprano voice and shared her musical talent generously here in the Pine Bluff community, particularly in the choir of St. John A.M.E. Church, where she was a devout member and organist, at one time. Her life was not outstandingly social, as we often narrowly use the word, but it centered mainly around her home, her church, and Merrill School ... She is typical of the teacher that a child will always want to remember—always interested in the child's welfare and thoroughly dedicated to the task of giving her best to those entrusted to her care.[171]

## MRS. JAMIE HENDERSON BARNES
### Teacher at Merrill School and Greenville Elementary School

Personal Data:
    Birth: 1885.
    Death: 1943.
    Parents: Tom and Emma Henderson.
    Birthplace: Pine Bluff.
    Siblings: The oldest daughter of eight.
    Spouse: Will Barnes, a Pine Bluff businessman.
    Children: No children.
Educational Data: Graduated from Merrill on June 1, 1903.
                In 1941, a bachelor of science degree in education at AM&N College.
Professional Experience: Her teaching career began at Merrill School on February 4, 1904, and continued to the year of her passing [1943]—with the exception of a brief stay at Greenville Elementary School.
Professional Affiliations: Arkansas Teachers Association.
Religious Affiliations: Barraque Street Baptist Church and First Baptist Church, where her husband held membership.

In 1968, Mrs. Lanier Callion Stevens said, "For the students living along the route from Miss Jamie Henderson's home on Scull Street to Merrill High School, clocks were almost unnecessary at two periods of the day, at 8:00 a.m. and at 4:00 p.m. They watched the daily comings and goings of Miss Henderson to her destination—Merrill High School. She was such a personification of punctuality and regularity that we, the younger teachers, called her 'Miss Never-Absent-Nor-Tardy.' To her students and others, she possessed a deep sense of responsibility to her profession ... For many years, she was the beloved teacher of the first grade, and many former Pine Bluff residents of the Merrill School community learned their *ABCs* under her care. Although she had no children of her own, she loved her little charges as if they were ... Complete dedication to family, church, and school characterized her life."[172] Her aspiration for greater efficiency in her work was recognized in 1941 when, after many summers of study, she was awarded the Bachelor of Science degree in education at AM&N College.

## MRS. MARY E. DAVIS MAYER
### Teacher at Merrill Elementary School

Mrs. Mary E. Davis Mayer
Teacher at Merrill Elementary School

Personal Data:
   Spouse: Mr. John Mayer, a Pine Bluff letter carrier.
   Children: Fannie E. Mayer, an adopted daughter.
Educational Data: Bachelor's degree from AM&N College.
Professional Experience: Webb Chapel Primary School in Battlesville (school in the Pine Bluff School district). Merrill Elementary School.
Professional Affiliations: Arkansas Teachers Association.
Religious Affiliations: St. James United Methodist Church.

From 1919 to 1942, Mrs. Mary E. Davis Mayer was a third-grade teacher at Merrill Elementary School. An effective teacher who taught" by precept and example." She put great emphasis on visualization in all of her teaching. The head teacher, she taught with three other primary teachers at Merrill Elementary School. Whatever activities the school engaged in, she enjoyed working with her children's parents and community affairs and encouraged parents to help in school.[173]

## Principal Floyd B. Brown
### Fargo Training School

Principal Floyd B. Brown
*Fargo Training School*

Personal Data:
    Birth: April 27, 1891.
    Death: September 11, 1961, Pine Bluff, Arkansas.
    Parents: Charles and Janie Brown; Mississippi tenant farmers.
    Birthplace: Stampley, Mississippi.
    Siblings: nine; second of ten children.
    Spouse: Married Miss Lillian Epps on March 5, 1921.
    Children: none.
Educational Data: Received a high school certificate in 1917 from Tuskegee Institute. Ordained as a Baptist minister after studies at Phelps Hall Bible School at Tuskegee Institute.
Professional Experience: Founder and Principal of Fargo Agricultural School in Monroe County. Principal of Fargo Training School for Negro Girls.
Awards and Honors: The Fargo Agricultural School Museum honors Brown. The museum moved to Brinkley, Arkansas later.
Residence at Death: Brown and his wife moved to Pine Bluff in 1955, living at 1401 Georgia Street.
Burial: P. K. Miller Cemetery of Pine Bluff.

As a youth, Floyd B. Brown worked with his father in the cotton fields of Mississippi and the cane fields of Louisiana. Encouraged by his mother, who had heard of Booker T. Washington, he entered Tuskegee Institute. Brown was a strong believer in providing a good education for those whose schooling was limited. Influenced by founder Booker T. Washington, Brown entered Tuskegee Institute when he was twenty-one years old. Having a passion for teaching and while selling biographies of Washington's *Up from Slavery* (1901), he discovered Fargo, Arkansas, a small farming community in eastern Arkansas. Moving to Fargo in 1919, after ordination as a minister, with $2.85 in his pocket, he established Fargo Agricultural School in Monroe County, which was a private school modeled after Tuskegee Institute, and one of the few private nondenominational schools for Black children ever recognized in Arkansas. Fargo and nearby Zent [Monroe County] were primarily African American communities that lacked school facilities.

Brown purchased twenty acres of land on credit and persuaded local supporters to donate mules, lumber, supplies, and labor for what was to become Fargo Agricultural School. Groundbreaking was on Thanksgiving Day in 1919. The school started with one teacher, Ruth Mahon, and fifteen students in a one-room building. His wife, Lillian Epps, taught classes as head of the Home Economics Department. The school's motto was, "Work Will Win." Students divided their time between academic and agricultural training, and they participated in various cultural and educational activities. A required weekly class was taught by Brown himself. It was a class in common sense, where he emphasized the virtues of hard work, service, self-help, thrift, and self-determination. Principal Brown traveled extensively to solicit donations for the school, which never turned away a student who could not pay. Brown accommodated himself to segregation and to "liberal" Whites in return for their support of the school. To his students, Brown shared that they must earn greater rights based on accomplishments, not confrontation, and he emphasized that they should not be ashamed to start at the bottom of the economic ladder, nor to work with their hands. Brown stressed, as had Booker T. Washington, what could be done rather than what should be done. [174]

The Great Depression produced severe challenges for Fargo Agricultural School, but the school was able to survive because of the farm. By 1945, the school owned 550 acres of land, twelve buildings constructed by faculty and students, and an enrollment of 180 day and residential students. None of the original campus buildings survive. Besides the day school,

Brown organized an annual Negro Farmers Conference for continuing education and groups to conduct annual maintenance of local cemeteries. In 1949, when the need for the school had diminished, Brown sold the campus to the State of Arkansas, which then used the campus for a new school, the Fargo Training School for Negro Girls. Brown served as principal until his retirement in 1954. In the 1990s, alumni and friends of Fargo Agricultural School created a museum at the school site for Fargo Training School for Negro Girls. The museum honors Brown.[175]

Floyd Brown (*standing, left of porch*) with friends and students in front of the first school building of the Fargo Agricultural School in Monroe County; 1920.
*Courtesy of the Arkansas History Commission*

# No Research Uncovered for These Educators

PRINCIPAL S. W. CRUMP
PRINCIPAL B. Y. HEAD
PRINCIPAL A. N. FREEMAN
MRS. A. T. STRICKLAND
Graduate of Alcorn College in Mississippi
PRINCIPAL J. B. SHORT

## Principal Oscar Lucious Douglass
### Missouri Street School

Personal Data:
    Death: 1942.
    Birthplace: Born in Conway, Arkansas, but reared in Clarendon, Arkansas.
    Spouse: Miss Blanche White of Clarendon, Arkansas.
Educational Data: Public schools of Clarendon, Arkansas. Branch Normal College.
Professional Affiliations: Principal of the only school for Blacks, serving three decades. Principal of Missouri Street School in 1918. NAACP.
Religious Affiliations: St. John AME Church.

Principal Oscar Lucious Douglass arrived in Pine Bluff near the end of World War I. His influence on the east side of town was in the growth and development of African American boys and girls in the Pine Bluff School System for almost three decades. As the principal of the Missouri Street School for twenty-four years, he was a firm believer in the effectiveness of good home-school relationships in the total school program. With the preceding, he worked endlessly to build a strong Parent-Teacher Association, which became a model program for other Pine Bluff schools.[176]

As a member of St. John AME Church, Principal Douglass served as the Sunday school superintendent for many years and was serving in this role at his passing.

## MRS. SARA JONES HOWARD
Teacher

Mrs. Sara Jones Howard
*Teacher*

Personal Data:
    Birth: December 18, 1886.
    Death: September 1987—one hundred years.
    Parents: Williams and Menerva Jones.
    Birthplace: Gethsemane, Arkansas.
    Spouse: Julius Harmon; George Howard Sr.
    Children: Vivian Malinda Harmon, Luther Lee Harmon, George Howard Jr., McClora "Pete" Howard, William M. Howard Sr., Andrew A. Howard Sr.

Educational Data: Public schools of Jefferson County. Branch Normal College. Teachers College of Emporia, Kansas. University of California at Los Angeles. University of Arkansas at Little Rock.

Professional Experience: Walnut Grove Elementary at Winchester. Jefferson County Training School, later became Coleman Elementary School (Colored). Jefferson Springs Elementary School at Jefferson Springs. Sherrill Elementary School at Sherrill. Barnett Chapel Elementary School at Pine Bluff. New Town Elementary School at Pine Bluff. Townsend Park Elementary School at Pine Bluff; where she formed the Brownie Girl Scout Troop.

Professional Affiliations: During the 1950s, State Health Chair for the Parent Teachers Association for the State of Arkansas. Arkansas Teachers Association. Volunteers in Service to America (VISTA) in North Carolina.

Church Affiliations: New Town Baptist Church. Sunday school teacher in the Children's Department; organized the first Vacation Bible School; organized the first Girl Scout Troop in the New Town Church community. Scout leader.

Funeral and Burial: New Town Baptist Church, Saturday, September 26, 1987; eulogy by Rev. Jerrold R. Brantley.

Pallbearers were grandsons and great-grandsons:

| | |
|---|---|
| George Howard III | William M. Howard Jr. |
| Willie K. Howard | Julius Harmon |
| Luther Harmon Jr. | Raymond A. Howard |
| Durwood J. Howard | Derrick Howard |
| Gregory Harmon | Corey Grant |
| Jerome Howard | William N. Cowan |
| George Howard IV | Christopher D. B. Howard |
| Gregory Harmon Jr. | |

Burial arrangements by P. K. Miller Mortuary Inc., and interred in Miller's Cemetery.

Awards and Honors: Established the Sara Howard Honor Society in the Dollarway School District.

Established the Sara Howard Scholarship Fund at New Town Baptist Church.

A teacher for more than fifty years before retiring to the nonprofit sector, Mrs. Sarah Jones Howard served at New Town Baptist Church in the Children's Department and the Girl Scout troop in the community. Her life connected with many of the African American 1960s-1970s activists in Pine Bluff: William Dove Sr., Ivey Anderson, and Sarah E. Smith. She was a part of the genesis of Townsend Park Elementary School, emerging from New Town School, Pine Hill School, and Barnett Chapel School. In 1952, she taught fourth-graders in what was then known as the Dollarway School District of Jefferson County (Colored). At that time, the Superintendent was Mrs. Hazel Watson. At Townsend Park Elementary School with Rev. M. L. Brantley were other inaugural school officers: Mr. Clyde N. Toney, Assistant Principal; Mrs. Evelyn Young Taylor Hatchett, secretary to both principals.

Her favorite songs were, "Sweet Hour of Prayer," "The Old Rugged Cross," "If I Could Hear My Mother Pray Again," and "What a Friend We Have in Jesus." Her favorite scripture was Psalm 91.

*Above*: Home of P. K. Miller (1887-1951) and Mrs. Vesta Miller (1897-1986), founders of P. K. Miller Mortuary, Inc., and The Great Protective Burial Association, located at 204-208 East Second Avenue, Pine Bluff. Business opened in 1926, serving Arkansas and adjoining States The house above is located on Pullen Street, one block from Pine Bluff Fire Station #2. President is Judith A. Miller. Photo by Bettye J. Williams

*Below:* Located at 1906 West Ninth Avenue, Pine Bluff, is a white, five-room frame house which wa owned by Professor William H. Zachary (1880-1980), who operated a full-time music school out of this house for nearly 69 years, retiring from full-time teaching in 1975, at the age of 95. He was found dead by his cousin, Mrs. Josephine Foster. Photo by Bettye J. Williams

*Above:* Home of Rev. M. L. Brantley (1888-1966) who lived on Blake Street ((U. S. Highway 79 South) in Pine Bluff. Besides being a teacher, Rev. Brantley was an administrator in the public schools of Pine Bluff and southeast Arkansas for more than 40 years. He is the first principal of Townsend Park Elementary School on 2600 Fluker Street. He was the pastor of Eighth Avenue Baptist Church in Pine Bluff.

*Below:* Home of Sara Jones Howard (1886-1987) who lived on the corner of West Barraque and Blake Streets (U. S. Highway 79 South), in Pine Bluff. Howard was a teacher for more than 50 years before retiring to the non-profit sector.

*Above:* 1950s residence of Jefferson County Training School Superintendent, C. P. Coleman. The school was renamed Coleman High School.

# PINE BLUFF/JEFFERSON COUNTY LEADERSHIP [1833—1892]

## CHIEF SARACEN (SARASEN)

Chief of the Quapaws

Born in 1735
Died in 1832
Friend of the Missionaries
Rescuer of Captive Children

The tombstone of Quapaw leader Sarasin (also spelled *Saracen, Sarasen, or Sarrasin*) at St. Joseph's Catholic Cemetery in Pine Bluff. *Courtesy of the Butler Center for Arkansas Studies, Central Arkansas Library System.*

The most famous of the Quapaws is Saracen.[177] He was born around 1735 of mixed parentage. His father is believed to be Cadet Francois Sarazin, which is listed on the 1744 Register of Arkansas Post. Sometime between 1744 and 1824, there occurred the incident that was the foundation for the legend of Saracen, rescuer of captured children. The popular version of the legend took place at Pine Bluff. A band of Chickasaws stole two children from a young mother, who implored Saracen to return her children. He agreed to make the rescue attempt and followed the Chickasaws downriver, overtaking them late at night. The Quapaw war whoop erupted out of the dark woods, echoing repeatedly, and drove off the

Chickasaws. Saracen then returned the children to their mother. The preceding version was used by T. B. Morton in his novel, *Daniel Hovey* (1901). In the novel, Daniel Hovey was one of the children rescued by Saracen, whose life was interwoven into the history of Pine Bluff and Arkansas.

In 1824, the Quapaws signed the treaty in which they abandoned all of their lands in Southeast Arkansas and moved to the Caddo country, near Texarkana. This exodus was led by Antoine Barraque and Saracen. A little later, most of the Quapaws quietly moved back to Jefferson County. He petitioned the Governor of Arkansas to be allowed to spend his remaining days on the river of his youth. The wish granted, Saracen was given acreage on the river where the Port of Pine Bluff is now located. A third and final treaty was signed by the Quapaws when, in 1833, they agreed to move to Oklahoma.

When he died, he was buried in the old town cemetery, located behind the Methodist Church at Fourth and Main in Pine Bluff. In 1888, the town cemetery was moved to Bellwood. The grave of Saracen was pointed out to Father J. M. Lucy, pastor of St. Joseph's Catholic Church. After obtaining permission from the bishop, Father Lucy had Saracen's remains buried in St. Joseph's Catholic Cemetery, where he lies today.

Drawing of Sarasin rescuing stolen children in 1824, from *Stories of the States: Makers of Arkansas History* (Silver, Burdett, and Company; 1905)

## White American Life in Pine Bluff/Jefferson County

Historical Overview

The area along the Arkansas River had been inhabited for thousands of years by indigenous peoples of various cultures. They used the river for transportation and for fishing.[178] Pine Bluff was founded by Europeans on a high bank of the Arkansas River heavily forested with tall pine trees. A man of French and Quapaw ancestry, Joseph Bonne settled on this bluff in 1819. Many other American settlers began to join Bonne on the bluff. In 1829, Thomas Phillips claimed a half section of land where Pine Bluff is located. Jefferson County was established by the Territorial Legislature, November 2, 1829, and began functioning as a county on April 19, 1820. In the August 13, 1832, county election, Pine Bluff was chosen as the county seat. The Quorum Court voted to name the village "Pine Bluff Town" on October 16, 1832. It was incorporated January 8, 1839, by the order of County Judge Taylor. At the time, the village had about fifty residents. Improved transportation facilities aided in the growth of Pine Bluff during the 1840s and 1850s. More and better steamboats increased river traffic.

A major slave-holding area, Pine Bluff was prospering by the outbreak of the Civil War, with wealth built on the commodity crop of cotton cultivated on large plantations by enslaved African Americans. Because of Union forces, Pine Bluff attracted many refugees and freedmen after the *Emancipation Proclamation.* Freed slaves working with the American Missionary Society started schools to educate African Americans, who had been prohibited from learning to read and write by southern laws. By September 1872, Professor Joseph C. Corbin opened the Branch Normal School of the Arkansas Industrial University. Branch Normal is a historically African American institution. It was founded as Arkansas' first Black public college.

Pine Bluff suffered lasting effects of defeat in the aftermath of the Civil War. Recovery was slow at first. Construction of railroads improved access to markets, and with increased production of cotton as more plantations became active again, the economy began to recover. The first railroad reached Pine Bluff in December 1873. Personal fortunes increased from the 1870s onward. Community leaders constructed large Victorian-style homes west of Main Street. Author of *Saracen's Country: Some Southeast*

*Arkansas History* (1974) and *Land of Cypress & Pine: More Southeast Arkansas History* (1976), historian James W. Leslie scripted that Pine Bluff entered its "Golden Era" in the 1880s, with cotton production, river commerce, and the lumber business helping the city draw industries and public institutions to the area. By 1890, it was the state's third-largest city. Pine Bluff depended on river traffic and trade. During a latter flood, the main channel of the river moved away from the city. River traffic diminished, even as the river was a barrier separating one part of Jefferson County from the other. In 1889, Jefferson County included Altheimer, Bankhead, Cornerstone, Dexter, Double Wells, English, Fairfield, Faith, Garretson's Landing, Greely, Greenback, Grier, Humphrey, Jefferson, Kearney, Linwood, Locust Cottage, Macon, Madding, New Gascony, Noble's Lake, Nubia, Pastoria, Pine Bluff, Plum Bayou, Rainey, Red Bluff, Redfield, Rob Roy, Sleeth, Swan Lake, Toronto, Wabbaseka, and Williamette.[179] After some years of wrangling, the county built the Free Bridge, which opened in 1914. For the first time, the bridge united the county on a permanent basis.

## White American Leaders in Pine Bluff and Jefferson County

| Leaders | Biography and/or Achievements |
|---|---|
| Joseph Bonne (or Boone) (First settler in Pine Bluff) | Joseph Bonne was born in Arkansas in 1794. In the autumn of 1819, Bonne made his way upstream from Arkansas Post. His possessions were a rifle, a canoe, and a dog. He built a crude cabin for his Quapaw wife and family on a high bluff with pine trees. Jefferson County was established in 1829. The first county seat was at Bonne's cabin. Becoming a cotton bale production center where steamboats could dock, Pine Bluff became the county seat in August 1832. At their first meeting in October 1832, commissioners recommended that the town be called "Pine Bluff Town." Pine Bluff was incorporated in January 1839, and the court authorized in October 1839 the construction of a brick courthouse that would become the city's architectural centerpiece. Bonne was the first White settler at the site of Pine Bluff. |
| James Scull (Trader) | Shortly after 1819, James Scull, from the Arkansas Post, arrived and set up an encampment on the north bank across from the future site of Pine Bluff. The encampment soon became a tavern and small inn. He was an immigrant from England, and kept a trading post for the Indians in Arkansas as early as 1809. |

| | |
|---|---|
| Antoine Barraque (Established New Gascony) | Born on April 15, 1773, in France, Antoine Barraque established the settlement called New Gascony, one of the oldest settlements in Jefferson County. He also served as a government agent with the Quapaw Nation, whom he guided to Louisiana in 1826, after the Treaty of 1824. He was educated in Paris and served in the French army under Napoleon Bonaparte. Following the end of Napoleon's empire, Barraque relocated to Arkansas in 1816. He married a Quapaw woman. Barraque was appointed by Governor George Izard as sub-agent to work with the Quapaw. Beginning his post in June 1825, he supervised the migration of 455 Quapaws in January and February of 1826. He was active in county politics, and the county records were held at his estate for five months in 1832. He was the first postmaster of New Gascony when the post office was established in November 1832. Barraque died on October 29, 1858. With the growth of Pine Bluff, and the increasing importance of railroads, New Gascony eventually faded into oblivion. |
| General James Yell (Lawyer) | A Confederate Major General and relative to Arkansas Governor Archibald Yell, James Yell (1811–67) came to Pine Bluff in March 1838, and began a long career as a jury lawyer. General Yell sponsored the original Ordinance of Secession, which was narrowly defeated in the Secession Convention's first session. The Arkansas Military Board removed Yell from command on July 23, 1861. He took no active part in the Civil War. During the war years, he moved to Texas. He died in 1867, having advanced large sums of his personal fortune to pay and equip Confederate troops. General Yell's son, Fountain Pitts Yell acquired Wiley Jones as a wedding gift when Jones was ten years old. Jones became a carriage driver to Fountain Yell's wife. General Yell is buried in Bellwood Cemetery. |
| Colonel Joseph W. Bocage (Early Businessman) | One of the pioneers of the city, Colonel Joseph W. Bocage was born on the island of St. Lucia (France), May 8, 1819. His paternal grandfather came to the United States, in company with others, in 1795, fleeing from the French Revolution. On the island of St. Lucia, he purchased a sugar and coffee estate and engaged in mercantile and shipping business, which proved lucrative, and he became very wealthy. Joseph Bocage came to Pine Bluff in 1837, when there was but eight log houses and one frame building in town. He entered the law office of General James Yell, studied law, and began practice in 1840. After the Civil War, he went into the lumber and building business. With others, he engaged in the cotton seed oil business, the foundry business, and manufactured steam engines and cotton presses. He was elected mayor in 1888.[180] |

| Colonel M. L. Bell<br>Lawyer and Businessman | Born in Wilson County, Tennessee, on July 27, 1829, Colonel M. L. Bell was a Pine Bluff attorney. Having come from a tobacco farm family in Tennessee, Colonel Bell was licensed to practice law in April 1852, and located to Pine Bluff from Little Rock. He started the law firm of Bell and Bridges. Besides town property, he owned fifteen hundred acres of land, with six hundred acres under cultivation. He was engaged in milling under the firm Bell and Bocage and also was in the foundry business.[181] |
|---|---|
| Joseph Merrill<br>(Founder of the Merrill Institute for young people) | Born in Rockingham County, New Hampshire, Joseph Merrill found his way to Pine Bluff in 1847. The next year, he opened a store of general merchandise for the next twelve years, and then he sold out. He was the postmaster during most of the time he was in business. He purchased lots and land, fully nine hundred acres of good bottom land. He became founder of the Merrill Institute, a $20,000 structure, three stories in height, with a tower, containing a lecture hall, a library, a gymnasium, and parlors for the use of the young people of the city, to improve them physically, morally, and spiritually. Merrill School is named in his honor.[182] |
| Harvey Crowley Couch<br>(Responsible for bringing Arkansas Power and Light Company (AP&L) to Pine Bluff, now named Entergy) | Born in Calhoun (Columbia County), near Magnolia, Arkansas, Harvey Crowley Couch (1877–1941) helped bring Arkansas from an agricultural economy in the early twentieth century to more of a balance between agriculture and industry. His persuasiveness with investors from New York and his ingenuity and energy influenced Arkansas' national reputation among businessmen. He owned several railroad lines and a telephone company and was responsible for what became Arkansas' largest utility, Arkansas Power and Light Company (AP&L), now named Entergy. |
| Robert Crittenden<br>(Engaged in Quapaw issues) | On March 3, 1819, President James Monroe named Robert Crittenden territorial secretary. Crittenden quickly set about exploiting the remaining Quapaws in southeast Arkansas to relinquish their last tract of land. The Indians signed away the last of their tribal lands on November 15, 1824. |
| John W. Pullen<br>(One of the first English settlers) | On November 2, 1829, Territorial Governor John Pope approved an act to establish Jefferson County, named for President Thomas Jefferson. John W. Pullen was one of the first English settlers in Jefferson County. |
| James T. Pullen<br>(One of the first English settlers) | Brother to John W. Pullen, James T. Pullen had served as county clerk since 1830 and postmaster since December 1834. He was shot and killed by John N. Outlaw on June 11, 1839. |

| Major Charles Gordon Newman (Founder of the *Pine Bluff Commercial)* | The *Pine Bluff Commercial* is the dominant source of news for Southeast Arkansas and has been since it was founded on April 18, 1881, by Major Charles Gordon Newman (1842?-1911), a military veteran and actor. He was born in Haverstraw (Rockland), New York. The paper stayed in the Newman family for more than a century. Newman edited and directed the paper without assistance until 1902, when he gave his son-in-law, E. W. Freeman, a half interest in the office and management of the business department. It enjoyed a wide prosperity and became one of the leading publishing houses of the state. The *Pine Bluff Commercial* grew out of the *Press-Eagle*. Newman had been connected with newspapers since 1868. Upon the death of Newman in 1911, full control of the *Pine Bluff Commercial* was passed to E. W. Freeman. During that time, a series of editorials on race relations in the South won a 1969 Pulitzer Prize for Editorial Writing—the only existing newspaper in Arkansas to have received such an honor.[183] |
|---|---|
| Freeman Harrison Owens Pioneering cinematographer | Born in Pine Bluff, Freeman Harrison Owens (1890–1979) constructed the first moving camera around 1908. In 1910, he worked for Universal Studios. An inventor, he worked with movie stars such as Charlie Chaplin, Mary Pickford, Douglas Fairbanks Sr., Wallace Beery, Gloria Swanson, and Ben Turpin. He developed a 16 mm projector with sound that was designed for use in schools, sales, and advertisements. In 1912, he worked with Essanay Studio, which was owned by former Pine Bluff resident Max Aaronsohol (a.k.a. "Bronco Billy" Anderson) and George Spoor.[184] |

## News in Pine Bluff

| Pine Bluff Newspapers | Founders or Editors | Date of Publication |
|---|---|---|
| *Press-Eagle* | | 1893 |
| *Jeffersonian* | W. E. Smith, who was succeeded by Wyatt and Luckie. The newspaper did not have a long existence. | 1847. The first paper established in Pine Bluff. |
| *Pine Bluff Republican* | Enoch H. Vance | 1850 |
| *Pine Bluff American* | Suspended in a short time. | 1850 |
| *Democrat* | Walter C. Dent | 1856 |
| *Jefferson Enterprise* | Wyatt and Luckie | 1856 |

| | Lee and Douglass | 1856 |
|---|---|---|
| *Jefferson Independent* | A July 1859 issue gave a synopsis of the contents of the tax books for the year [1859], showing that the slaves in the county were valued at considerably more than the land. It was an influential newspaper. | There were 397,864 acres of land assessed at a value of $2,132,525, while 4,899 slaves were valued on the tax books at $2,471,870. Miscellaneous personal property brought the value up to a half a million.[185] |
| *Pine Bluff Bulletin* | H. B. Worsham | About 1862. The city's first daily newspaper. It was about war news. |
| *Pine Bluff Dispatch* | Judge T. B. Morton and John L. Bowers | 1865 |
| *Orthopolitan* | Lee and Williams | 1865 |
| *Southern Vindicator* | A triweekly, replaced the *Orthopolitan* | 1865. Suspended after a year. |
| *Jefferson Republican* | J. L. Bowers | About 1868 |
| *Bluff Press* | Wyatt C. Thomas and Major Charles Gordon Newman, sole editor and proprietor | 1868. It continued until 1878. In September 1878, it became a daily, but that edition was suspended in January 1879. |
| *Daily Press* | Ryan continued it. | 1881 |
| *Weekly Eagle* | W. F. Bell. He died the following August [1880]. | February 26, 1880. Bell was succeeded by his brothers, D. C. and J. C. Bell. Arthur Murray joined them in November 1880. |
| *Press-Eagle* | Arthur Murray and Ryan Murray | 1881 |
| *Pine Bluff Commercial* | Major Charles Gordon Newman | May 1878. Published at first as a weekly, but in August 1887, it became an evening daily, although no Sunday issue was published. |
| *Pine Bluff Graphic* | Fletcher Bass | 1886 |

**Only two newspapers established in Pine Bluff have survived. They are the *Pine Bluff Graphic* and the *Pine Bluff Commercial*.[186]**

## *Portraits of White American Leaders*

Reverend Evander McNair

Colonel Joseph W. Bocage

Samuel Calhoun Roane

Powell Clayton

*Second row:* John Selden Roane. Pine Bluff (Jefferson County) early in the twentieth-century. The Jefferson County courthouse can be seen to the right. *Courtesy of the Arkansas History Commission*

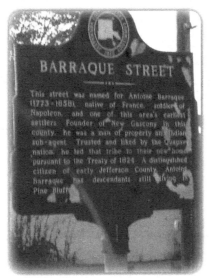

Bettye J. Williams

## Transportation Vehicles

Postcard: Horse and wagon.

Postcard: An advertising truck.

Postcard: Traveling by ship.

266

*Travel by Railway: 1860–1950s*

Train Postcard
Early 1900s

Train Postcard
Early 1900s

Train Postcard
Early 1900s

The railroad had its largest impact on United States transportation during the second half of the 1800s. For businesses, rail travel decreased transportation costs and transported new products and goods to commercial markets. The First Transcontinental Railroad in the United States was built across North America in the 1860s, linking the railroad network of the eastern United States with California on the Pacific coast. Rail travel led to the rapid cultivation of new farm lands. Railroads concentrated their efforts on moving freight and passengers over long distances.

## *Travel by Railway: 1860–1950s*

*Above*: **Engine 819**, a steam locomotive. This train was built by the St. Louis Southwestern | Railway Company (Cotton Belt Route) at its Pine Bluff, Arkansas shops in 1942. The | Mighty locomotive ruled the rails for a dozen years before being replaced by diesel locomotives. The engine was donated to the city in 1965 and "Old 819" placed in Oakland Park until 1983 when the Cotton Belt brought it out of the park for restoration by the Cotton Belt Historical Society, Inc. The engine's home is now in the Arkansas Railroad Museum which is located at the place of its birth, the Old Cotton Belt Shops in Pine Bluff.

Train Postcard
Early 1900s

Train Postcard
Early 1900s

## *Travel by Cars: 1900s to the 1950s*

Postcard: A Street Scene of
Model T cars

Postcard: 1921 Model T
Suburban

## *Travel by Cars: 1900s to the 1950s*

Postcard: 1910 Ford Model T

Postcard: 1915 Ford Model T
Touring

Postcard: 1926 Ford Model T,
New Jersey Auto Museum

Postcard: 1924 Model T
Coupe

Postcard: 1931 Ford Model A
Deluxe, Henry Ford Steel,
Parade Car

Postcard: 1911 Model T. Ford
Torpedo Roadmaster

Postcard: 1911 Model T

Postcard: 1910 Ford Model A

Postcard: 1915 Model T
Couplet

Postcard: 1929 Ford Model A

## JEWISH LIFE IN PINE BLUFF/JEFFERSON COUNTY

### Historical Overview

With the county of Jefferson, the legacy of Pine Bluff as a Jewish center is substantial and lives on. Pine Bluff had the second-largest Jewish community in Arkansas with Little Rock being the first.[187] Jews first arrived in Pine Bluff in the 1840s. By 1865, there were about ten Jewish families in the city and several Jewish-owned businesses. Cotton farming was king in the rural areas around Pine Bluff. In 1866, the German Jews organized a local *B'nai B'rith* lodge, and the following year, they founded a congregation Anshe Emeth. By 1878, 250 German Jews lived in town. By 1879, there were three *B'nai B'rith* lodges in town, together with branches of other fraternal organizations, including Kesher Shei Barzel (Bond of Iron) and the Free Sons of Israel. There was also a Ladies Aid Society and a Ladies Relief Society, both of which provided charity to members of the Jewish community. They formed purely social organizations and their own social club, called the *Entre Nous Eucre Club*. In 1872, Jewish men founded the Bluff City Club, which later became the Harmony Club.

Immediately after the Civil War, it took farsighted men to envision what Pine Bluff could become, considering its depressed economy, rutted streets, frame buildings, and low-lying lands that tended to flood in the spring. Among the visionaries who helped develop Pine Bluff were a number of Jewish merchants who had settled in town prior to the early 1860s. Linked to Little Rock by railroad in 1881, Pine Bluff developed industry and grew into the third-largest city in the state by 1900. The Jewish community grew significantly in the late nineteenth century as many Jews moved to Pine Bluff to open stores, relying on the area's farming economy. These merchants included, among others: Isaac Althschul, Max Weil, Charles Weil, Colonel Solomon Franklin, Captain Samuel Franklin, members of the Bluthenthal family, Gabe Meyer, David Aschaffenberg, and John Bloom. When the prosperous tide of business took a downturn in the 1890s, businessmen in the Pine Bluff area were solely affected, which included Isaac Altschul, Joseph Altheimer, Colonel Solomon Franklin, and Captain Samuel Franklin.[188]

In 1881, there were thirty Jewish-owned businesses in town. They were retail stores specializing in dry goods, groceries, clothing, jewelry, or odds and ends. Show windows at toy and gift stores showcased eye-catching dolls and dishes. By 1905, an estimated 425 Jews lived in Pine Bluff. Following the same economic path as the earlier German immigration and forming their own separate Orthodox congregation, B'nai Israel, a wave of Eastern European Jews came to Pine Bluff in the early twentieth century. Both groups concentrated in retail trade. By 1970, the farming economy in the Pine Bluff area began to change as mechanization reduced the number of farm workers needed. As those people left, so did the customer base of the stores of Anshe Emeth congregants.[189] Also, the families that owned stores—Barre, Baim's, Burt's, Cohen's, Levine's, Kahn's Jewelers, and Rosenwigs's—were aging, and the next generation did not want to live in a small town and put in the long hours in retailing. Most Jewish-owned stores closed in Pine Bluff around 1985.

The Ben Pearson block included a mix of Black and White residences, which also included Branch Normal College [1872], Trinity Episcopal Church [1859], and Anshe Emeth [1867], a Jewish synagogue—all within blocks of each other.

## Jewish Leaders in Pine Bluff and Jefferson County[190]

| Leaders | Biography and/or Achievements |
| --- | --- |
| Isaac Altschul (Merchant and community leader) | A very successful businessman who worked the counter himself, Isaac Altschul (1825–98) opened a dry goods store outside Pine Bluff in 1852. The store was in the midst of several slave plantations, which Altschul catered to. In addition to serving plantation owners, he would remain open on Sundays to be able to trade with slaves on their day off. In 1860, he had $10,000 in personal property, which included one slave. Being a merchant and foreign-born [Germany], Altschul and other Jewish merchants were considered outsiders to the planter elite in the rural plantation economy of the antebellum South. With the rise of the new, commercial South after 1865, Jews in Pine Bluff and the rest of the South led the way and emerged as community leaders. Altschul moved to Pine Bluff after the Civil War, and many of his relatives joined him as they became one of the most prominent Jewish families in town. |

| | |
|---|---|
| Samuel Altschul<br>Solomon Altschul<br>Adolph Altschul<br>Charles Altschul<br>(Members of Isaac Altschul family)<br><br>Joseph Altschul (son of Isaac Altschul) | A number of the Altschul family settled in Pine Bluff and became a vital part of the business and civic community. They included Samuel (1816–78), Solomon (1824–1910), and Adolph (1841–1901). Charles Altschul (1859–1922) served as vice president of the Citizens Mortgage and Security Company. Isaac Altschul's son, Joseph (1845–1923), opened the first confectionary store in Pine Bluff in 1868, and handled fancy groceries, tobacco, toys, and sporting goods.[191] |
| Gabriel Meyer<br>(City official and father of public schooling in Pine Bluff)<br><br> | Born on July 4, 1836, in Bavaria, Germany, Gabriel Meyer sailed from his native home to New Orleans and then to Quachita, Louisiana. Stranded in Pine Bluff by the flood of 1856, Meyer was one of several Jewish traders passing through Pine Bluff before the Civil War. His extended stay in town convinced him to remain. He soon opened a store. Meyer owned nineteen plantations, "all of which were successfully cultivated." Serving in local government, Meyer was city alderman for ten years and spent much of his time working to restore the fiscal health of the city. Devoted to the public schools and serving on the school board for twenty one years in the 1860s when the city did not have funds to pay its teachers, Meyer paid them out of his own pockets. He then negotiated a loan from an East Coast bank to cover the schools' shortfall. Known as the father of the Pine Bluff school district, an elementary school [Gabe Meyer] was named in his honor. |
| David Blumenthal<br>(Hotel owner) | Arriving in 1860, David Blumenthal opened a hotel that catered to traveling traders passing through Pine Bluff. |
| Colonel Solomon Franklin<br>(Land owner and businessman) | Once having owned two riverboats, both of which sank, Solomon Franklin (1827–95) decided to try his luck with cotton and purchased a plantation. By 1878, he owned nineteen hundred acres of land and eventually became the most prominent businessman and citizen in Pine Bluff. Relying on local people to work his land, Franklin realized an economic fortune. By the 1890s, his fortune and health had declined. He died of a heart attack on the same day he sold his plantation to pay off debts, amounting to $65,000. He was survived by ten children, many of whom became leading businessmen and citizens of Pine Bluff. |

| | |
|---|---|
| Captain Samuel Franklin<br>Businessman and writer | Captain Samuel Franklin (1836–93) served in the Confederate army and then settled in Pine Bluff. He purchased a sawmill east of Pine Bluff. He, together with W. B. Ragland and M. L. Bell, established the Pine Bluff Gas Works and laid gas pipes on Barraque Street. Coal was used to make the gas used in homes, businesses, and street lamps. Samuel Franklin erected one of the first cotton oil mills in the South and became known as a leading financier of the area. He was a gifted writer. In 1880, he served as president of the Hancock and English Club of Pine Bluff, an organization that encouraged harmony between the races and included African American members. He suffered financial losses in the 1880s. |
| W. B. Ragland<br>M. L. Bell<br>Pine Bluff Gas Works | Helped establish the Pine Bluff Gas Works and laid gas pipes in Pine Bluff. |
| L. E. Goldsmith<br>(Mayor and cotton grower) | Pine Bluff Jews were very involved in civic affairs and politics. L. E. Goldsmith served as mayor and was elected by a large majority in 1895. |
| Simon Bloom<br>(Mayor and cotton grower) | A Pine Bluff cotton grower and successor to L. E. Goldsmith, Simon Bloom served three terms as mayor [1913–19]. |
| David Aschaffenberg<br>(City clerk and businessman) | This prominent and much-respected citizen was born in Albersweiler, Rhine Bavaria, Germany, on September 27, 1831, and was one of twelve children of Henry and Nanett (Meyer) Aschaffenburg. David Aschaffenberg left his native country at the age of nineteen, and arrived in Pine Bluff in 1854 with the post quartermaster and remained as chief clerk for the quartermaster's department until after the close of the Civil War. He was occupied in merchandising, and then was appointed justice of the peace of Jefferson County. In 1871, he was elected city clerk.[192] |
| David Aschaffenberg<br>Nathan Cook<br>Charles Weil<br>Ben Weil (son of Charles Weil)<br>(City council members) | The preceding four citizens served on the city council. A prominent merchant and planter, Charles Weil (1840–1914) was a longtime director of the Merchants and Planters Bank. Charles Weil was president of the Anshe Emeth congregation for thirty years and was active in the B'nai B'rith lodge, which was renamed in his honor after he died. [193] |
| Max Weil<br>Charles Weil | Max Weil (1829–1908) continued the bakery he established in the 1850s. His brother, Charles Weil (1840–1914), joined Max in the bakery business and opened a furniture store after the Civil War. Max built up an extensive trade with farmers. Charles served as acting mayor. |

| | |
|---|---|
| Irving Reinberger<br>(Attorney) | Moving to Pine Bluff in 1882, Irving Reinberger was an attorney and served as assistant district attorney and city attorney. His two sons became lawyers and joined the family firm in Pine Bluff. Maurice Reinberger became a successful criminal defense lawyer who specialized in death penalty cases. |
| Sam Hilzheim<br>(Politician) | Manager of the Pine Bluff Opera House, Sam Hilzheim served in the state legislature in the 1890s. |
| Frank Silverman<br>(Sheriff and collector) | Born in Wooster, Ohio, January 6, 1843, son of a Germany father and a Berks County, Pennsylvania, mother. In 1871, he traveled to Pine Bluff, where he became editor of the *Jefferson Republican*. He purchased the business and ran the newspaper for two years. He next engaged in the mercantile business, was elected as a delegate to the Republican Convention, and became a land commissioner and deputy sheriff. |
| Sam Levine<br>(Lawyer) | Born in 1891, in Louisiana, Sam M. Levine was an attorney. He served in both the state House of Representatives and the state Senate, beginning in the 1930s. He distinguished himself in a long legal career and was said to have had the biggest vocabulary in Pine Bluff and the poorest clients. He was ahead of his time. |
| Meyer Solomon<br>(Journalist) | Meyer "Boy" Solomon (1880–1938) became a reporter for the *Pine Bluff Daily Graphic* at age seventeen and became managing editor of the newspaper at age twenty-one. Solomon built an excellent reputation in journalism in Pine Bluff, and from there, he worked with a St. Louis newspaper. He then became managing editor of the *New York Morning Telegram* and was editor of the theatrical publication *Variety*. He was a district Tammany leader and became acquainted with noted political leaders of the time. He also was a publicity agent for William Jennings Bryan's presidential campaign. |
| Joseph Altheimer<br>(Owner of nineteen plantations and founder of Altheimer, Arkansas) | The Altheimer brothers are members of the oldest and most influential business houses in Pine Bluff. Born in 1842 in Eberstadt, South Germany, Joseph Altheimer settled in Pine Bluff in 1868. Joseph and Louis invested every dollar in real estate and plantation lands. They opened up the land out of the forests, cut immense ditches to drain the water off, and converted many swamps into productive and blooming farms. They are the founders of Altheimer, Arkansas.[194] |

| Louis Altheimer (Owner of nineteen plantations and founder of Altheimer, Arkansas) | Born in 1847 in Eberstadt, South Germany, Louis Altheimer and his brother, Joseph, erected a depot in Altheimer, and donated all necessary grounds for side tracks for the St. Louis, Arkansas and Texas Railroad. Being farsighted, Louis and Joseph contributed to the wealth and prosperity of Jefferson County and Pine Bluff. Louis was nominated by the Republican Party in 1886 as treasurer of the state. [195] |
|---|---|
| Henry Marx (Retailer) | Henry Marx (1873–1950) came to Pine Bluff as a lad of sixteen, worked for a relative, then opened a men's and boy's clothing store. He also accumulated some twelve thousand acres of cotton land. He served as a director of the Cotton Belt Trust Company and was active in the civic life of the city. |

*Jewish Merchants and Businesses in Pine Bluff*
Courtesy of the *1940 Lion Yearbook* and the *1950 Lion Yearbook*

Pine Bluff's Fastest Growing

Department Store

Shop With Confidence at

## Cohen's Department Store

Pine Bluff, Arkansas

## American Clothing Store

A. Meyer, Proprietor

Men's & Young Men's Tailor-made Clothing

Outfitters For Your Entire Family

329 Main     Ph. 5658     Pine Bluff

## Black & White Store

Main Street                    Pine Bluff

If You Want to Be Well-Dressed

Shop With Confidence at

COHEN'S

DEPARTMENT STORE

205 Main Street          Pine Bluff, Ark.

STORE FOR MEN

502 Main

New MaRu

## Baims Eagle Store
## And
## Baims 401 Supply Store

Main St.                         Pine Bluff

*Jewish Merchants and Businesses in Pine Bluff before the 1950s*
*Courtesy of the 1940 Lion Yearbook and the 1950 Lion Yearbook*

SINCE 1910

Kahn's Jewelers

415 MAIN • JE 4-1931

PINE BLUFF, ARKANSAS

Arkansas' Only Elected

Member of the Diamond

Council of America

Compliments

of

SILBERNAGEL & CO.

WHOLESALE

Pine Bluff, Arkansas

Compliments of

**F. G. SMART
CHEVROLET CO.**

Sales CHEVROLET Service

Colored Salesmen:
E. D. Peebles        Phones
S. B. Adams          50—51

**THE PERDUE CO.**

OFFICE SUPPLIES

PRINTING

207-209 W. 2nd      Phones 218-219

**John A. Pope
Furniture Company**

423 Main Street

WE WILL NOT BE UNDER SOLD

PINE BLUFF, ARK.

In Pine Bluff Always

**Shop
Froug's
First**

Southeastern Arkansas' Finest
Department Store

"QUALITY AND DEPENDABILITY"

Complements
Of
W. A. KIENTZ GROCERY CO.
Pho. JE 4-2161 - 218 State St.
Pine Bluff, Arkansas

HENRY E. REYER JEWELER
Ph. JE 409006
308 Pine Street
Pine Bluff, Arkansas

## Jewish Merchants and Businesses in Pine Bluff before the 1950s

Courtesy of the *1940 Lion Yearbook* and the *1950 Lion Yearbook*

SERVING SOUTHEAST

ARKANSAS SINCE 1895

Location at 500 Main in the heart of Downtown Pine Bluff, we continue to offer such famous brands as Florsheim Shoes; Stetson Hats; Hart Schaffner and Marx Clothing; Arrow Shirts; and many more. See our new department with the college or career man in mind.

COMPLIMENTS

We carry a complete line of well-known brands in every department.

EITHER YOUR MONEY'S WORTH OR
YOUR MONEY BACK

3rd and Main Sts.      Phone 343

## Jewish Merchants and Businesses in Pine Bluff before the 1950s
Courtesy of the *1940 Lion Yearbook* and the *1950 Lion Yearbook*

Bettye J. Williams

284

## Chain Stores in Pine Bluff in the Early Twentieth Century

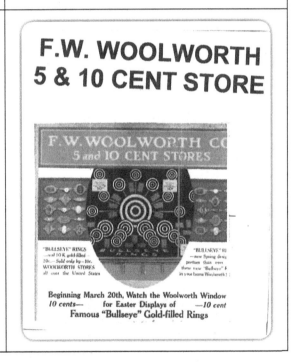

*Merchants and Businesses in Pine Bluff*
Courtesy of the *1924–25 Merrill Yearbook*

COTTON BELT BANK

SERVICE WITH A SMILE

UNDER BOTH FEDERAL AND STATE

SUPERVISION

THE SIMMONS NATIONAL BANK

OF

PINE BLUFF, ARK.
Capital, Surplus and Profits Over $600,000.00
Resources Over $6,000,000.00
U. S. Government Supervision.

Whenever You Think of Banking

Service . . . Think First

of

PEOPLES SAVINGS BANK & TRUST
COMPANY

OF

PINE BLUFF, ARK.
UNDER STATE and FEDERAL SUPERVISION

Resident Phone 126

Capital Assets Over $2,850,000.00

*Businesses in Pine Bluff before the 1940s*
Courtesy of the *1940 Lion Yearbook*

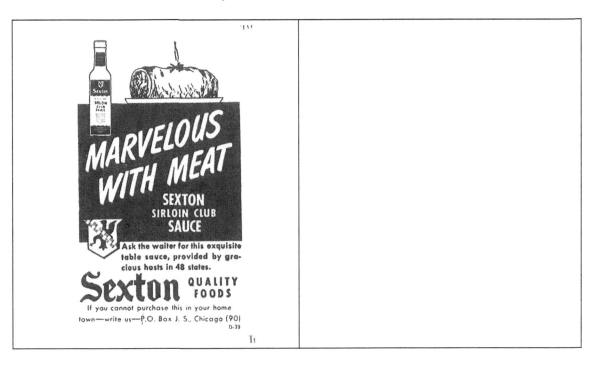

Compliments of

O. K. Ice Cream & Candy Co.

721-725 Main Street—Phone 104

PINE BLUFF, ARK.

## Ferguson's Refrigeration & Furniture Co.

*Servicing All Makes of Refrigerators*

1306 Main                    Phone 3162

PINE BLUFF

*Merchants and Businesses in Pine Bluff*

Courtesy of the *1940 Lion Yearbook* and the *1950 Lion Yearbook*

## FOX BROTHERS HARDWARE CO.

*"Your Frigidaire Dealers"*

415 Main Street               Phone 880

Pine Bluff, Arkansas

## THE B. F. GOODRICH STORE

"B. F. Goodrich Tires"

Geo. W. List, Pres.    R. C. List, Vice-Pres.

## LIST LAUNDRY DRY CLEANERS

201 East Barrique            Phone 146

Pine Bluff, Arkansas

## KOBERLEIN BAKERY CO.

210 Walnut Street               Pine Bluff

## Merchants and Businesses in Pine Bluff before the 1950s

Courtesy of the *1940 Lion Yearbook* and the *1950 Lion Yearbook*

All Illustrations for "THE LION"
were made into cuts at the
modern plant of
COMMERCIAL PRINTING &
LITHOGRAPHING CO.

Pine Bluff, Ark.

DEPEND ON US
to fill Your
PRESCRIPTION
Exactly as your Doctor Prescribed
Lowest Prices on Drugs, Tobacco, Toiletries
and Prescriptions in Town

Reed's Cut-Rate Drug Store
220 Main St.          Pine Bluff, Ark.

Congratulations to Class of '40

322 Main Street          Phone 100

For a Lasting Pleasure
AN RCA VICTOR RADIO

TAYLOR ELECTRIC
COMPANY

Everything Electrical

718 Main St.          Pine Bluff, Ark.

SHELL-ROSS COMPANY

GARDEN—
FIELD— SEED
FLOWER—

Fertilizer, Sprayers, Spray Materials
Poultry Feed and Supplies

PINE BLUFF, ARK.

WAYMACK'S

LAUNDRY & DRY CLEANERS

304 N. CEDAR

*Merchants and Businesses in Pine Bluff before the 1950s*
Courtesy of the *1940 Lion Yearbook* and the *1950 Lion Yearbook*

15 W. 5th.     *"Since 1906"*     JE 4-8122

W. D. Wells
Office Equipment Co.

Typewriters

Calculators - Adding Machines
Rental - Purchase Plan

Ph. 7266     Pine Bluff     627 - 29 Main

# STREET SCENES: 1911 AND 1918 CABLE TRACKS IN PINE BLUFF

*Above*: A 1911 street scene with vehicles and a cable car on the street. Cable tracks line the street. Observed is a horse and cart on the street. A postcard. *Below*: Barraque Street in 1918, east from Pine Street. A postcard.

## *Early City Hall and First United States Post Office*

*Above*: Until the construction of the Civic Center, this building served as the first City Hall in Pine Bluff. A postcard. *Below*: Built in 1909, this building served as the Post office until the construction of the Federal Building on 100 East 8th Street. A postcard.

## *Pine Bluff Courthouse and Street Scene*

COURT HOUSE, PINE BLUFF, ARK.——6

### JEFFERSON COUNTY COURTHOUSE

Named for Former President Thomas Jefferson, Jefferson County makes up the towns of Altheimer, Humphrey, Pine Bluff, Redfield, Sherrill, Wabbaseka, and White Hall. Located at 101 West Barraque Street, it was constructed in 1838. The 1838 courthouse is the only one known to have caused a river to be changed. During the 1908 flood of the Arkansas River, the Judges' chambers, jury room, part of the courtroom, and the Sheriff's and Assessor's offices were purposely torn off and dumped into the river to keep the rest of the building from caving into the river. It was destroyed by fire in 1976, and rebuilt. A postcard.

Main Street Looking South from Court House, Pine Bluff, Ark.

A Main Street scene looking South from the Court House. Pictured on the right is the Merchants and Planters Bank which is located across the street from the Court House. The bank building currently is owned by the Hood family. A cable car is on the track. A postcard.

## Pine Bluff Banks

Simmons Bank

On March 23, 1903, a local physician became a bank president. Dr. John Franklin Simmons, with some paid employees, first opened the doors to what was then called Simmons National Bank. The word "First" was added in 1960, making it Simmons First National Bank. In 1967, Simmons First opened its investment department and became the first bank in Arkansas to offer customers the Bank America Card (now VISA). Effective April 1, 2016, Simmons First National Bank changed its name to Simmons Bank. It has branches and ATM locations in Arkansas, Kansas, Missouri, and Tennessee.

National Bank of Commerce

Located on Fifth and Pine Street, National Bank of Commerce was established as a National Bank on January 1, 1934. On March 3, 1991, it was renamed Worthen National Bank of Pine Bluff. On July 1, 1995, it was renamed Boatmen's National Bank of Pine Bluff. On July 16, 1997, Boatmen's Bank was acquired by NationsBank of N.A., and became a branch of Bank of America, National Association.

## *1910 Main Street and Cotton Belt Railroad Yard*

*Above*: 1910 Pine Bluff—Main Street Looking South, horses and buggies.  A postcard.

### PINE BLUFF COTTON BELT RAILWAY YARD

*Below*: In 1883, the Texas & St. Louis Railroad was completed through Arkansas.  The purpose of the railroad was to connect St. Louis with the cotton fields of the southwest, nicknamed "Cotton Belt."  About 1895, the St. Louis Southwestern built a new passenger and freight depot at the southeast corner of Third and Alabama Streets (no longer in existence). Later, the St. Louis Southwestern built a separate freight depot at the SE corner of Third and State. The Cotton Belt Railroad shops, including a roundhouse and car-making facility, were located near downtown. The roundhouse was dismantled in the 1970s, and the shops closed in the 1990s.  The Arkansas Railroad Museum is housed in what was once the locomotive fabrication building. From Rachel Silva, "Walks through History: Pine Bluff Commercial Historic District," August 10, 2013.  A postcard.

## *Public Buildings*

### HOTEL PINES

Located on the corner of West Fifth and Main Streets, the Hotel Pines is a six-story U-shaped masonry structure, with a two-story section filling the center of the U. The center section has a portico projecting over the sidewalk, with Classical Revival detailing and paired columns for support. Built in 1913, and in operation as a hotel until 1970, it was Pine Bluff's grandest hotel. The building was listed on the National Register of Historic Places in 1979. A postcard.

*Public Library, Pine Bluff, Ark.*

### PINE BLUFF LIBRARY

The Pine Bluff Library was established in 1913, with the help of the local Pine Bluff Chapter of the Daughters of the American Revolution. Located on Fifth Street, this building is an earlier site for the Pine Bluff Library. In 1979, an agreement between the city and Jefferson County created the Pine Bluff Jefferson County Library System. Presently, the library is located in the Civic Center, at 200 East 8th Street. A postcard.

# Pine Bluff Properties on the National Register of Historic Places

### MERCHANTS AND PLANTERS BANK BUILDING

The Merchants and Planters Bank building is a historic commercial structure at 100 Main Street in Pine Bluff. It is a two-story brick building with a hip roof and a turret at the northeast corner. Designed by Thomas A. Harding of Little Rock and opened in 1892, the building is a distinctive local example of Victorian Romanesque architecture. It was listed on the National Register of Historic Places in 1978. A postcard.

Located at 116 West 6th Street in Pine Bluff, the Arkansas Louisiana Gas Company was listed on the National Register of Historic Places on May 10, 2001.

*Your future will be better in Arkansas because nuclear power is on the way from AP&L*

**ARKANSAS / POWER & LIGHT COMPANY**
HELPING BUILD ARKANSAS

## *Pine Bluff Properties on the National Register of Historic Places*

### MASONIC TEMPLE

Built in stages during 1902, 1903, and 1904 by the Sovereign Grand Lodge of Free and Accepted Masons of the State of Arkansas, the state's Black Masonic order, the Masonic Temple was the tallest building in Pine Bluff when it was completed. The Masonic Temple was designed by Little Rock architects Frank Gibb and Theo Sanders in the Romanesque Revival style with arched window openings on the top floor and stone columns at the storefront. The first floor housed a variety of retail shops. The second floor was used as office space for the Grand Lodge as well as doctors, dentists, and other professionals. The third and fourth floors were the lodge rooms/lodge hall. The Masonic Temple is listed on the National Register of Historic Places, 1978. Photo by Bettye J. Williams, founder of *Oak and Ivy: African American Museum and Cultural Center*, 2016. .

UNION STATION

Union Station was built in 1906 to serve both the Cotton Belt and St. Louis, Iron Mountain & Southern Railroad Lines. Iron Mountain became Missouri Pacific in 1917 and is now Union Pacific. The depot housed a ticket office, baggage room, waiting rooms, and the far eastern end of the building was the Wells Fargo Railway Express office. The depot currently houses the Pine Bluff/Jefferson County Historical Museum. From Rachel Silva, "Walks through History: Pine Bluff Commercial Historic District," August 10, 2013. Union Station is listed on the National Register of Historic Places, 1978. A postcard.

SAENGER THEATER

The southeast corner of West Second and Pine Street has been the focal point of entertainment in Pine Bluff since 1912, when O. C. Hauber converted an old store building into a movie theater which he called Hauber Theater. In May 1920, Hauber sold the theater to the Bohlinger Amusement Company of New Orleans for $40,000. The Bohlinger Company sold the theater two months later to the Saenger Amusement Company of New Orleans. This latter company, a subsidiary of Paramount Films, renamed the theater "The Saenger." In October 1922, plans were made to remodel the theater to accommodate stage performances in addition to movies. But the latter structure burned. Designed by Emile Weil, the Saenger Theater opened in November 1924 and closed in 1975. In 2012, the Saenger Theater was given to the city of Pine Bluff. From Rachel Silva, "Walks through History: Pine Bluff Commercial Historic District," August 10, 2013. The Saenger Theater is listed on the National Register of Historic Places, 1995. A postcard.

## *Pine Bluff Properties on the National Register of Historic Places*

Du Bocage House
Also known as the Judge William Joseph Bocage House, the Du Bocage House, at 1115 West 4th Street in Pine Bluff, is an example of late Greek Revival architecture in Arkansas. Completed in 1866, it was added to the National Register of Historic Places on June 24, 1974.

PINE BLUFF SCHOOL OF AVIATION
Located at Grider Field and opened in April 1941, this building was the Ground School at Pine Bluff School of Aviation. College professors with the highest qualifications taught United States Army Air Corps flying cadets. The facility was inactivated on November 30, 1944, with the withdrawal of the pilot's training program. It was declared surplus and eventually discharged to the War Assets Administration. The airport became a civil airport. A postcard.

# Pine Bluff Properties on the National Register of Historic Places

The Rosenzweig House
The Rosenzweigs lived in this Queen Anne Victorian-style house at 717 West Second Street. It was sold by Irene Rosenzweig in 1970, and placed on the National Register for Historic Places on December 12, 1976. William M. Rosenzweig emigrated from Lithuania (Kovno), Russia in 1889, and opened the Good Luck Store, later Rosenzweigh's Department Store in Pine Bluff, which was the city's largest mercantile and farm supply store. A postcard.

Rosenzweig Store at 3rd and Main Streets in Pine Bluff (Jefferson County); circa early 1930s. *Courtesy of the Butler Center for Arkansas Studies, Central Arkansas Library System*

## *Pine Bluff Properties on the National Register of Historic Places*

**Caldwell Hall**

Caldwell Hall occupies a central position on the campus of UAPB, formerly Branch Normal College. It is a large, T-shaped two story brick building with Late Gothic Revival features. It was built in 1928 to a design by the Arkansas architectural firm of Thompson, Sanford, and Ginnochio. Its central entrance has Art Deco features in stone panels above the entrance, and fluted stone piers that rise to streamlined finials. The building was listed on the National Register of Historic Places in 1982.

**CHILDRESS HALL**

The Works Progress Administration (WPA) library named Childress Hall was completed in 1939. It served as the campus library until 1969. This structure now houses the University Museum and Cultural Center. Arriving at Branch Normal College in 1889 as an assistant instructor of mathematics and library science, Rufus C. Childress was the first graduate of Philander Smith College.

## Historic Hotels in Pine Bluff

*Above*: The Jefferson Hotel in Pine Bluff was opened on May 16, 1909. *Below*: Lobby of the Jefferson Hotel. Vintage postcards.

## Historic Motels in Pine Bluff

Above: Kotton Kort Tourist Motel in Pine Bluff, Arkansas, 1950s. Tri-view of the hotel site. Vintage postcard. *Below*: Admiral Benbow Inn in Pine Bluff. 1960s cars in the parking lot. Vintage postcard.

## Historic Motels in Pine Bluff

*Above:* Pine Bluff Motel & Plantation Embers Restaurant. Twenty-six units on six acres with beautiful trees. Air conditioned, telephones, televisions, beauty rest mattresses. Located on Highway 65 North. Vintage postcards.

*Pine Bluff Motel*
HIWAY 65 NORTH - PINE BLUFF, ARK.

# WORKS CITED

Allsopp, Fred W. *History of the Arkansas Press for a Hundred Years and More*. Little Rock: Parke-Harper, 1922, 207–15.

*Biographical and Historical Memoirs of Central Arkansas*. Chicago, Nashville, St. Louis: Goodspeed, 1889.

*Biographical and Historical Memoirs of Jefferson County, Arkansas*. Chicago, Nashville, St. Louis: Goodspeed, 1889.

*Biographical and Historical Memoirs of Pulaski County, Arkansas*. Chicago, Nashville, St. Louis: Goodspeed, 1889.

Carroll, Joe Barry. *Growing Up: In Words and Images*. Joe Barry Carroll Publishing, 2013.

Chambers, Frederick R. "Historical Study of Arkansas Agricultural, Mechanical, and Normal College, 1873–1943." EdD diss., Ball State University, 1970.

Corbitt, John H. *Black Churches Reaching College Students*. Nashville: Townsend Press. 1995.

*Educating the Mind and the Spirit: The Unfolding History of Black School Administrators in Arkansas, 1900–2000*. C. Calvin Smith, editor. Linda Walls Joshua, contributing editor. University of Arkansas Press, 2003.

*The Encyclopedia of Arkansas History and Culture*. Central Arkansas Library System, 2015.

Gordon, Fon Louise. *Caste and Class: The Black Experience in Arkansas, 1880–1920*. Athens, GA: University of Georgia, 1995.

Hanley, Steven, and Ray Hanley. *Images of America: Arkansas County*, 2008.

Johnson, Ted Dean. "History of Arts Education at the University of Arkansas at Pine Bluff, 1873–1973." EdD diss., University of Oklahoma, Norman, OK, 1985, 16.

Kilpatrick, Judith. *Extra-Ordinary Men: African American Lawyers and Civil Rights in Arkansas Before 1950*, 2000.

Lankford, George E., ed. *Bearing Witness: Memories of Arkansas Slavery. Narratives from the 1930s, WPA Collections,* Fayetteville: University of Arkansas Press, 2003.

Leslie, James W. *Land of Cypress and Pine: More Southeast Arkansas History*, 1976.

———. *Saracen's Country: Some Southeast Arkansas History.* Little Rock: Rose, 1974.

*Life in Arkansas: The First 100 Years.* Arkansas State Society, Daughters of the American Revolution, 1990.

Litwack, Leon F. *Trouble in Mind: Black Southerners in the Age of Jim Crow.* New York: Alfred A. Knopf, 1998, 345.

Logan, Rayford W., and Michael Winston. *Dictionary of American Negro Biography.* New York: W. W. Norton, 1982.

McMurry, Linda O. *To Keep the Waters Troubled: The Life and Times of Ida B. Wells,* 120–23.

Martin, Josephine, and Hames Ware, eds. *A Selected History of Pine Bluff Public Schools.* Pine Bluff, AR, 1971.

Meir, August, *Negro Thought in America, 1880–1915*, 1963.

Murry, Linda O. *Recorder of the Black Experience: A Biography of Monroe Nathan Work.* Louisiana State University Press, 1985.

Perry, Ivory. *Pine Bluff: The Moral Resources of a Southern Community.* Temple University Press, 1988.

———. *A life in the Struggle and the Culture of Opposition.* Temple University Press, 1995.

*Pine Bluff, Arkansas: A Visual History.* From the *Pine Bluff Commercial,* 1992.

*Post Card History of Jefferson County.* Pine Bluff/Jefferson County Historical Museum.

Rothrock, Thomas. "Joseph Carter Corbin and Negro Education in the University of Arkansas." *Arkansas Historical Quarterly* 30 (Winter 1971): 277–314.

Simmons, William J. *Men of Mark: Eminent, Progressive, and Rising.* Chicago: Johnson Pub., 1970.

"UAPB Founding Father Honored with a Headstone on Memorial Day," *Pine Bluff Commercial,* Sunday, June 2, 2013, 2B.

Williams, Bettye J. "Names and Naming," *Oxford Companion to African American Literature.* William Andrews, Frances Smith Foster, Trudier Harris, eds. Oxford: Oxford University Press, 1997, 523–26.

Williams, C. Fred. "Introduction," *Life in Arkansas: The First 100 Years.* Arkansas State Society, Daughters of the American Revolution, 1985, i-iii.

# ENDNOTES

1  Augmenting visual records not ordinarily available, postcards advance glimpses of places and illustrate popular culture. They provide important visual information, as postcards provide authentic insights into daily activities and appearances of neighborhoods, individuals, and objects.

2  "Unearthing History," *PRIDE:* University of Arkansas at Pine Bluff, Summer 2014, 20.

3  http://enwikipedia org/wiki/Pine_Bluff_Arkansas.

4  http://enwikipedia/wiki/Pine-Bluff_Arkansas_Civil_War.

5  http://en Wikipedia.org. wiki Pine_Bluff_Arkansas_Civil War_and_Reconstruction_ 28186.

6  http://en Wikipedia.org. wiki Pine_Bluff_Arkansas_CivilWar_and_Reconstruction_ 28186.

7  The Newberry Store and most of the stores on Main Street were targeted for not hiring Blacks.

8  http://en.wikipedia.org./wiki/Historyof Arkansas.

9  http.//www.encyclopediaofarkansas.netCarl H. Moneyhon.

10  http.//www.encyclopediaofarkansas.netCarl H. Moneyhon.

11  http.//www.encyclopediaofarkansas.netCarl H. Moneyhon

12  http.//www.encyclopediaofarkansas.net Russell E. Bearden.

13  http://ncpedia.org/sites,1790-1860.

14  *Biographical and Historical Memoirs of Central Arkansas.* (Chicago, Nashville, St. Louis: Goodspeed, 1889).

15  http://www.encyclopedofarkansas.com.

16  http.//www.encyclopediaofarkansas.netCarl H. Moneyhon.

17  http://www.encyclopedia ofarkansas.net.

18  Read full article, Bettye J. Williams, "Names and Naming," *Oxford Companion to African American Literature*, William Andrews, Frances Smith Foster, Trudier Harris, eds. (Oxford, Oxford University Press, 1997), 523–26.

19  Jennifer Hallam, "Slavery and the Making of America: The Family." A production of Thirteen/WNET New York, 2004. Educational Broadcasting Corporation

20  Heather Andrea Williams, "How Slavery Affected African American Families," University of North Carolina at Chapel Hill, National Humanities Center Fellow.

21  John Simkin (john@spartacus-educational.com) September 1997.

22  From Reginald Washington, *Sealing the Sacred Bonds of Holy Matrimony.* Freedmen's Bureau Marriage Records.

23  From Annie L. Burton, *Memories of Childhood Slavery Days,* 1909.

24 Leon F. Litwack. *Trouble in Mind: Black Southerners in the Age of Jim Crow.* (New York: Alfred A. Knopf, 1998), 345.

25 http://www. wikipedia.org. slave_health_on _plantations.

26 http://www.enwikipedia,org/wiki/"Free People of Color."

27 http://www.encyclopediaofarkansas.net/Ashlee Perry.

28 http://www.encyclopediaofarkansas/James Loewen.

29 Linda O. Murry, *To Keep the Waters Troubled: The Life and Times of Ida B. Wells*, 124.

30 Will Cowen, "Lori Walker Sees Treasured Past in Pine Bluff Neighborhoods," *SEA Life*, published by *Pine Bluff Commercial*, February 2016, 22–23.

31 http://www.encyclopediaofarkansas.net.

32 Linda O. Murry, *To Keep the Waters Troubled: The Life and Times of Ida B. Wells*, 2. Images of African Americans at the end of the nineteenth century were most disturbing—chimpanzees, gorillas, monkeys, apes.

33 http://www.familypedia.wiki.com.

34 http://www.encyclopediaofarkansas/Brent E. Fiffel.

35 "A Fatal Blow," *Arkansas Gazette*, February 11, 1892, 1–2; "Expiation," *Pine Bluff Commercial*, February 15, 1892, 3; "Two Brutal Murderers Lynched Sunday Night at Pine Bluff," *Arkansas Gazette*, February 16, 1892, 1.

36 http://wwwencyclopediaofarkansas.net Nancy Snell Griffith.

37 "A Mob's Victim," *Lowell (Michigan) Journal*, February 17, 1892, p.1; "Lynched in a City," *Sedalia (Missouri) Weekly Bazoo*, February 23, 1892, p.7; "Two Were Lynched," *Chicago Tribune*, February 15, 1892, 2.

38 "Two Brutal Murderers Lynched Sunday Night at Pine Bluff," *Arkansas Gazette*, February 16, 1892, 1.

39 http://www.encyclopediaofarkansas.net/James Loewen.

40 Read Allen W. Jones, "The Black Press in The 'New South': Jesse C. Duke's Struggle for Justice and Equality," *Journal of Negro History* 64. no. 3 (Summer 1979), 215–28.

41 http://wwwencyclopediaofarkansas.net.

42 From Fred W. Allsopp, *The History of the Arkansas Press for a Hundred Years and More* (1922), 207–15.

43 August Meir, *Negro Thought in America, 1880–1915* (1963). 150–62.

44 Mississippi was the worst state in the United States. Arkansas was next. Leon F. Litwack, *Trouble in Mind: Black Southerners in the Age of Jim Crow.* (New York: Alfred A. Knopf, 1998).

45 Litwack, 170–72.

46 Homer Plessy, a light-skinned African American, chose to challenge the Thirteenth and Fourteenth Amendments.

47 In May 1954, *Brown v. Board of Education*, 347, United States 483 (1954) was a landmark United States Supreme Court case in which the court declared laws establishing public schools for Black and White students to be unconstitutional. This decision ended legal segregation in public schools.

48 The judicial system—lawyers, judges, sheriffs, constables, policemen, wardens, and prison guards—worked against African Americans. One person says that no clear line divided the lawless lynchers from the legal lynchers.

49 Litwack, 233–77.

50 http://www.trocadero.com /stores/stonegate/items.

51  Interview with Doris Caldwell. She recounted information that happened on March 25, 1960, in Pine Bluff, Arkansas. The article appeared in the *Arkansas Gazette* on June 10, 1983.

52  Will Cowen, "Lori Walker Sees Treasured Past in Pine Bluff Neighborhoods," *SEA Life*, published by *Pine Bluff Commercial*, February 2016, 22–23.

53  75–76.

54  Tom Baskett Jr., ed., *Persistence of the Spirit: The Black Experience in Arkansas*. (Little Rock: Arkansas Endowment for the Humanities, 1986) 27. See Gordon's *Caste and Class*, 76.

55  http://www.cityofpinebluff.com.

56  Will Cowen, "Lori Walker Sees Treasured Past in Pine Bluff Neighborhoods," *SEA Life*, published by *Pine Bluff Commercial*, February 2016, 22–23.

57  http://www.encyclopediaofarkansas.net.

58  James W. Leslie, *Land of Cypress and Pine: More Southeast Arkansas History* (1976), 124–37.

59  http//:www.encyclopediaofarkansas.net, "The Epic Story of Race and the American Media," Juan Gonzalez and Joseph Torres.

60  http://arkansasblacklawyers.uark.edu/branton.html.

61  Letters from the Booker T. Washington Papers.

62  George E. Lankford, ed., *Bearing Witness: Memories of Arkansas Slavery. Narratives from the 1930s, WPA Collections* (Fayetteville: University of Arkansas Press, 2003).

63  Bill Bowden, "Mule Sale Barn Among Nine Sites Pitched for Historic List," *Arkansas Democrat Gazette*, Friday, April 8, 2016, B1–2.

64  http://www.slideshare.net/daily life of a slave.

65  Joe Barry Carroll, *Growing Up: In Words and Images*, 43–45.

66  *Encyclopedia of Arkansas History and Culture*, Aristotle Web Design, Central Arkansas Library System.

67  C. Fred Williams, "Introduction," *Life in Arkansas: The First 100 Years*, Arkansas State Society Daughters of the American Revolution, 1985, i-iii.

68  http://www. American Missionary School in Pine Bluff.

69  *Biographical and Historical Memoirs of Central Arkansas* (Nashville, Chicago, and St. Louis: Goodspeed, 1889).

70  John H. Corbitt, *Black Churches Reaching College Students* (Nashville: Townsend Press, 1995), 2–3.

71  Corbitt, 3–4.

72  Corbitt, 30–31.

73  Arkansas Baptist College, http:// www. blackpast.org.

74  *Pine Bluff Weekly Press-Eagle*, January 8, 1883, 8.

75  *Pine Bluff Commercial*, May 18, 1980, 15.

76  Linda O. Murry, 10.

77  C. Calvin Smith, ed., *Educating the Mind and the Spirit: The Unfolding History of Black School Administrators in Arkansas, 1900–2000*.

78  http://www.chermsidedistrict.org.

79  http://www.chermsidedistrict.org.

80  http://www.chermsidedistrict.org.

81  http://www.encyclopediaofarkansas.net.

82  George E. Lankford, ed., *Bearing Witness: Memories of Arkansas Slavery. Narratives from the 1930s, WPA Collections* (Fayetteville: University of Arkansas Press, 2003).

83  "Negro Boys Industrial School Fire in 1959," http://www. encyclopediaofarkansas, net.

84  See "Arkansas Locked In." *TIME,* Monday, March 16, 1959.

85  https:// en. Wikipedia.org/wiki/Arkansas_Negro-_Boys Industrial School. "KTHV Extra: Arkansas' Secret Holocaust," March 9, 2011.

86  Josephine Martin and Hames Ware, eds. *A Selected History of Pine Bluff Public Schools.* (1971). Pine Bluff, Arkansas.

87  Martin and Ware, *A Selected History,* 11–13.

88  Martin and Ware, eds., *A Selected History of Pine Bluff Public Schools,* 14–15.

89  Martin and Ware, *A Selected History,* 22–25.

90  Bowden, B2.

91  Linda O. Murry, *Recorder of the Black Experience: A Biography of Monroe Nathan Work* (Louisiana State University, 1985), 14.

92  Melody Moorehouse, "Early Times: Numerous Settlements Once Dotted Grant County," *Pine Bluff Commercial*, Sunday, June 30, 2002, 2C. The information was shared with the newspaper from George Cooper, San Jose, California.

93  Andrea Isaac Adams, "Bookman Generations," *Sheridan Headlight*, Wednesday, November 12, 2003, 1, 12.

94  http://www.cityofpinebluff.org.

95  Moorehouse, "Early Grant County Settlements," *Sheridan Headlight*, Wednesday, November 12, 2003, 2D.

96  http://www.cityofpinebluff.com.

97  From *Life in Arkansas: The First 100 Years*, Arkansas State Society, Daughters of the American Revolution, 1990.

98  http://ltc4940.blogspot.com/2008/09/pine-bluff-ar.html.

99  Obituary, *Pine Bluff Commercial*, August 28, 1918, 11.

100  James W. Leslie, "Ferd Havis: Jefferson County's Black Republican Leader," *Arkansas Historical Quarterly* 37, no. 3 (Autumn 1978), 240–51.

101  *Pine Bluff Press-Eagle*, June 20, 1872, 3.

102  http://www.encyclopediaofarkansas.net.

103  http://www.encyclopediaofarkansas.net.

104  *Press Eagle*, February 1, 1890, 5; "Ferd Havis: Jefferson County's Black Republican Leader," *Jefferson County Historical Quarterly* 8, no. 1, 1979.

105  "Ferd Havis: Jefferson County's Black Republican Leader," *Jefferson County Historical Quarterly* 8, no. 1, 1979, 25.

106  *Pine Bluff Weekly Press-Eagle*, February 1, 1890, 3.

107  *Pine Bluff Commercial*, August 26, 1918, 3

108  Parks tombstone, Block 155, Lot 2, Bellwood Cemetery, Pine Bluff, Arkansas.

109  James W. Leslie, "Dave Parks: A Political Wannable," *Jefferson County Historical Quarterly* 25, no. 1, 1997, 4–16.

110  Allen W. Jones, "The Black Press in the 'New South': Jesse C. Duke's Struggle for Justice and Equality," *Journal of Negro History* 64, no. 3 (Summer 1979), 215–28. Fon Gordon, *Caste and Class*, 71.

111  Linda O. McMurry, *To Keep the Waters Troubled: The Life and Times of Ida B. Wells*, 120–23.

112 McMurry, 120–23.

113 McMurry, 123.

114 http://www.peace,saumag.edu/swarkarticles/ahq/arkansas/black_ark_legislators/ blacklegislators.

115 "St. Paul Missionary Baptist Church to Celebrate 135th Year," *Pine Bluff Commercial*, Saturday, December 4, 2004, D1.

116 James Leslie, *Saracen's County, Some Southeast Arkansas History* (Rose Publishing) 1974, 144.

117 Read Fon Gordon, *Caste and Class: The Black Experience in Arkansas, 1880–1920* (Athens: University of Georgia Press, 1995), 71–72.

118 *Biographical and Historical Memoirs of Central Arkansas* (Goodspeed, 1899), 804.

119 Martin and Ware, *A Selected History,* 82–83.

120 Judith Kilpatrick, *Extra Ordinary Men: African American Lawyers and Civil Rights in Arkansas before 1950.* (2000).

121 *Chicago Daily Tribune,* June 5, 1892, 10; *Chicago Daily Tribune,* July 19, 1896, 4; *The Broad Ax* V, September 1, 1900, 1, CHIPS column; *The Broad Ax,* February 17, 1906, CHIPS column.

122 Judith Kilpatrick, *Extra Ordinary Men: African American Lawyers and Civil Rights in Arkansas before 1950.* (2000).

123 Judith Kilpatrick, *Extra Ordinary Men: African American Lawyers and Civil Rights in Arkansas before 1950.* (2000).

124 Judith Kilpatrick, *Extra Ordinary Men: African American Lawyers and Civil Rights in Arkansas before 1950.* (2000).

125 "UAPB founding Father honored with a headstone on Memorial Day," *Pine Bluff Commercial*, Sunday, June 2, 2013, 2B.

126 *The Encyclopedia of Arkansas History and Culture,* from the Central Arkansas Library System (2015).

127 James W.Leslie, *Saracen's Country,* 199–208.

128 *Saracen's Country,* 206.

129 "UAPB founding Father honored with a headstone on Memorial Day," *Pine Bluff Commercial*, Sunday, June 2, 2013, 2B.

130 Read "Dissertation of Frederick R. Chambers," *Historical Study of Arkansas Agricultural, Mechanical, and Normal College, 1873–1943,* (1970), 155–235.

131 Frederick Chambers, "Dissertation," 183.

132 Booker T. Washington, *Up from Slavery* (1883).

133 Frederick Chambers, "Dissertation," 204.

134 See Ted Dean Johnson, "History of Arts Education at the University of Arkansas at Pine Bluff, 1873–1973," EdD dissertation, University of Oklahoma, 1985, Norman, OK, 1985, 16–22.

135 *Pine Bluff Graphics,* March 24, 1908; Frederick Chambers, "Dissertation," 213.

136 Frederick Chambers, "Dissertation," 219.

137 Frederick Chambers, "Dissertation," 229.

138 See Ted Dean Johnson, "History of Arts Education at the University of Arkansas at Pine Bluff, 1873–1973," EdD dissertation, University of Oklahoma, Norman, OK, 1985, 16–22.

139 See Ted Dean Johnson's dissertation, 29–31.

140 Fon Louise Gordon, *The Encyclopedia of Arkansas History and Culture*, http://www. encyclopediaofarkanas.net.

141 John Brown Watson Papers, John Hay Library, Brown University, Providence, Rhode Island.

142 Fon Louise Gordon, *The Encyclopedia of Arkansas History and Culture*, http://www. encyclopediaofarkanas.net.

143 Read Fon Gordon, "'A Generous and Exemplary Womanhood': Hattie Rutherford Watson and NYA Camp Bethune in Pine Bluff, Arkansas," *The Southern Elite and Social Change: Essays in Honor of Willard B. Gatewood, Jr.,* edited by Randy Finley and Thomas A. DeBlack, Fayetteville: University of Arkansas, 2002; John Brown Watson Papers, John Hay Library, Brown University, Providence, Rhode Island.

144 Read Judith Kilpatrick, *Extra Ordinary Men: African American Lawyers and Civil Rights in Arkansas before 1950,* 53; Arkansas Law Review, 299, 381, n630, 394, (2000); A'Lelia Bundles, "An Outline of Marion Perry, Jr.'s *Negro Progress in the United States (from 1835 to the present),* at www. ABundles@aol.com; *Who's Who in Colored America* 411(1933–37); Colored Classified Section. *Arkansas Democrat,* 5/16/1927, 10; James W. Leslie, "1867 Legislation Established Public Schools in County," *Pine Bluff News,* 6/12/1986, 1D; from Henri Linton, UAPB, African American Database, 4/19/1999' "20th Century Club," Directory, est., 1927, 52.

145 *Educating the Mind and the Spirit: The Unfolding History of Black School Administrators in Arkansas, 1900–2000.* C. Calvin Smith, ed.. Linda Walls Joshua, contributing editor. (2003): University of Arkansas Press, 22.

146 Martin and Ware, *A Selected History,* 81.

147 Martin and Ware, *A Selected History,* 117–18.

148 Martin and Ware, *A Selected History,* 118.

149 Heather Register, staff of the *Encyclopedia of Arkansas History and Culture.*

150 *Educating the Mind and the Spirit: The Unfolding History of Black School Administrators in Arkansas, 1900–2000.* C. Calvin Smith, ed.. Linda Walls Joshua, contributing editor. (2003): University of Arkansas Press, 22.

151 Phyllis Stokes, "Owner of P. K. Miller Cemetery accused of Mismanagement, defends his position," *Pine Bluff, Commercial,* June 6, 2014.

152 Interview with Ruth Frances Duvall, Arkansas State University, February 15, 1939.

153 Remarks made by Ruth Frances Duvall in 1939.

154 Interview with Ruth Frances Duvall, Arkansas State University, February 14, 1939.

155 Interview with Ruth Frances Duvall, Arkansas State University, February 14, 1939.

156 Interview with Ruth Frances Duvall, Arkansas State University, February 14, 1939.

157 Obituary of Mrs. Vester Miller, *Pine Bluff Commercial,* September 19, 1986, 1.

158 "W. H .Zachary," *Pine Bluff Commercial,* Saturday, Aug. 9, 1980, 1; *Pine Bluff Commercial,* Thursday, Aug. 14, 1980, 4.

159 See "W.H. Zachary," *Pine Bluff Commercial,* Aug. 14, 1980, 4.

160 See Obituary of Nanette Coggs, *Pine Bluff Commercial,* Tuesday, Sept. 3, 2013, 3A.

161 See http:// www. coggs-granville.com/ tandy-washington-coggs.

162 See http:// www. coggs-granville.com/tandy-washington-coggs, 2.

163 Memorial, *Jet,* March 30, 1987, photo of Dr. Coggs with family.

164 Ted Dean Johnson, "History of Arts Education at the University of Arkansas at Pine Bluff, 1873–1973," EdD.dissertation, University of Oklahoma, Norman, OK, 1985, 16.

165 The newspaper article appears in the collection of Archie Lee Moore Jr., of Little Rock, AR.

166 From the Archie Lee Moore Jr. collection in Little Rock, AR.

167 Martin and Ware, *A Selected History,* 103–6.

168 Martin and Ware, *A Selected History,* 104.

169 Martin and Ware, *A Selected History,* 105.

170 Martin and Ware, *A Selected History,* 84.

171 Martin and Ware, *A Selected History,* 85.

172 Martin and Ware, *A Selected History,* 95–96.

173 Martin and Ware, *A Selected History,* 110.

174 *The Encyclopedia of Arkansas History and Culture,* http://www.encyclopediaofarkansas.net.

175 Read Floyd Brown, *He Built a School with Two Dollars and Eighty-Five Cents: His Friends Tell the Story in this Book*, Fargo, AR, 1956. Helaine R. Freeman. "Fargo School Museum Cultivates Memories of Many Past Glories," *Arkansas Democrat-Gazette*, Feb. 20, 1996, 14D.

176 Martin and Ware, *A Selected History,* 108–9.

177 http://www.arkansasties.com/Saracen.

178 Information from *Settlements Established in 1832.* Books LLC: 2010. Memphis, TN, 139–49.

179 *Biographical and Historical Memoirs of Central Arkansas,* (Chicago, Nashville, St. Louis: Goodspeed, 1889).

180 *Biographical and Historical Memoirs of Jefferson County, Arkansas.* (Chicago, Nashville, St. Louis: Goodspeed, 1889).

181 *Biographical and Historical Memoirs of Pulaski County, Arkansas* (Chicago, Nashville, St. Louis: Goodspeed, 1889).

182 *Biographical and Historical Memoirs of Jefferson County, Arkansas* (Chicago, Nashville, St. Louis: Goodspeed, 1889.

183 Reported by Bob Lancaster, a former *Pine Bluff Commercial* reporter.

184 *Encyclopedia of Arkansas History and Culture.*

185 Fred W. Allsopp, *History of the Arkansas Press for a Hundred Years and More* (Little Rock: Parke-Harper 1922), 207–15.

186 All information in this chart came from Fred W. Allsopp, *History of the Arkansas Press for a Hundred Years and More* (Little Rock: Parke-Harper, 1922), 207–15.

187 *Encyclopedia of Southern Jewish communities,* http://www.arkansas-encyclopedia, html.

188 *Corner of the Tapestry: A History of the Jewish Experience in Pine Bluff.* Https://books, google.com.

189 See Goldring/Woldenburg Institute of Southern Jewish Life.

190 The information about Jewish life in Pine Bluff came from the *Encyclopedia of Southern Jewish Communities* and *Corner of the Tapestry: A History of the Jewish Experience in Pine Bluff.*

191 *Corner of the Tapestry: A History of the Jewish Experience in Pine Bluff,* http://www.books, google.com.

192 *Biographical and Historical Memoirs of Jefferson County, Arkansas* (Chicago, Nashville, St. Louis: Goodspeed, 1889).

193 *Corner of the Tapestry: A History of the Jewish Experience in Pine Bluff,* https://books, google.com.

194 *Biographical and Historical Memoirs of Jefferson County, Arkansas.* Chicago, Nashville, St. Louis: Goodspeed,, 1889).

195 *Biographical and Historical Memoirs of Jefferson County, Arkansas* (Chicago, Nashville, St. Louis: Goodspeed, 1889).

Bettye J. Williams resides in Pine Bluff, Arkansas. After forty-three years [1969–2012] of teaching literature, grammar, and rhetoric in the Department of English, Theatre and Mass Communications at the University of Arkansas at Pine Bluff, she retired to devote full time to the public, nonprofit sector. *The Pioneers: Early African American Leaders in Pine Bluff, 1833–92* is her first book, published for the benefit of Oak and Ivy African American Museum and Cultural Center.

All proceeds from the sale of this book will benefit the museum.

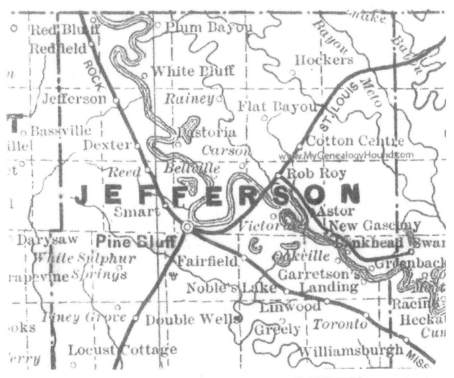

1898 MAP OF JEFFERSON COUNTY